AFRICAN SAGA

AFRICAN SAGA

a brief introduction to african history

STANLAKE SAMKANGE

ABINGDON PRESS
nashville · new york

AFRICAN SAGA: A BRIEF INTRODUCTION TO AFRICAN HISTORY

ISBN-0-687-009537 (paper)
ISBN-0-687-009545 (cloth)

Library of Congress Catalog Card Number: 70-162457

MANUFACTURED BY THE PARTHENON PRESS AT NASHVILLE, TENNESSEE, UNITED STATES OF AMERICA

Kuna Amai

PREFACE

This book is what its title proclaims it to be: an introduction to African history. It is not, in any measure, intended to be a comprehensive or in-depth study. Its aim is merely to introduce the student with no previous training or background to the study of African history. It is also intended for the general reader who, while he does not wish to take a course in African history, wants to be knowledgeable and informed on the subject.

I am indebted to Fisk University for arranging a teaching load that enabled me to devote considerable time to research and writing, to my very efficient assistants, Miss Brenda Bass and Miss Thurma McCann, who typed the manuscript, and to my students with whom I discussed the contents of this book in the History of African Civilization course.

S. J. T. Samkange

CONTENTS

INTRODUCTION

It is Hugh Trevor-Roper, Regius Professor of History at Oxford University who said: "Undergraduates, seduced, as always, by the changing breath of journalistic fashion, demand that they should be taught the history of black Africa. Perhaps, in the future there will be some African history to teach. But at present there is none, or very little: there is only the history of Europeans in Africa. The rest is darkness. . . . And darkness is not a subject for history. Please do not misunderstand me." Prof. Roper hastened to add that "men existed even in dark countries and dark centuries," but to study their history, he maintained, would be to "amuse ourselves with the unrewarding gyrations of barbarous tribes in picturesque but irrelevant corners of the globe." [1]

Although the progress made within the last decade in the study of African history—particularly in Africa, Europe, and America—clearly indicates that the distinguished professor belongs to an academic species now fast becoming extinct; his attitude is still, unfortunately, all too common. Consequently, African historians find themselves having to beat the drum and to make the claim (a claim which we hope will become clearer, stronger, and more valid with each successive page of this book) that Africa has a history that is certainly longer and just as proud as that of any continent on the face of this earth. So, if there is any darkness about, it is not on the African continent but in the minds of those who proclaim that Africa lacks history.

The attitude of some non-Africans is also exemplified by Sir Phillip Mitchell, the former British colonial governor of Kenya, who declared: "The forty-two years I have spent in Africa—forty of them in public service—cover a large part of the history of sub-Saharan Africa, for it can hardly be said to extend much further back than about 1870." [2] As far as such people are concerned, until the advent of the white man, Africa had no history. To them the history of Africa is the story of the white man in Africa, for Africa has only "his story" and no history. Nothing could be further from the truth.

The history of Africa begins with the origin of man, for it is in Africa that man first became man. The true garden of Eden—albeit, without the apple and the snake—was there. The oldest culture known to, and associated with, man has been discovered in Africa. Scholars are now beginning to realize that for an understanding of the behavior of man, a thorough study of his African genesis is a prerequisite. There is no longer any doubt that African history will attract the attention of more and more scholars throughout the world.

In studying, trying to understand, and interpreting African history, however, it is important that scholars should endeavor to look at things through African eyes. They should, of course, remain free to draw any conclusions they deem fit, but greater accuracy will be attained if an effort is made to look at events in the context of African culture and society. The following story will illustrate the wisdom of such an approach.

In 1888 Lobengula, second king of the Amandebele (part of present-day Rhodesia), sent two of his *induna* ("chiefs") on a diplomatic mission to England. Before they left, the king warned his envoys about the impropriety of an ambassador's showing amazement at things in a foreign land and thus indicating that such things did not exist in his own country. When the indunas arrived in Cape Town and beheld, for the first time, the sea with mountains of angry white foam lashing upon the shores, one of them was heard to remark nonchalantly, "Ah, today the river is in flood!" The indunas refused to look at wax figures in a clothier's window because they believed them to be dead children on show before burial.

The king's envoys spoke about their voyage in what they called the "floating kraal" (i.e., village), and described the sea as being "like the blue vault of heaven at noon and the floating kraal was as the sun in the centre; the water was smooth, thus calmly blue, the kraal being pushed through it by its steamer from behind. Sometimes the sea was full like the boisterous rivers in the rainy season; then the floors of roofs of the kraal rocked till the Whitemen danced. . . . London," they later told their king, "is the place all Whitemen must come from; people, people everywhere; all in a hurry, serious of face and always busy like the white ants. There was no room for everyone above the ground in this great kraal, for we could see men and horses moving in a stage below, just as they live in houses built one above the other (referring to Holborn Viaduct). The free carriages, too (train) . . . have to burrow in the earth under the streets for fear of being stopped by the crowd. Their little boys, the sons of headmen, all learn to fight like men (referring to Eton boys). Their generals corrected all faults; they won't pass a man who is out of time as they dance by in line coming from the fight (the march past)." [3]

Lobengula's ambassadors told of a place (Madame Tussaud's) where they saw bodies of all the kings and queens who had been conquered by kings of England including the body of Cetewayo, king of the Zulus, whose *assegai* was at the end of the corridor.

Of Queen Victoria herself one of them reported, "When she entered the room where we were waiting, I was nervous and stricken with fear and I crouched on the floor with my hands on the stomach and the Queen laughed and said: "Rise, O Babiyane!" And I stood up and saw, hau! She was very small, very, very small, no higher than that calabash of beer but terrible to look at—a great ruler." [4]

The indunas were invited to inspect the vault in which gold of the realm was kept. The ambassadors were impressed, so impressed, in fact, that they could not understand why the English still went to Africa in search of more gold when they already had so much. "The English must indeed be wretched misers, . . . fancy, not even asking us if we would like to have one of those gold bars to take home! What Matebele would take a distinguished guest to his kraal to show him his herd of cattle and not offer the guest at least one beast?" [5]

However, before they left England, the indunas did ask one of the queen's ministers for an English wife to take to their king, this being the usual way in which neighboring states in Africa demonstrated their friendship for each other. "When we tell the men at home," we can hear the indunas argue, "that we were well received by the English and that they are now our friends, the men will ask us, 'But where are the wives for the King?—to show this friendship?' What shall we say in reply?" [6]

The description of England by Lobengula's envoys is, in some ways, very perceptive. Nevertheless, it shows serious limitations. It is couched in the language, concepts, and culture of 1890 Matabeleland where, for instance, people never marched but danced only; cities the size of London were beyond comprehension; the pace of life was leisurely and anyone who was busy was bound to attract attention. To a Ndebele, a queen is an *indhlovukaz* ("cow elephant"). She is expected to be huge, fat, and literally, terrible to behold. For a queen to be small and no taller than a calabash of beer was unthinkable.

The indunas looked at English society through Ndebele eyes and found that society wanting. The Europeans were pronounced stingy misers whose cupidity made them go to the utmost ends of the earth in search of more and more gold to hoard and display to visitors.

As for the failure of the English to offer them a wife or wives for their king, in accordance with the most elementary rules of intertribal etiquette, we can imagine that the English were justly condemned as barbarians and savages who knew no better.

Any non-African historian who tries to describe and interpret African history without a sound knowledge of, or regard for, African culture and society cannot escape showing in his work the defects and limitations of the Matabele indunas' account of England. And yet many books about Africa have been written by people who saw things only through Western eyes. And some are still being written today.

How then, should one who knows little or nothing about African culture or society prepare for a career in African history? The spectacular progress made in this field in the last decade is due not only to the contribution of historians but also to the labor and research of non-historians. The best preparation that one can have for a career in African history seems to be, first and foremost, a good liberal education, strong in the sciences as well as in the humanities. This should enable one to be conversant with the general principles of the other disciplines to which historians must turn for confirmation of their findings. It is appreciated, of course, that more than one lifetime would be required for one to be an expert in all these disciplines. So most students will be content to follow, intelligently, the research and findings of these disciplines so as to compare, relate, and correlate them with conclusions of the historian.

Archaeology, anthropology, anatomy, linguistics, biology, musicology, physiology, and sociology are only some of the disciplines whose researches the African historian must try to be conversant with. A trained historian who is also competent in one of these related fields will find this additional expertise very useful in his own research.

How do these disciplines actually contribute to our knowledge of African history? Well, much of the evidence on which the growing store of African history is based was unearthed, literally, by archaeologists. They dug up the evidence. When the discovery was a skull or a bone, an anatomist was brought in; when it was a coin, a numismatist was consulted. A piece of paper or stone with a strange inscription was submitted to a paleographer to decipher. Sometimes the artifacts were buildings with tools, weapons, furniture, and implements. From these, anthropologists are able to tell us something about the people and the kind of life they led.

Through the dating methods known as carbon 14 and potassium argon, physicists are able to estimate the age of some artifacts. This gives us fairly reliable dates. Historians study the written records as well as the oral tradition of the people. The biologists tell us whether the crops grown in the area are indigenous and, if not, suggest where, when, and how they came to the area. Migration trends are thus studied.

Linguists tell us which groups of people speak languages originating from a common tongue and suggest how long the various users have been separated from each other. The musicologists compare the music of these peoples for similar trends. It is abundantly clear, therefore, that the sum total of the body of knowledge we call

African history is not the product of the historian laboring alone, but the contribution of a number of disciplines. It is the historian, however, who gathers, sifts, and finally pieces the evidence together.

In trying to acquire a more intimate knowledge of African society and culture it is important to bear in mind that Africa is a large continent of some 11,700,000 square miles larger, in fact, than the United States, China, and Russia put together, and that it has a population of about three hundred million, grouped in tribes speaking hundreds of different languages. There is no single language common to the whole of Africa even though Hausa, Swahili, and Arabic enjoy wide usage. Therefore, while one must of necessity generalize about African culture and society there is a great diversity.

There is hardly anything one can say about Africa or Africans, as a whole, for which an exception cannot be adduced. A student of African society and culture will, obviously, do well to confine himself to a specific region, people, tribe, or clan. There is now available a fair amount of literature on a number of these.

A relatively new source of information is the African novel, and quite a few are now being published every year. Some of these authors have depicted the pre-European society of their land as only Africans can and have provided non-Africans with an easy and enjoyable way of inbibing the culture.

There are also readily available a number of good films on African societies. Carefully selected, they can be used to great advantage.

NOTES

1. H. Trevor-Roper, *The Rise of Christian Europe* (New York: Harcourt, Brace & World, 1965), p. 1.
2. Sir Phillip Mitchell, "Africa and the West in Historical Perspective," in *Africa Today,* ed. G. C. Haines (New York: Greenwood Press, 1968), p. 3.

3. *Royal Geographical Society and Monthly Record of Geography,* 13 (1891), 6-8.
4. *Royal Geographical Monthly* as quoted by Stanlake Samkange in *On Trial for My Country* (New York: Humanities Press, 1966), p. 77.
5. Oral tradition as quoted by Samkange in *Origins of Rhodesia* (New York: Praeger, 1969), p. 127.
6. Oral tradition as quoted by Samkange in *Origins,* p. 130.

ATLANTIC OCEAN
MEDITERRANEAN SEA
Morocco
Algeria
Tunisia
Libya
United Arab Republic (Egypt)
RED SEA
Spanish Sahara
Mauritania
Mali
Niger
Chad
Sudan
Gambia
Senegal
Upper Volta
Guinea
Port Guinea
Sierra Leone
Ivory Coast
Ghana
Nigeria
Liberia
Togo
Dahomey
Cameroon
Central African Republic
Ethiopia
Gulf of Aden
Uganda
Somali
Equator
Equatorial Guinea
Gabon
Congo
Republic of the Congo
Ruanda
Kenya
INDIAN OCEAN
Tanzania
Burundi
ATLANTIC OCEAN
Angola
Zambia
Malawi
Rhodesia
Mozambique
South-West Africa
Botswana
Swaziland
South Africa
Lesotho
AFRICA

CHAPTER 1
Africa

Many geologists believe that about three hundred million years ago, Africa was united with other continents of the world in one vast landmass they have given the name Gondwanaland. Geologists hold this view because of the remarkable similarities in the geological record of different continents, as well as important biological links found among them.

It is believed that some time in the distant past Gondwanaland gradually split up and separated into land masses, similar to the continents we know today. In this separation, Africa, which lay near the center, emerged as a continent with a high plateau in the middle and sides steeply falling to sea level. Erosion subsequently altered this coast line, depositing soil at the foot of the slope and gradually leaving the escarpment farther and farther away from the sea. In places, however, the steep rise or fall of the terrain, depending on whether one is looking at it from the sea or from the land, is still a feature of Africa. It has been likened to an inverted saucer.

The importance of the Gondwanaland theory to students of history lies in the suggestion it offers about how the ancestors of man and, indeed man himself, may have migrated from one area—Africa—to the rest of the world. If the earth was once a single landmass, then seas and oceans were not at that time formidable and effective barriers to the migration of prehistoric animals, apes, and men. We have reason to believe such a migration took place millions and millions of years ago.

The split up of Gondwanaland and the separation of continents had another effect on Africa: It disrupted the river systems. The emergence of a high plateau resulted in some rivers' being deprived of their former lower courses to the sea and having to make an abrupt exit to the new coast line. In finding this new egress many of them flowed over protruding rock shelves exposed by later continental uplifts. Consequently, most major African rivers have waterfalls or cataracts which reduce their value as waterways and means of communication. Their waters can, however, be harnassed for hydroelectric power and irrigation schemes.

Another result of the uplift occurring in the split-up of Gondwanaland is the existence, in the interior of the African continent, of great basins separated by gently rising uplands. These basins have become repositories for erosion from the surrounding high areas. The Congo Basin, the Chad Basin, the Kalahari Basin are such areas.

The chain of rift valleys, which includes the Red Sea trough and extends from Syria in the north to Lake Malawi in the south, is another result of the split-up of Gondwanaland. The valleys are, on average, twenty-five to thirty miles wide with walls frequently rising to a height of over six thousand feet, while some of the lake floors in this area may be as much as two thousand feet below sea level. The area is also volcanic. Ethiopia and the region of Mount Kenya and Mount Kilimanjaro are dotted with extinct volcanoes while the area west of Lake Victoria is believed to have still active craters. These basins and rift valleys are especially important in the study of African history because this is the location of many of the fossils and artifacts which have contributed most to our knowledge of our ancestors. Important also is the extension of the Rift Valley trough as far as Syria, linking by the Suez Isthmus the continents of Africa and Asia, and forming of North and East Africa, Arabia, and the Middle East a cultural and technological unit.

From the break up of Gondwanaland Africa emerged, a great compact landmass stretching five thousand miles from north to south. It is four thousand miles across at its widest girth. Africa covers an area of 11,700,000 square miles. In size it is second only to Asia. It is "four times the size of the United States; and the whole of Europe, India, China, and the United States could be held within its borders." [1]

Africa has a population in excess of three hundred million and over eighty percent of its people live in rural areas and depend on agriculture for subsistence. There is, nevertheless, a rapidly growing urban population.

Africa is almost bisected by the equator. Consequently, it is the most tropical of continents with nine million square miles of its land lying within the tropics. This has had an important bearing on the course of human history, for scientists tell us that the congenial climate and rich vegetation of the interlacustrine area—about Olduvai Gorge, for instance—was an ideal cradle for the development of man.

Africa has three desert regions: the Sahara, Somali, and Kalahari. The Sahara region has featured prominently in the continent's history. It has often been used to divide Africa into North Africa and sub-Saharan Africa, and it has been claimed that Europe terminates at the Saharan border. But the Sahara has not always divided the people of the north from those of the south. Even when it became a desert, it did not form a complete barrier, but rather a porous one, minimizing rather than forbidding intercourse between north and south Africans.

Once considered almost useless, deserts have suddently become very valuable since oil and minerals were discovered in their sandy wastes. The economies of countries like Libya, Algeria, and Botswana and the lives of their people have been affected accordingly. Forest areas have played no mean role in the history of Africa. It is the forests that have supported the great variety of animals whose ivory and hides have, throughout the ages, been valuable articles for intercontinental trade. There have been minerals in other areas, particularly gold, which have attracted outsiders from prehistoric times to this day.

We have already referred to the existence of Gondwanaland over three hundred million years ago—a long, long span of time to get into perspective. As a help in getting a proper historical view of events, scientists have divided the time into various eras. Generally, the last three million years are given the name Pleistocene;

from three to twelve million years ago, Pliocene; and from twelve to thirty million years ago, Miocene. Between thirty to forty million years ago is known as Oligocene, and from forty to sixty million years ago is the Eocene era. Each era is further subdivided into lower or earlier, middle, and upper or later, periods.

NOTES

1. W. E. B. DuBois, *The World and Africa* (New York: Viking Press, New World, 1965), p. 82.

CHAPTER 2

Miocene Era to Pleistocene Times

Prior to 1924, most scientists believed Asia to be the original home of man and large sums of money were spent on the river banks of central Java where the famous Java Man named *Pithecanthropus* was found; in excavating the caverns of Choukoutien, home of *Sinanthropus,* the Peking Man; and in sifting the sands of the Gobi Desert for the missing link which, it was believed, joined apes and men to a common ancestor. It was also thought that *Homo sapiens* was the first toolmaker and that it was the capacity to think well enough to make tools that made him superior to other beings.

That year, Miss Josephine Salmons, a young student in anatomy at the Witwatersrand University in Johannesburg, South Africa saw, one Sunday evening, a fossil baboon skull on the mantel piece of a friend's home. A fossil is that hard portion of a creature, whether bone or shell, which has resisted rot long enough to be transmuted into stone by natural process. The skull had come from the works of a local lime company. She decided to take it to her teacher, Prof. Raymond A. Dart. Her action was to have a profound effect on the study of the origins of man and was the first intimation of the existence of fossil primate remains in Africa, south of Egypt.

From the fossil-laden rock, blasted out on a site near the Kalahari Desert, not far from a railway station called Taungs, Professor Dart found a complete cast of the interior of a skull. This fitted another rock from which emerged "the complete facial skeleton of an infant only about five or six years old, which looked amazingly human. It was the first time that anyone had been privileged to see the complete face and to reconstruct accurately the entire head of one of man's extinct ape-like relatives. The brain was so large and the face so human that I was confident that here, indeed, was one of our early progenitors that had lived on the African continent; and as it had chosen the southern part of Africa for its homeland, I called it *Australopithecus africanus,* i.e., the South African Ape." [1]

From geological and other evidence, Dart deduced that *A. africanus* had lived about a million years ago in the early Pleistocene era, walked erect, weighed about ninety pounds, had a small brain like that of a gorilla, possessed teeth no longer than those of a man, was carnivorous, and led a hunting life. Dart concluded, therefore, that *A. africanus* was a transitional being, enjoying all significant human attributes except man's large brain. Africa's claim to possess the secrets of the evolution of man had been staked.

But scientists the world over, still believing Asia to be the original home of man, were interested in *Pithecanthropus erectus* and Peking Man. They firmly rejected Dart's claims on the grounds that no fossil background for his Australopithecine had ever been found in the whole of Africa, and flesh-eating Primates were unknown, anyway. Furthermore, scientists believed at this time that man's large brain had preceded, rather than followed, all his other human characteristics, such as, his posture, diet, and way of life. These characteristics were thought to be the result of man's possession of a large brain. Dart's *Australopithecus,* with the body of a man and the brain of an ape, appeared, therefore, to have the order in reverse.

Fortunately for Dart, in 1936 one of the world's leading zoologists was attracted by the controversy raging over *Australopithecus.* South African Robert Broom, who had successfully demonstrated the emergence of the mammal from the reptilian background, decided to emerge from retirement at the age of seventy in order to investigate the emergence of man from the mammalian background. Within eight days, Broom had discovered an adult man-ape in a cave at Sterkfontein near Johannesburg. The scientific world could not ignore him. Even though World War II intervened and work stopped at Sterkfontein, by 1940 there were few scientists in the world who still treated Dart's claims with derision. Before long men like Sir Arthur Keith, then regarded as the most outstanding English anthropologist, were retracting their long held opposition to Dart's claims.

After the war, Broom resumed his digging, even blasting rocks among precious fossils because at the age of eighty he could not afford to wait any longer. Fossils were unearthed by the dozen, and Dart's projections from his single infant specimen were confirmed. A French Jesuit philosopher and anthropologist, Teilhard de Chardin, a specialist in the Far East, visited the australopithecine sites in South Africa and in 1952 reported to the New York Academy of Science that the occurrence of the *Australopithecinae* in Africa, between five hundred thousand and a million years ago, "offered an additional argument, that this continent was the main birthplace of the human group."[2] Asia had withdrawn its claim in favor of Africa. Also, Darwin's prophecy of 1871—made in his *Descent of Man* after a study of the distribution of the great apes, old-world monkeys, and *lorisides*—that Africa would eventually be proved to be the birthplace of man, had been fulfilled.

Unfortunately, the South African scientists' success in unearthing numbers of australopithecine specimens tended to make confusion worse confounded. When Broom discovered an adult specimen of Dart's infant *A. africanus* in 1936, he took it into his head to name it *Plesianthropus,* providing it with a brand new species and genus. When Dart later found more specimens of his South African Ape at a different site in the Makapan Valley, he christened them *A. prometheus* and claimed that they used fire. When Broom discovered a new creature at another site, Swartkrans, he called it *Paranthropus.* John Robinson, one of Brooms's assistants, found another creature at Swartkrans and called it *Telanthropus.* On July 17, 1959, Mary Leakey found a fossil skull on the oldest bed of Olduvai Gorge, and her illustrious husband, Dr. L. S. B. Leakey, named him *Zinjanthropus* and created for him a new genus. The ease with which scientists create a new species every time they make a discovery, instead of shedding light, sometimes intensifies darkness. We shall return to these discoveries later.

After the war Raymond Dart found, in peculiarly cracked skulls from a cave at Makapan, evidence leading him to conclude that

A. africanus was a hunter who used a weapon: the humerus bone, or upper foreleg bone, of the common antelope. Nevertheless, some hundred anthropologists attending the 1955 Pan-African Congress in Prehistory at Livingstone in present-day Zambia, rejected Dart's thesis that *A. africanus* was a predator using a weapon. They claimed that hyenas had collected the bones. The "hyena alibi," as it was called, has now been attacked in a stinging twenty-four points catalog by Robert Ardrey in his *African Genesis* [3] and need not concern us here. Ardrey turns to irony and chides the scientists who refused to accept Dart's thesis that man came from a line of plundering predators dependent upon the use of weapons and that "weapons preceded man." Ardrey spots as the cause of the opposition, Dart's profound violation of man's age-old, fundamental assumptions about himself inculcated by poets like Wordsworth, who sang of his innocent birth:

> Not in entire forgetfulness,
> And not in utter nakedness,
> But trailing clouds of glory do we come
> From God, who is our home:
> Heaven lies about us in our infancy!
> Shades of the prison-house begin to close
> Upon the growing boy.

Philosophers like Rousseau had spoken of the noble savage, Ardrey pointed out, and had taught that "God made all things good. Man meddles with them and they become evil." This has led to a great welter of conclusions: "that babies are born good; that in innocence resides virtue; that primitive people retain a morality which civilized people tend to lose; that a man's moral worth declines in rough proportion to his distance from the soil; that civilization must be held accountable for man's noteworthy catalogue of vices; that human fault must therefore have its origin in human institutions, relationships and environments." [4] The scientists' rejection of Dart's plundering Australopithecine was, according to Ardrey, an obeisance to man's romatic fallacy about his own innocence.

So far, Kenya has turned out the largest number of fossils we know. Over six hundred specimens have been identified from this area. So, it is to East Africa in the Lake Victoria region we must turn in our search of man's ancestors. Scientists now believe that in Miocene times the ape came into being in this area. This was about twenty million years ago and at that time the East African plateau was cool, with large well-watered forests and plains in which fruit and vegetables abounded. In these almost ideal circumstances, the ape appeared. Perhaps it is not even correct to call him an ape, for that word brings to our minds the picture of a creature specialized for brachiating, or limb swinging, with arms rather longer than his legs. The East African Miocene being, however, had arms like ours, shorter than his legs, and he lived on the ground as well as in the trees. Although his skull looks more like that of a man, he had the specialized canine teeth characteristic of the forest ape. Scientists have called him *Proconsul*. It has been argued that because of these large canine teeth, which man does not have, *Proconsul* could not be man's ancestor. This argument lost weight when it was realized that man has, in fact, vestiges of not only canine teeth, but also a tail. *Proconsul* is now believed to be ancestral to the ape as well as the human stock.

During the Miocene era, with its ample rainfall, thick forests, and spreading prairies, some apes extended their domain to Europe and Asia. They preferred the forest environment, and gradually became more adapted to this life. Their arms lengthened, their legs became shorter, and brachiating was now their specialty. They became forest apes. Other apes, tending to be more terrestrial than arboreal, depended on the bush prairies and riversides for fruit. The terrestrial ape showed no great specialized characteristics, but remained a generalized creature.

Then a great change took place in the climate of Africa. Slowly, the plentiful rainfall of the Miocene era diminished. The Pliocene drought began. Rivers dried up, forests shrank, food became scarce. The arboreal ape, trapped in the dwindling forests because he had become a specialized creature, retreated to those areas where forests still flourished: to the Congo, to the hills of India, and to the jungles of Southeast Asia. Fortunately for him, the forests never quite disappeared.

For the terrestrial ape, this was a time of crisis. As the Pliocene drought increased; rivers, woodlands, prairies disappeared, and he faced extinction. He could not return to the forests, for there the forest ape, enjoying the advantage of specialized features for brachiating, would defend his territory with all his strength. The terrestrial ape would be no match for him there. For him, there was only the brush with its berries, shoots, leaves, and roots. So the terrestrial ape turned to a grubbing existence. During this time in the brush, the capacity to stand and move in an upright position, even for a short while, would have been a great advantage. The terrestrial ape developed agility and became a biped, freeing the hands.

The terrestrial ape was now able to use his hands for self-defense and to use them with such skill—skill in wielding a weapon, a stone or a stick—that his canine teeth became useless. They atrophied, and he lost them. According to Ardrey, the creature Robert Broom discovered at Swartkrans, named *Paranthropus* (but now generally known as *A. robustus*) with his small brain, reduced canine teeth, and erect posture, represented the terrestrial ape during the Pliocene era. And, Leakey's famous *Zinjanthropus,* has now also been recognized as a variant of *A. robustus* and certainly not a new species or genus.

But around *Zinjanthropus* on Bed I at Olduvai Gorge were found simple pebble tools, the simplest of all stone implements. Usually about the size of a man's hand, they are rounded pebbles chipped at one end to form a cutting edge. Rudimentary though this may be, it symbolizes the capacity to create, to fashion something in nature to a new design, a design that is only in the mind of the maker. Anthropologists have regarded the pebble tools as the beginning of human culture and the inventiveness that created them as probable evidence that the maker now had a large brain—the brain that distinguishes men from apes. An Australopithecine, therefore, was the first toolmaker.

Ardrey maintains that it was after *A. robustus* had developed that—by a process of mutation—a terrestrial ape, or Primate-carnivore, was born. This meant that an ape with a small brain, reduced canine teeth, erect posture, free hands, and the ability to wield a weapon of some sort now existed. This stage, according to Ardrey, is represented by Raymond Dart's *A. africanus* who was carnivorous and who developed and used, with devastating effect, the antelope's humerus bone as a weapon. Only the small brain separated him from man.

For millions and millions of Pliocene years there was nothing but drought in Africa. Rain fell only rarely on a few scattered places. Hunting Primates fought over water holes. They killed and were killed by other carnivorous animals. Indeed, being slow and small of stature, enjoying no protective hide, claws, fangs, or camouflage, the Primate was much more a prey than a predator. He survived because of the primate wits, which enabled him to learn things faster than other animals, and because of his social instinct, which enabled him to organize himself into bands and perhaps to communicate in a rudimentary form of language. He survived because his hands were free.

Then the rains came. The Pliocene era ended and the Pleistocene began. For thousands and thousands of years the rains came early and lasted longer. Lakes formed, rivers ran, forests grew, and the savanna flourished. But then, the rains dwindled and drought returned to Africa in the first of a series of wet and dry spells, which correspond to the time of the glacial periods. The wet spells have been named, the Kageran, Kamasian, Kanjeran, and Gamblian pluvials. These were followed by two post-pluvial wet phases, the Makalian and Nakuran. Between the great rains, there were dry spells, or interpluvials. During this time Primates migrated to other parts of Africa and the world, following the dwindling forests in search of water and game. This accounts for the existence of Australopithecines in southern Africa, and in West Africa, where the facial portion of a skull was found in the Republic of Chad.

Southeast of Lake Victoria lie the vast Serengeti plains. Just as today, thousands upon thousands of animals find water, food, and shelter among its trees, bushes, grass, and valleys; Pleistocene animals of all kinds roamed and found sustenance there. As thousands of years of rainfall were succeeded by thousands of years of drought, Lake Victoria, together with the lakes and rivers of the Serengeti plains, filled and dried up alternately. In Miocene times Mount Homa, which stands by the lake shore, was volcanic. So the clays and sandstones of the area are mingled with volcanic ash. Chemical ingredients in this ash may have given the waters of the lake a preservative quality, for insects, birds, and animals that fell into it were embalmed. The lake filled and dried up, filled and dried up, and filled again through thousands of years. Remains of the living creatures of the plain were buried in successive layers on its shores. Time has turned them into fossils. Fortunately for us, a geologic disturbance uplifted the land enabling the Olduvai River to cut a long narrow gorge through it, with the result that one can see here, as nowhere else on the face of the earth, layer after layer of ancient deposits exposed. Five layers, or beds, roughly corresponding with the pluvials have been determined. It is in these layers that the secrets of the evolution of man are preserved. It is in these beds that archaeologists and anthropologists seek to unlock them.

Let us bear in mind that man is classed in the order of Primates, and this order also includes apes, monkeys, lemurs, tarsiers, and tree shrews. Together with apes and monkeys, man is grouped in the suborder Anthropoidia and, with apes, belongs to the super family Hominoidae. This super family is subdivided into Hominidae and Pongidae. Hominidae walk on two legs and comprise both modern and extinct forms of man, while Pongidae are anthropoid apes who walk on all fours and, therefore, are dependent on their arms for locomotion. Hominidae are further divided into two subfamilies: Australopithecinae and Homininae. Homininae begin with *Pithecantropus. Australopithecines* are ape-men, while *Pithecanthropines* are true men.[5]

Although anthropologists are certain man progressed from a tool-using to a toolmaking stage, and still regard the inventiveness that created tools as probable evidence that the maker had a large brain distinguishing him from apes; modern apes have been observed to use and to make tools. As Posnansky says: "There is at present no ideal way of demonstrating when an advanced hominid with erect posture walking on two feet can be called Man except by pointing to the regular manufacture of tools for preconceived purposes. . . . The size of the brain was formerly suggested as an indication of Man but the brain size of the australopithecines falls within the range of the great apes and not of modern man." [6]

As we have seen, at the bottom of the oldest layer at Olduvai Gorge, *Zinjanthropus* was found with pebble tools.

Between Beds I and II, Leakey found little silicate formations, called desert roses, that come about as a result of extremely dry conditions. These indicate that a dry spell followed the rainy era marked by Bed I. How long it lasted is not known, but it is believed that the specimens of *A. africanus* found in South Africa migrated there during this dry spell.

About six hundred thousand years ago, the rains came once more, and the wet period marked by Bed II began. Lakes filled up, rivers flowed, and brush grew once more. The specimens of *A. robustus* which were found in South Africa probably migrated there during this period, and this was before any sign of ape or pre-man or any semblance of human culture appeared anywhere else on earth.

At the bottom of Bed II hand axes have been found which scientists are certain evolved directly from pebble tools found in Bed I. The pebbles had simply been chipped to make an edge at the end, hand axes had been chipped right round the edges to create a shape. While the pebble could have been used only for scraping and scratching, the hand ax was an all purpose tool.

Bed II covers a period of roughly two hundred thousand years. Olduvai Gorge shows that during this period the hand ax developed in four stages. First, they were crude, thick, oblong implements called *Chellean 1*. In the second stage, known as *Chellean 2*, they are slimmer and not quite pointed. In the *Chellean* 3 stage they are pointed. Pebbles and Chellean hand axes were made by striking one stone with another. In the fourth stage, however, a piece of bone or hard wood was used as a chisel, a tool to make a tool, and these hand axes are known as *Acheulean*.[7]

After man had improved his weapons in Africa, he moved northward following game during the mild interglacial periods. The earliest stone implements found anywhere outside Africa are in France. They are Chellean in type. The first human fossil found outside Africa was in Germany—the Heidleberg jaw. It also belongs to this period.

In 1961 Leakey discovered in Bed II the maker of Chellean 3 hand axes. He was a Pithecanthropine.

Six representatives of this creature with a larger brain than Australopithecines, have been found in Beds I and II. The creature has been named *Homo habilis,* "skillful man," and was the first systematic toolmaker. Some authorities consider *H. habilis* the direct ancestor of modern man, while others maintain that he represents only a more developed Australopithecine. So the Java Man, a Pithecanthropine, and the Peking Man, who was to develop his own characteristic tools and establish early mankind in Asia, had his cultural start in the pebble tools of Bed I at Olduvai. Even a Neanderthal specimen was found in Africa at Haua Fteah, in Cyrenaica and at Jebel Irhound in Morocco. Evidently at the time man was establishing his Asian branch, the hand-axe makers of Olduvai Gorge were already using tools to make Acheulean tools.

About four hundred thousand years ago, the rains ceased falling again. The Serengeti Plains dried up, as did the lakes and rivers. Drought returned to Africa. The hand-axe makers of East Africa migrated again. They went everywhere. *Atlanthropus,* a Pithecanthropine with Acheulean weapons, appeared in North Africa. And, in the gravel of the river Thames, was found Swanscombe Man, also with Acheulean weapons.

About thirty-five to forty thousand years ago, man with a large brain, *H. sapiens* appeared. Exactly how the brain of man became large is still unknown. What is generally accepted, however, is that the brain developed in response to man's environment and culture, or as Ardrey puts it, the brain "came about when it did in an evolutionary instant as an ultimate answer to Pleistocene's unprecedented demands." [8] Howells suggests that man's braincase emerged as the brain itself increased, by natural selection, in connection with the toolmaking and the development of culture generally. By the process of selection the brain's housing tended to become efficient and economical.[9] And Grahame Clark believes that "the earliest men of *Homo sapiens sapiens* type appeared in the context of Advanced Paleolithic culture." [10] By a process of natural selection, therefore, man's environment and culture contributed to the development of his brain and the emergence of *H. sapiens.*

But *H. sapiens,* as we see him today, can be classified into various racial groups. How did these races of man emerge? Unfortunately the most important features by which racial differences are distinguished: color of the skin and hair form, for example, cannot be studied from skeletal remains. It seems likely, however, that racial differences "arose as a result of gradual genetic diversification following on the widespread migrations and colonization of new territories. . . ." The differences of pigmentation, for instance, seem to be adaptive to the environment, "as blond fair-skinned people tend to go with a cool, cloudy habitat; brunettes with the strong sunlight and bright skies of climates like that of the Mediterranean area; the darkest skinned with the hottest, non-forested regions (for example, the savannah of Africa); and those with yellowish skin and crinky hair with the typical rain forests of Africa and south-east Asia." [11]

We have seen that over millions and millions of years man evolved and, in response to his needs and the dictates of his environment, migrated and spread to various parts of the earth. All the same, man came from one source and has one original home—Africa. The brotherhood of man is, clearly, something real.

We have also seen that for hundreds of thousands of years, the important steps in the evolution of man and his culture, took place in Africa, and that until about 2000 B.C. Africa was the leading continent in the world. In answer to those who ask: What has Africa contributed to world progress? We can say that Africa gave birth to man and is man's original home, that the oldest culture on earth evolved in Africa. It was in Africa that man took the most important steps toward domesticating himself, thus increasing his chances for the continuation of his kind. It was also in Africa, as rock paintings clearly show, that the concept of coloring in art, was born.[12] This, then, is Africa's proud contribution to world progress.

NOTES

1. R. A. Dart as quoted by Robert Ardrey in *African Genesis* (New York: Dell Books, 1961), p. 176.

2. Teilhard de Chardin as quoted by Ardrey in *African Genesis,* p. 179.
3. Ardrey, *African Genesis,* pp. 293-317.
4. Ardrey, *African Genesis,* pp. 147-48.
5. Sonia Cole, *The Prehistory of East Africa* (New York: Macmillan, 1969), pp. 103-5.
6. M. Posnansky, "The Prehistory of East Africa," in *Zamani,* ed. B. A. Ogot and J. A. Kieran (New York: Humanities Press, 1969), p. 53.
7. Ardrey, *African Genesis,* pp. 276-77.
8. Ardrey, *African Genesis,* p. 329.
9. William Howells, *Back of History* (New York: Natural History Press, 1963), p. 89.
10. Grahame Clark, *World Prehistory,* 2nd ed. (London: Cambridge University Press, 1969), p. 13.
11. Clark, *World Prehistory,* p. 14.
12. L. S. B. Leakey, *The Progress and Evolution of Man in Africa* (New York: Oxford Press, 1961), pp. 1-8.

CHAPTER 3
The Stone Age

The Paleolithic or Early Stone Age

For over half a million years, the hand ax served as a tool all over the continent of Africa, some parts of Asia, and western Europe. It was in such general use, and its manufacture so standardized, that it would be impossible to tell in what place a given specimen was made. Judging by the beautiful finish of hand axes made during the later stages of the Acheulian culture, the makers of the tools attained a very high standard of proficiency as stone craftsmen. As time went on, flakes produced in the making of hand axes were used for working wood, scraping skin, as weapons for hunting, and perhaps even for war. No doubt many points were hafted to bone or wooden handles, and gummed or bound with sinews to form daggers, spears, and arrows.

It was during this time that man in Africa became a regular user of fire. Several sites with evidence of the use of fire, charred logs and charcoal, have been found. There are sites which date between fifty thousand to sixty thousand years ago, which is later than fire is known to have been used in the Far East. With fire men were able to sharpen sticks for digging, shape clubs, and to make edges on lifelike wooden tools.

As a result of his use of fire, man gained increased ability to make better tools and gather more food, and he spread into equatorial forest regions he had not previously occupied. He moved into the forest areas lying in the basins of the Congo and Zambezi rivers, near Lake Victoria and into the rain regions of West Africa. In these areas, man developed heavier tools, such as picks, scrapers, and cores to use in woodworking, grubbing, or extracting raw materials from the earth. This culture was first observed at Sango Bay in Uganda, and so is known as *Sangoan culture*. It was dominant throughout the Congo and West Africa. Spreading to East Africa, it extended west of the eastern rift in Uganda and western Kenya, down into Zambia, Rhodesia, and into southeastern Africa as far as Natal.

In other parts of southern and eastern Africa on the high plateau pans and grasslands, where conditions were favorable for the continuation of the Acheulian culture, the old hand-ax tradition lingered on; but cleavers, stone balls, tools made from flakes with faceted platforms, including scrapers and chisels, made their appearance. This culture has been called *Fauresmith*. It was widespread in southern Africa, from Natal to the Cape and to the highlands of Kenya and Ethiopia. Both Sangoan and Fauresmith cultures are associated with *Homo rhodesiensis*, the Rhodesian Man, represented by skulls found at Broken Hill in Zambia, Saldanha Bay in the Cape Province, Lake Eyasi in northern Tanzania, Singa in the Sudan, Kanam in Kenya, and Dire Dowa in Ethiopia.

In North Africa Acheulian culture was replaced by flake industries similar to those found on the Levantine coast and in the Near East. These included implements with points made on faceted platforms, side scrapers, burins or gravers, and hand axes made by step-flaking. This culture is known as *Levalloisian-Mousterian* and is associated with the Neanderthal physical type, fire-using cavemen whose remains have been found at Haua Fteah in Cyrenaica and Jebel Irhoud in Morocco. In the Maghreb, the Levalloisian-Mousterian culture developed into what is called *Aterian culture*, after a site at Bir-el-Ater in Tunisia. This culture is characterized by tanged flakes and points which could well have been used as arrow tips. In the east and as far south as the Horn, however, Levalloisian-Mousterian culture continued. Sangoan, Fauresmith, and Levalloisian-Mousterian cultures were contemporaneous.

The Mesolithic or Middle Stone Age

From about 35,000 B.C. to about 8000 B.C. is regarded as the Mesolithic, or Middle Stone Age period. In place of the Fauresmith culture of the savanna and grasslands in southern and eastern Africa, the *Stillbay culture* evolved with mainly light cutting or piercing, projectile tools of stone. In the forest areas, the Sangoan culture was replaced by the *Lupemban culture* characterized by many axes and chopping tools and knives with stabbing points.

As a result of natural selection during the Middle Stone Age, *H. sapiens* began to appear and the Rhodesoid type to disappear. Also at this time, man began to bury his dead—proof that he now had religious beliefs—and to use paint and ornamentation in his art—a sign that he now had an aesthetic sense.

Responding to the necessity to adapt himself to his environment, *H. sapiens* began to develop various types. In Africa the dominant type that emerged after the Rhodesoids was the "Big Bushman" of Bushmanoid stock, ancestral to Bushmen and Negro races. Resembling present-day Bushmen in appearance, Big Bushman occupied most of the dry and open parts of the continent, from the Sahara right across to the Ethiopian highlands, on to the East African plateaus, and down into southern Africa. Their skeletal remains have been found in places as far apart as the Nile Valley and West Africa. Posnansky concludes "that they formed the basic stock of Africa from whom the present-day African races of Negro and Bushmen have developed in the last ten thousand years."[1] The *Wilton culture,* found in southern and eastern Africa, is believed to be associated with descendants of these people.

In the forest regions of the Lupemban culture, a distinctly Negroid type ancestral to the Mande people of West Africa, the Bantu, and the Nilotic people evolved. Also, from these areas emerged Pygmanoid people ancestral to Pygmies who, though more closely akin to the Negroid than to other stock, show differences significant enough to justify their being classified separately. Three distinct races evolved in Africa, therefore, the Bushmanoid, Negroid, and Pygmanoid.

Between 10,000 B.C. and 8000 B.C., as the Middle Stone Age was drawing to a close, the Aterian people of North Africa were joined by two groups of people who entered the area from outside the continent. Both these groups were of Caucasoid stock. One consisted of tall, large-brained people, a type known as Cro-Magnon, and came from Europe; and the other, associated with what is known as North African *Capsian culture,* came from southwestern Asia.

Capsian culture, is also found in East Africa, a type being known as Kenya Capsian. Capsian culture has been attributed to people of Caucasian stock known as Erythriotes or Proto-Hamites.

There was considerable movement of people and ideas within the continent of Africa, itself. The Aterian people of the Maghreb, for instance, were able to travel as far as the southern and eastern Sahara and the Nile. As a result of such movement, tanged projectile heads and other tools characteristic of Aterian culture appeared as far afield as the Congo, Rhodesia, and South Africa during the final stages of the Middle Stone Age. Similarly, the influence of tools associated with Lupemban cultures of the equatorial forest regions is found in Aterian implements of this period.

People often ask, Why is North Africa not as "black" as the rest of Africa? Why is there a mixture of races in this area? Were early Egyptians black or white? The entry into North Africa of Caucasoids eight thousand years before the birth of Christ and their mingling with native stock of Aterian, Bushmanoid, Negroid, and Pygmanoid people provides part of the answer to such questions. There are other reasons as we shall see.

The presence of Caucasians in Africa at such an early stage in the history of man on the continent has enabled some European historians to conclude that most significant progress in Africa has emanated from these people of Caucasian stock, the so-called Hamites.[2]

The Late Stone Age

From about 5500 B.C. to 2500 B.C. there occurred in Africa, one of those wet phases we have mentioned. This is known as the Makalian wet phase and lasted three thousand years. During this period water was plentiful. People of Pygmanoid, Negroid, Bushmanoid, and Caucasian stock moved about and mingled in the Sahara. The Sahara was a rich land with forests, lakes, and rivers and not the desert it is today.

During this wet phase, rivers and lakes increased in importance, not only in the Sahara but throughout the whole continent. For they contained a permanent supply of food, fish, shellfish, and water plants. Because these foods were plentiful man began to occupy these areas around the waters permanently, instead of visiting them seasonally.

As a result, when the Makalian wet phase came to an end, man had developed highly specialized and successful hunting and gathering societies and also groups that were competent fishermen, using barbed bone points as spears or harpoons.

Early in his history, man relied chiefly on hunting for his food supply. From the Australopithecine using bone weapons to Neolithic man armed with a bow and arrow, man regarded hunting as his main source of food.

At Olduvai Gorge, on the Pithecanthropine living floors, bones have been found of several species of giant pig, huge sheep, hippoptamus, rhinoceros, one- as well as three-toed horses, antelopes, gazelles, hyenas, felines, rodents, birds, reptiles, and ostrich eggshells. Most of these bones had been broken to extract marrow and the skulls crushed to obtain brains.

To hunt such quarry, man obviously needed a technique different from that of *A. africanus* at Makapan, who appears to have come quite close to his victims before swinging his bone weapon and cracking their skulls. To solve this problem, makers of the hand ax culture in Africa developed the bolas, the first weapon for attack from a distance. And as Leakey observes, "Once the bolas was developed, early man became a much more proficient hunter than he had been and we find the remains of many large animals on his living floors. Creatures that could not be hunted by mere stalking and clubbing from now on fell relatively easy prey to hand-axe man." [3]

Other weapons were needed for hunting big game, and Leakey assures us that during the Middle Stone Age period "makers of the Sangoan culture in Africa were producing beautiful spear-heads of stone," [4] which marked an important step in human progress long before this type of weapon appeared in Europe and Asia. Stone spearheads could be attached to long wooden handles and thrown at animals some yards away or used to stab them at close quarters.

Some fossils of animals at Olduvai Gorge have been found standing upright, a fact which suggests that the animals had been driven into a swamp and then pelted with stones, stabbed with stone spearheads, or beaten with sticks before being killed. Then the parts not immersed in water were hacked off and eaten. This seems to indicate that weapons alone were not the complete answer to man's hunting needs. Because of the gigantic size of most animals of this period, hunting man had to rely on his wits, ingenuity, and resourcefulness. His social organization also supplemented his weapons. He not only drove animals into swamps but also used game pits to trap and catch them. Both feats suggest that he hunted in groups and showed a high degree of cooperation and coordinated effort.

During the Mesolithic period man learned to make use of dogs to help him in hunting and still later to round up young goats and sheep which had been added to man's domesticated stock. Man's life had become more settled, and he was, at least in some degree, a pastoralist.

The invention of the bow and arrow was a great forward step in man's progress. Exactly, how, when, and where this weapon was first used, is still uncertain, although the Aterians of the Sahara and North Africa are considered by many scholars as the most likely inventors because their smaller tanged points could have been used as arrowheads.

Stone Age hunters and gatherers still continued to roam over parts of Africa for centuries. "Some of these late hunters," Sonia Cole tells us, "were directly ancestral to the present Bushmen, and their way of life must have been essentially the same as that of these fascinating Stone Age survivals. Bushman hunting bands generally consist of up to a hundred individuals, each group having its own rights over a particular stretch of territory and its water supplies. They have few possessions other than bows and arrows, throwing sticks and spears, digging sticks for grubbing up roots, ostrich eggshells, and gourds for use as containers. Their shelters are simple affairs made of branches and grass, and frequent house moving presents no problems."[5] Such, then were man's successful hunting societies that emerged from the Makalian wet phase.

Fishing was almost as important to man as hunting. Early in his development, man became a fisherman. We know, for instance, that *H. habilis,* the "skillful man" and a systematic toolmaker, ate catfish which he scooped out of shallow water. Scooping fish was apparently not the only way early man caught them. He also trapped them, for small fish weirs and dams, like those still being built in Africa today, have been found by the shores of former lakes where fish were trapped as water receded at the end of the rainy season.

Bones appear to have been used as arrowheads and spearheads, and fish were shot at as well as speared. When later, a line was attached to a notch in the bone, spearhead harpoons had been invented. On the shores of Lake Edward, Bushmanoids with Negro affinities may have been the inventors of the harpoon during the Mesolithic era. Along the Upper Nile and the Congo, this method may be observed for fish are still shot with bow and arrow.[6] In course of time, the canoe was developed, and it facilitated the use of nets and fish traps.

A community known as "Nile Fishermen of Khartoum" and identified by Sonia Cole as the "earliest recognizable Negroes in Africa," may have invented pottery and thus initiated a new era in man's storage and cooking of food.[7]

Rock paintings and engravings depicting early man's art have been found all over the African continent, from the Mediterranean shores to the Cape, from the Sahara in the west, to the coastal lands of East Africa. The warm climate of Africa enabled man to move with ease from one plain to another, and so we find widely distributed specimens of man's art. The rock paintings of the Sahara, Tanzania, Rhodesia, and South Africa have become quite well known.

Although these paintings have been exposed to the elements for centuries—the earliest in eastern Africa, for instance, have been dated to 4,300 B.C.—they have withstood exposure to the sun and rain extremely well and remain remarkably clear, even though the earliest examples are invisible unless the silica film covering them is made transparent by spraying water on it.

Believed to be the work of Bushmanoid people, these paintings generally depict game of all kinds—antelopes, elephants, giraffes, rhinoceroses, ostriches. The style is sometimes naturalistic, and the animals are very well drawn. Others are crude and stylized. When portrayed, the human figure is generally stylized. As a rule, the animals are single figures, superimposed one on top of the other. Often, however, they are arranged in groups. At least sixteen styles are distinguishable. In Rhodesia and South Africa, a number of the paintings are polychromes. There are also engravings of schematic lines and patterns believed to be associated in some areas with initiation ceremonies.[8]

Why did man paint? we may ask. Perhaps it was to decorate the walls of his shelter, to achieve self-expression, to beautify his home, merely to "doodle," or to pass an idle hour. Even gorillas, chimpanzees, and monkeys have been observed to draw, tracing with a finger the outline of a shadow on the wall or the outline of a hand in the dust. It may be that man drew out of "wishful thinking," hoping that he would obtain what he drew—a successful hunt, cattle, or good weapons. Some drawings may have grown out of a belief in "sympathetic magic," i.e., a belief that by action directed toward its image, something or someone could be made to suffer or be influenced to act in a certain way. It may be man drew because he wanted to commemorate an outstanding event, perhaps, one that had a religious significance.[9] For whatever reasons, it is clear that man drew and painted on rocks thousands of years before the birth of Christ.

For painting materials, mineral pigments mixed with urine, animal fats, or marrow were used. Heated to various temperatures, iron oxide gave colors ranging from yellow, to dark red and brown. Rotted ironstone or ochre mixed with urine or fat gave red. Manganese and charcoal were probably used for black, while white was obtained from kaolin or bird droppings. Sharpened bird bone was used to apply the paint; and feathers, fur, beaten sticks, or fingertips were used as brushes.

Many rock paintings superimposed one over the other have been found. A study of the styles and colors used has led scholars to conclude that the paintings are the work of several generations of artists. But why should generations of artists choose to use the same canvass? Why should later generations paint over the masterpieces of their predecessors? We can only guess—perhaps suitable rocks with smooth surfaces were not easily found. Perhaps the very fact that these rocks had been used by a former generation enhanced their significance and, in course of time, were associated with magical or religious practices.

Man probably also painted on bone and skin, barkcloth and wood, "but except for one decorated bone from Nyero in Uganda the rest have vanished." [10]

The Neolithic Era

In some parts of Africa as man also emerged from the Makalian wet phase he achieved what is known as a Neolithic way of life. In point of time, Neolithic refers to the New Stone Age, generally, the same period as the Late Stone Age. The term Neolithic has, however, come to be associated not only with an era but also with a way of life, one which signified a change from the gathering, hunting, and fishing economies of the Paleolithic and Mesolithic periods to an economy producing food through the cultivation of plants. In southern Africa, because the chances of the preservation of grain cereals are remote, evidence of food production is much later than in North Africa. This is not to say that some form of food production, or vegeculture, did not exist in southern Africa at this time. It may have existed, but there is no way of telling whether plants were cultivated or gathered wild. So we can only say that people in southern Africa passed through the Late Stone Age without leaving evidence of the great Neolithic change to agriculture, while in North Africa there are many indications that the Late Stone Age was the period during which such a way of life did develop.

It was once thought that the use of pottery and the polishing of stone tools were evidence of a Neolithic way of life since they implied a settled mode of living in villages or towns and a certain amount of leisure time during which tools could be polished. But as we have seen, Mesolithic man used pottery and had domesticated animals. He is also known to have polished his tools and lived in sizeable villages and towns.

Food-growing or vegeculture is generally considered the distinctive characteristic of Neolithic life. The oldest known food-growing site is in the Middle East and existed before 7500 B.C. in a region where wheat and barley grew wild and sheep and goats were also found wild. In Africa, the earliest agriculturists, i.e., people who grow crops and keep domestic animals, were in West Africa. Perhaps as early as 5000 B.C. before the Makalian wet phase, people there were cultivating sorghum and pearl millet.[11] This conforms with George Murdock's contention that agriculture was invented "independently on the upper Niger long before it had diffused from Asia to the lower Nile, though doubtless later than its earliest development in the Near East." [12] It is, therefore, not surprising that Davidson finds in the *Nok culture* of northern Nigeria evidence of the transition between a Stone Age food-collecting culture and one that cultivated food.[13]

In North Africa, about 4500 B.C. the Neolithic way of life spread from the Middle East to Fayum in Egypt and later to Esh Shaheinab near Khartoum in the Sudan. Arkell, who discovered the latter site, believes both Fayum and the Shaheinab sites received Neolithic influences from an area that lay west of the Nile and probably included Tibetsi and Lake Wanyanga. The traditional view is that food production spread to the rest of the world from the Middle East. It is Murdock's contention, however, that there are four areas in the world where food production through the cultivation of plants, was discovered independently, and by innovators belonging to four distinct races. "Along with the Caucasoids, who developed the southwest Asian complex, the Mongoloids who achieved the southeast Asian complex, and the American Indians who elaborated the middle American complex, we must now align the west African Negroes as one of mankind's creative benefactors." [14]

From about 2000 B.C. the Sahara, as well as its eastern extension across Egypt and the Sinai peninsula area, began to lose rainfall and dry up. There was progressive dessication until desert conditions formed, gradually changing it into the Sahara of sand we know today. Further south, papyrus swamps, known as the Sudd, developed along the Nile and minimized communication in this corridor. The drying up of the Sahara had important repercussions on the continent of Africa. First, most of the people who occupied that region moved out. Some went north, others south. Second, as it became difficult to cross the dry waste, people on either side of it were separated from each other. They could no longer communicate frequently or exchange ideas and techniques as easily as they had done before. Consequently, some important developments that took place in North Africa, such as the development of food production through the cultivation of plants, remained unknown in parts of southern Africa until the advent of the Iron Age thousands of years later. But for the barrier to communication caused by the drying up of the Sahara, the cultivation of crops in southern Africa might have taken place earlier than it is known to have done. Nevertheless, there was still communication between northern and southern Africa, even though it had been reduced to the barest minimum. Raiding and trading bands and migration groups were still able to find their way to and from the Fezzan in the north and the Niger in the south or along the Red Sea and round the Horn of Africa in the east. The Sahara not only reduced to a minimum contact between African people on the continent but it also virtually isolated subsaharan Africa from the rest of the world. As Leakey says, "At just about the time that major developments in cultural evolution were taking place in Egypt, Syria, and Mesopotamia, the deserts became more extensive and then cut off Africa from the rest of the world, except for a narrow passageway down either bank of the river Nile. Some southward movements of the effects of civilization did penetrate down this passage into the Sudan; but on either side the desert conditions prevented any extension either to the east or to the west. Further south even this narrow corridor formed by the Nile was completely closed by the swamps of what is called 'the Sudd.' "[15]

So from this time onwards, most of Africa became virtually isolated from the rest of the world. It was then that Africa lost its position as the leading continent in the world. Up until this time, nearly every important and significant step in the development of man had taken place in Africa, but now, to use Leakey's words, "Africa ceased to play the dominant role in world progress, after having led for something like 600,000 years."[16]

NOTES

1. Posnansky in *Zamani,* p. 64.
2. J. E. G. Sutton, "The Settlement of East Africa," in *Zamani,* pp. 96-97.
3. Leakey, *Man in Africa,* p. 9.
4. Leakey, *Man in Africa,* p. 9.
5. Cole, *Prehistory,* p. 199.
6. Cole, *Prehistory,* p. 248.
7. Cole, *Prehistory,* p. 45.
8. Cole, *Prehistory,* pp. 220-24.
9. Cole, *Prehistory,* p. 226.
10. Posnansky in *Zamani,* p. 65.
11. Cole, *Prehistory,* p. 274.
12. G. M. Murdock, *Africa* (New York: McGraw-Hill, 1959), p. 68.
13. Basil Davidson, *A History of West Africa to the Nineteenth Century* (New York: Doubleday, 1966), pp. 17-20.
14. Murdock, *Africa,* p. 65.
15. Leakey, *Man in Africa,* p. 12.
16. Leakey, *Man in Africa,* p. 9.

CHAPTER 4
Ancient Egyptians Black

Before we embark upon an examination of the Neolithic way of life in Egypt, it may be useful to pause briefly and scrutinize the people who inhabited Africa at this time. We have observed three racial types: the Bushmanoids, Negroids, and Pygmanoids as being indigenous to Africa. A fourth type, the Caucasoids, arrived in Africa from Europe and Asia around ten thousand years before the birth of Christ. Thousands of years later, the Mongoloids occupied Malagassy to make Africa a continent inhabited by all races of man.

The migration of Caucasoids from Europe and Asia into Africa in prehistoric times was by no means a one-way traffic, as the remains of Negroids found at Mentone in France, Landes and Wellendorf in Lower Austria, and in other parts of Europe testify. In *The World and Africa,* DuBois cites several authorities who agree with him that there was once a belt of Negro culture extending from Central Europe to South Africa. These people were probably very numerous in Europe at the close of the Paleolithic Age and their remains have been found in Brittany, Switzerland, Illrya, Bulgaria, as well as other locations. They are, of course, universal throughout Africa and Melanesia, and the Botocudos and the Lagoa Santa skulls of East Brazil show where similar folk penetrated to the New World. This and similar evidence leads to the conclusion that "The one sole race that can be traced among the aborigines all over the earth or below it is the dark race of a dwarf, Negrito type." [1]

In Europe it may well have been Negroid people who introduced the art of sculpture to the Caucasians. Some of their works, such as the Wellendorf Venus cut in a limestone block, have been found intact. The migration of people to and from the African continent occurred at a time when it was still possible to pass from Africa to Europe on dry land because Sicily was then part of the Italian mainland, and the Straits of Gibraltar did not exist.

Although the presence of Negroid remains in Europe has not caused black historians to make extravagant claims on their behalf, white historians have attributed to the people of Caucasoid stock in Africa—whom they now refer to as Erythriotes or Hamites—every worthwhile innovation that has taken place on African soil.*

It is interesting to note that before descendants of Caucasoids came to be called Hamites, this name referred to black people. So Hamites are the only people in history who have undergone a metamorphosis, changing their race from Negro to Caucasian, without even trying.

From the sixth century, when a collection of Jewish oral traditions, known as the Babylonian Talmud, appeared stating that the descendants of Ham are cursed, being black because Ham was a sinful man and his progency degenerate, Hamites were identified with Negroes. Throughout the Middle Ages and right up to the end of the eighteenth century, the Negro was seen by Europeans, as a descendant of Ham bearing the stigma of Noah's curse and destined to be, forever, the white man's drawer-of-water and hewer-of-wood. This view suited Europeans very well indeed because it absolved them from any sense of guilt they might nurse concerning the enslavement of fellow human beings and enabled them to exploit and treat Negroes with brutal cruelty without compunction, since it was not for them—good Christians—to interfere with what God had ordained: that Hamites would be servants of servants forever.

As Europeans grew richer and richer from the institution of slavery, they became more and more reluctant to regard the Negro as a human being and yearned for scientific proof to show that the Negro did not share a common ancestry with them. The status of

* I am indebted to Edith R. Sanders for the arguments which underlie the basic thesis of this chapter. Her excellent article, "The Hamitic Hypothesis," in *Journal of African History* 10 (1969), 521-32, traces the development and transformations in the theory of the Hamites.

the black man deteriorated in direct proportion to his value as chattel, and the Negro was held to be either depraved and degenerate from his environment or a separate subhuman creation. DuBois notes that "in the usage of many distinguished writers there really emerged from their thinking two groups of men: Human Beings and Negroes." [2] And his thesis was that this extraordinary result came from the African slave trade to America in the eighteenth century and the capitalistic industry built on it in the nineteenth.

This was Europe's attitude to the Hamites until Napoleon invaded Egypt in 1798, and his archaeologists and scientists found ancient monuments, well-preserved mummies, evidence of the beginnings of science and art. They came to realize that the origins of Western Civilization were much earlier than the Greeks or Romans. Even though the population which Frenchmen found in the country was racially mixed, Napoleon's scientists came to the conclusion that the ancient Egyptians were Negroid. One member of that expedition, Baron Denon, described the people as having "a broad and flat nose, very short, a large flattened mouth . . . thick lips, etc." [3]

Their conclusions coincided with the opinion of a famous French traveler who earlier had spent four years in Egypt and Syria. Constantin Volney wrote, "How are we astonished . . . when we reflect that to the race of negroes, at present our slaves, and objects of our contempt, we owe our arts, sciences, and . . . when we recollect that, in the midst of these nations, who call themselves the friends of liberty and humanity, the most barbarous of slaveries is justified; and that it is even a problem whether the understandings of negroes be of the same species with that of white men." [4] But how could Negroes, the cursed sons of Ham, be originators of a civilization older than that of the West? What justification had Europeans to enslave such people or regard them as a separate race?

It was at this point that white scholars, on both sides of the Atlantic, began their efforts to prove that Egyptians are not Negroes until "it came to pass that Egyptians emerged as Hamites, Caucasoid, uncursed and capable of high civilization. This view became widely accepted and it is reflected in the theological literature of that era." [5] After this Hamites ceased to be black and became Caucasoids—

whites, even though some people so designated are as black as six midnights put together. Egypt was completely left out of African history, and to the Hamites was ascribed not only the civilization of Egypt but also anything worthwhile that ever happened in Africa.

Consequently, today "The term 'Hamitic' is highly confusing, and also hedged with racist overtones. It has been used in a variety of ways to denote linguistic, physical and cultural traits, and often more vaguely, reflecting European presumptions that light-skinned peoples are more intelligent than dark-skinned. For the Hamites have commonly been envisaged as the 'more European-like' of Africans—in other words those peoples with lighter skins, thinner lips and straighter noses inhabiting most of northern and north-eastern Africa. To these 'Hamites' have been attributed any remarkable technological feat, any notable political organization, any trace of 'civilization' in black Africa." Old irrigation systems, drystone walling, rock-cut wells, the coming of ironworking, the origins of the interlacustrine kingdoms, have all been ascribed to "Hamitic" invasions or influences. J. H. Speke and C. G. Seligman invented theories of vanished "Hamitic" civilizations, of "conquest of inferior by superior peoples," of Negroes being raised from barbarism by intermarriage and interaction with Hamites, and of Negroes improving themselves by copying the example of Hamites. In fact, Seligman claimed that the civilizations of Africa are the civilizations of the Hamites and the history of Africa could only be written in terms of Hamites and their influences. This, of course, is nonsense.

As Sutton points out, among the so-called Hamites are the least cultured or "civilized" peoples in Africa, pastoralists whose seasonal movement in search of pasture and water does not encourage the development of advanced material cultures of political systems. But the pastoralist, especially if he is light-skinned, has been hailed as innately superior to the Negro.[6]

But what race were Ancient Egyptians? Negro—of course! Even though there were Caucasians in Egypt at this time, there is nothing to suggest they were more numerous than, or drove away, the native black population they found in the country. On the contrary, all the evidence points to the black population's having remained dominant. This was not only the opinion of Napoleon's scientists, it was also the view of contemporaries like, Diodorus, Strabo, Pliny, Tacitus, and Herodotus, who visited the country. As Cheik Anta Diop argues, "To show that the inhabitants of Colchida were of Egyptian origin and that they should be considered as a part of the army of Sesostris that settled in this region Herodotus said: 'The Egyptians think that these people are the descendants of a part of the troops of Sesostris I would suppose the same for two reasons: the first is that they are black and have crinkly hair." [7]

Diop charges that many Negro skeletal remains and mummies were destroyed by white scholars because the facts were too disconcerting, and it was necessary to make them confirm to previously fixed assumptions. Those that have survived, together with paintings and reliefs, confirm the views of ancient writers that the Ancient Egyptians were Negro. DuBois also concludes "that the Egyptians were Negroids, and not only that, but by tradition they believed themselves descended not from the whites or the yellows, but from the black peoples of the south. Thence they traced their origin, and toward the south in earlier days they turned the faces of their buried corpses." [8] We are, therefore, talking about black people, Negro Africans, when, in the following pages, we discuss the civilization of Ancient Egyptians.

It is because Ancient Egyptians were black that some people believe Moses and Jesus were black. For, "how could the Jewish people be exempt from having Negro blood? During the four hundred years in Egypt they would have increased from seventy individuals to about 600,000 in the midst of a Negro nation which dominated them during that period," argues Diop. "If the Negroid characteristics of the Jews are less apparent today, this is due, it would seem, to their mixing with European elements since their dispersion." [9]

The black man's own experience of slavery in a white-dominated society in America supports Diop's contention. Few black people, if any, in America today can claim to have no Caucasian blood, while their skin color ranges from black to white. This must have been the case with the Jews when they left Egypt and, under such circumstances, it is quite likely Moses and Jesus were black. What we know for certain, however, is that Moses chose a black woman, an

Ethiopian, to be his wife (Numbers 12:1). His choice is quite understandable since Moses had been brought up and educated as an Egyptian prince. In a country where the aristocracy was black, it is only natural, in view of his social and cultural background that he should have had more in common with the black aristocratic classes than members of his own enslaved Jewish race. It was presumably because his wife was, by religion, a Gentile and not a Jew that there was opposition to his marriage among some members of his family, opposition which, we are told, did not escape the wrath and punishment of the Lord.

Evidence which points to Jesus' having been black also comes from Europe where black statues of the Virgin Mary are found in several countries, and the author of *Roman Rolland Intermediare des Chercheurs et des Curiex* asks, "Why are the majority of the Virgins that are revered in the celebrated pilgrimages black? At Boulogne-sur-Mer the sailors carry a Black Virgin in the procession. At Clermont, Auvergne, the Black Virgin is revered as also at Einsiendeln, Switzerland, near Zurich, to which thousands of pilgrims—Swiss, Bavarians, Alsatians go to pay her homage. The famous Virgin of Oropa, in the Piedmont, is still a negress, as well as the not less legendary one of Montserrat in Catalonia which receives 60,000 visitors a year. I have been able to trace the history of this one to the year 718 A.D. and it was always black. Tradition says St. Luke, who personally knew the mother of Christ, carved with his own hand the majority of these Black Virgins. It is highly interesting to know, therefore, if the mother of Christ was not a Negro woman; how it happens that she is black in France, Switzerland, Italy and Spain?" [10]

If Mary was black, it stands to reason that Jesus was also black. As a matter of fact, Eisler tells us that according to Josephus, a Jewish historian of the first century, Christ "was a man of simple appearance, mature age, dark skin, short growth, three cubits, hunchbacked, . . . with scanty hair, . . . and with an underdeveloped beard." The prophet Isaiah had said of the Messiah, "He hath no form or comeliness; and when we shall see him, there is no beauty that we should desire him" (53:2), and Eisler maintains that this pen picture of Christ, which appeared in the reconstructed original (*Halosis* 2.174 ff.), was accepted by early Christians, including

Tertullian and Augustine. But the picture changed when the Halosis underwent the usual corrections at the hands of Christian copyists who embellished it. For when Christians gained power and possessed authority, Christ became King. It was, therefore, no longer fitting to portray him as unimpressive in appearance. Eisler indicates that because it was feared the original text would give offense to believing Christians and their Hellenistic idea of male beauty the pen picture of Christ was changed to make him "ruddy, six feet tall, well-grown, venerable, erect, handsome . . . blue eyes, beautiful mouth, copious beard." [11]

There is thus evidence indicating that both Moses and Jesus were not the blue-eyed blondes white people have pictured and painted them. There is more than humor in the story of a black man who complained to Jesus that white Christians were refusing him admission to a certain church because of his color, and Christ replied, "Don't I know it? I have been trying to enter that church myself all these years. They won't let me in."

NOTES

1. J. A. Rogers as quoted by DuBois in *World and Africa,* p. 88.
2. DuBois, *World and Africa,* p. 87.
3. Baron V. Denon as cited by Sanders, "Hamitic Hypothesis," p. 525.
4. Count Volney as cited by Sanders, "Hamitic Hypothesis," p. 525.
5. Sanders, "Hamitic Hypothesis," p. 527.
6. Sutton in *Zamani,* pp. 96-97.
7. Cheik Anta Diop, "Negro Nations and Culture," in *Problems in African History,* ed. R. O. Collins (Englewood Cliffs, N. J.: Prentice-Hall, 1968), p. 12.

8. DuBois, *World and Africa,* p. 106.
9. Diop, "Negro Nations," pp. 12-13.
10. G. K. Ogsai, "Fifty Unknown Facts about the African," p. 5.
11. Robert Eisler, *The Messiah Jesus* (London: Methuen & Co., 1931), pp. 411-21, 425-29.

CHAPTER 5
Egypt

As we have seen, about 4500 B.C. the Neolithic way of life spread from the Middle East to Fayum in Egypt. How did this happen? Well, during the Makalian wet phase the Nile was a vast inland lake, extending from its present valley as far south as the Sudan and in a westerly direction to the southern margin of the Sahara. In this lake fish, crocodiles, and hippopotamuses flourished. As the gradual desiccation leading to the formation of desert conditions in the Sahara continued, the Nile lake progressively dried and shrank to its present bed leaving behind eight terracelike formations along the hills of the Libyan and Arabian deserts. On the lower four of these terraces, evidence of human habitation has been found in stone tools characteristic of the Early Stone Age.

In their search for water, the inhabitants of the region were steadily forced to occupy areas along the verges of the shrunken lakes. Judging by their equipment—flint arrowheads of winged form and barbed, bone harpoon heads—these people had become advanced hunters and fishermen with domesticated animals. It was here, along the banks of the Nile, that a transition from a hunting and fishing way of life to food production through the cultivation of plants, took place.

In the valleys, swamps, and shallows left by the Nile flood each year, the inhabitants found an abundance of water creatures while the meadows and shrubs along the wadis that flanked the Nile supported lions, asses, wild cattle, sheep, ibex, antelopes, and other game. With plenty of water foods and game, edible roots such as, the papyrus rhizome or plants, and fruit; life was easy. So these people had no incentive to change their ways. But immigrants came among them, presumably from Palestine, and started the practice of sowing barley or wheat in the ground which was ploughed, manured, and watered—all in one process—by the inundation of the Nile. It turned out to be fruitful work for the seed, planted by merely treading it in with foot or hoof, quickly germinated, grew, and ripened in the gentle heat of winter and spring. Abundant crops were raised. Just as important, was the fact that the grain could be stored indefinitely, especially near the dry desert areas. Neolithic sites have been found at Deir Tasa, el-Badari, and el-Amra in the south, and Fayum and Merimda in the north.

The large-scale growing of food that could be stored indefinitely greatly reduced man's dependence on hunting and fishing as a source of his food supply. It had other results. It gave man leisure, leisure to think, to specialize in arts and crafts, and to try to influence his future. As more and more people took to growing crops, the population in areas suitable for agriculture increased, making it highly desirable that the annual inundation by the Nile should be harnessed and made to flow over wider areas. The Egyptians learned that such work could be done better as a cooperative effort, organized on a wide scale.

To inspire, organize, coordinate, and direct such undertakings, political and religious institutions developed. Families grouped themselves in villages, which were in turn grouped in *nomes,* or provinces, worshiping a local variant of one of the universal gods. A powerful headman assumed the leadership of the nome. Many centuries later, in historic times, the whole country came under one government.

To facilitate our study of early Egyptian history, some Egyptologists have divided it into three periods—the Early Prehistoric or Early Pre-Dynastic, Later Prehistoric or Later Pre-Dynastic, and the Dynastic period which is subdivided into the Archaic, Old Kingdom, Middle Kingdom, Late, and New Kingdom periods.*

* In this chapter the chronology and general division into historical periods employed by Cyril Aldred in *The Egyptians* (New York: Praeger, 1963) has been followed.

The Early Prehistoric period ended about 3600 B.C. Egyptians were at the end of this period building houses of reed and mud, growing wheat and barley which they harvested using wooden knives with flint blades set in slots. The harvest was stored in pits lined with mats. From the grain, they cooked porridge and bread in hand-made vessels of monochrome pottery. They also made stone bins or silos in which they stored edible roots and wild fruit.

Their clothes were made of linen as well as soft, tanned animal skins. They wore rings, bracelets of ivory, necklaces, girdles and anklets of shell, perforated stone and shell disc beads. They also used cosmetics, eye-paint ground from green malachite or a red pigment and cleansing oils expressed from the wild castor plant. Men were, generally, clean shaven but wore their hair long. Women plaited their hair and wore ivory combs decorated with carvings of animal heads.

Although copper was known, it was used only in its native form for small objects such as pins. Their tools and weapons were generally made of wood, bone, stone, or flint. They used a throw-stick with a head of stone and arrows tipped with chert points or bone barbs. Their axes and adze blades were of polished flint or stone.

They buried their dead. The body was made to lie crouched on its side—as though awaiting rebirth while pots, weapons, cosmetic palettes, clay or bone figurines of women were buried along with the males. This mode of burial suggests that Egyptians of this period already believed in a life after death.

The Late Prehistoric period lasted from 3600 B.C. to 3200 B.C. It is typified by a culture found at el-Gerza. During this period, Egyptians became more and more wealthy as they based their society on farming. Hunting and fishing declined. Stone tools were perfected. The people lived in more substantial rectangular houses built of sun-dried mud bricks and fitted with a wood-framed doorway in the side.

To travel or carry goods from one part of the country to another on land, they used the ass as a beast of burden. Their boats, large enough to have cabins, were built of reeds and were propelled by oars along the Nile. Some vessels were fitted with sails. Wooden ships began sailing the tideless Mediterranean Sea at this time. In this way, Egypt came into greater contact with her neighbors in other parts of North and East Africa and along the eastern Mediterranean. She influenced them and was, in turn, influenced by them. There was thus contact between Egypt and her neighbors as a result of which Egypt shared a common trade, technology, and material culture with her neighbors.

Contact with her neighbors fertilized and invigorated Egyptian culture. Her copper industry grew. Flat axes, ribbed daggers, and flat knives were made out of copper. More copper was brought from the eastern desert while other raw materials, such as silver and lead, were imported from Asia.

Egyptian graves of this period show a greater range of wealth in burial offerings placed on shelves or in separate compartments attached to the grave. Palettes and mace-heads of the time show rudimentary hieroglyphs indicating that Egyptians now had a written language.

The Dynastic era refers to the time when a single ruler or pharaoh claimed sovereignty over the whole country. The first six hundred years of this period, from about 3200 B.C. to 2600 B.C. when two dynasties rules over the country, is called the Archaic period.

Egyptian tradition, recorded by Manetho their earliest known historian and also by Herodotus, ascribes the unification of the twenty-two *nomes* of Upper Egypt with the twenty nomes of Lower Egypt to Menes, the first pharaoh. This ruler is said to have diverted the course of the Nile at the junction of Upper and Lower Egypt, built a white-walled city, later called Memphis, for his capital, and undertaken large irrigation schemes in its vicinity. From studying various archaeological objects, however, scholars believe that the process of unification took longer than one generation and was accomplished only after much fighting. Egyptologists, nevertheless, identify Menes with King Narmer or Merinar, whose monuments have been found in Upper Egypt at Hierakonopolis and Abydos, where his dynasty originated.

The Nile made it possible for Upper and Lower Egypt to be united and governed as one country. Pharaohs strove to maintain this unity. They ruled as divine kings symbolizing the whole nation.

It was their unchallenged sovereignty, supremacy, and well-being that engendered confidence and stability in the state.

To administer the state, the pharaohs delegated authority to the governors of *nomes* or to officials of the central government whose duties included the supervision of public works and collection of taxes. The pharaohs also promoted an official religion, centered on the worship of Ra-Atum, the sun god, whose black and woolly-haired son Osiris was lord of the regions of the dead. The idea of life after death greatly influenced the lives of ancient Egyptians. Because they believed that the spirit could only survive if the body was properly preserved and provided with the necessities of afterlife, Egyptians embalmed their dead and buried them in richly furnished graves. In the First and Second dynasties, structures of sun-baked bricks, called *mastabas,* were erected over graves of prominent people.

During the Archaic period, the working of ivory, wood, stone vessels, pottery, and copper utensils continued. Egypt can also claim a number of inventions for this period as Aldred points out, The first is a plastic substance, usually referred to as Egyptian faience. It was a material made of crushed quartz pebbles which could be carved and shaped, then fired to a brilliant blue or green on the glazed pottery vessels. Egypt also left her unique mark on stone working. Beginning in the Archaic age special rocks were sought for making objects of beauty as well as utility, and great blocks of granite were cut into sills, lintels, jambs, and other constructional items. Artistic sculptures were also made from granite and slate as well as the softer limestones.

Perhaps the most important material for which Egypt is noted is papyrus. This is a fine, flexible paper made from the pith of the reedy papyrus plant, and it has been known from the very beginning of historical times at least. In addition to papyrus, leather rolls were often used for more durable records. Other writing tools were developed also; a pen made of rushes and colored inks. Their system of cursive writing was designed to permit rapid copying, and the art of writing underwent a continuous development as long as the Egyptian language was spoken. The ancient Egyptians thus had, from the start, a reliable means for keeping records of their affairs.

They also made impressive strides in the science of calculation. They employed a decimal system which had existed in Pre-Dynastic times, and during the Archaic period it is probable that most of later Egyptian mathematics was raised on this foundation. Linear measure was based on various dimensions of the human body; the finger, palm, forearm, and so forth. Measures of quantity also existed and were used by merchants in assessing the amount of corn, wine, and oil harvests.

There was an institute for the study of astronomy at Heliopolis. This city was also the center of the sun cult in which great emphasis was placed on determining the movement of the heavenly bodies. A calendar based upon twelve months of thirty days, plus five scattered feast days, was introduced during the Archaic period. By 2500 B.C. an even more accurate calendar had been developed.

"During the . . . Archaic Period, . . . some scholars . . . detect . . . a fumbling towards a scientific attitude on the part of the Ancient Egyptian in an organized world which he was having to establish as much by processes of rationalization as by trial and error. Two literary works, which from internal evidence are thought to originate in the time Dynasty I, are the warrant of this view point. The first is a treatise upon surgery, especially fractures, known as the Edwin Smith papyrus, which is remarkable for its empirical approach. . . . Manetho records that the second King of the dynasty was a noted physician and wrote works on anatomy. The other work is a theological composition ascribing the creation of the universe to Ptah in which a novel search for first principles is evident."[1]

Thus by the time the Archaic period came to an end about 2600 B.C. Africans already excelled in spinning and weaving linen cloth, in masonry, and in making cosmetics. They had invented faience, writing, paper, leather rolls, pens, and ink. They had established mathematics, a standard of linear measure, capacity measure, computed time, and devised a twelve-month calendar. They also studied astronomy, medicine, and surgery.

The period from 2660 B.C. to 2180 B.C.—a period of four hundred and eighty years, during which the Third through the Sixth Dynasties ruled Egypt—is known as the Old Kingdom. One of the most remarkable things about the Old Kingdom was the prominence during the Third Dynasty, not of the king, but of a king's man named Imhotep. Wise, learned, and steeped in the tradition of Heliopolis, Imhotep rose to the rank of vizier, or prime minister, to King Djoser. "In Imhotep," writes Aldred, "we can recognize the first known genius of historic times whose thought and imagination transcended his age and steered the course of human culture into new channels. In later periods he was celebrated as an astronomer, architect, writer, sage, and above all as physician, being eventually deified as the god of medicine whom the Greeks called Imuthes."[2] And as Sweeting reminds us, "Imhotep of Ancient Egypt, was the real Father of Medicine. He lived about 2300 B.C. Greece and Rome had their knowledge of medicine from him. In Rome he was worshipped as the Prince of Peace in the form of a black man. He was also Prime Minister to King Zoser, as well as the foremost architect of his time. The saying, 'Eat, drink and be merry, for tomorrow we die,' has been traced to him. Hippocrates, the so-called 'Father of Medicine,' lived 2,000 years after Imhotep."[3]

Tradition also credits Imhotep with developing the art of building entirely in stone, for it was during the Old Kingdom period that Egyptians built massive structures as eternal habitations for the royal dead. Imhotep's architectural revolution came about as an attempt to ensure that King Djoser would be buried in a tomb enduring forever. When Djoser died, he was buried in a tomb set beneath a giant stone staircase rising in six stages to a height of over two hundred feet. This stepped pyramid was set in the midst of numerous courts and buildings, and around all this a thirty-foot wall was built, having a perimeter of over a mile. It amounted to a "city" for the dead king. That tomb has, indeed, endured.

By 2590 B.C., when construction on the Great Pyramid of Cheops at Giza was probably begun, over two million blocks of limestone weighing, in some cases, over fifteen tons each, were quarried on the spot or cut some distance away and ferried over the river during the high tide of the Nile. There can be no doubt that the Ancient Egyptians had mastered the art of building in stone.

From the reliefs and statues of the period made of *mastabas* we learn that Egyptians worked in the fields, hunted, fished, enjoyed picnics on the river, music, dancing, feasting, and children's games.

We also learn that Egypt was in contact with Nubia and present-day Sudan—the Ethiopia of biblical times—from where she recruited some of her fighting men. Her traders traveled to the land of Punt—believed to be somewhere on the Somali coast of today—for incense gums and resins required for religious purposes. There is also evidence that Egypt conquered some parts of Palestine during the reign of Phiops I, assaulting positions as far north as Carmel.

Unfortunately, the highly centralized administrative machinery, structured around officials closely related to the king and built up over centuries, began, for several reasons, to crumble. First, the provincial governors and officials who received gifts of land exempt from taxation were expected in return to further the interests of the king and give him a decent burial when he died. Instead, the officials and governors came to regard their posts as hereditary and paid little attention to the king's interests. Some no longer sought to be buried near the king at all but built tombs of their own in the provinces, as if they were monarchs. Second, a large part of the nation's resources were spent on unproductive activities such as building and maintaining vast silent cities around the pyramids, forever free from taxation, whose function was to chant funerary prayers. Furthermore, the respect for the pharaoh diminished as the Heliopolitan sun cult spread. Another blow was dealt when the divine king condescended to marry women without royal blood.

By the middle of the Sixth Dynasty each provincial potentate was governing on his own behalf and at the end of the ninety-year reign of Phiops II, the central government was too weak to withstand the centrifugal and anarchical forces surging around it.

Although Egypt remained under the titular rule of a pharaoh for the next hundred years, power really lay in the hands of provincial governors. This period between 2180 B.C. and 2080 B.C., is known as the First Intermediate period. In general, the country experienced a decline in order and prosperity. Poverty, anarchy, internecine strife, famine, plague, and sterility stalked the land. The restoration of the old unity, order, peace, and glory of Egypt became the aim of certain responsible citizens. Among these was a powerful family at Herakleopolis who succeeded in uniting the Delta and Middle Egypt under their sway and in forming the Ninth and Tenth Dynasties.

The Herakleopolitans expelled the Asians who had straggled into the Delta, fortifying the eastern border to prevent further incursions. Then they set about to improve irrigation works, reopen trade with Byblos, and reestablish Memphis as the main city. However, they were decisively defeated by a southerner from Upper Egypt, the Theban prince Menthuhotep I Nebhepetre, who eventually reunited Egypt under his rule as pharaoh.

From the trials and tribulations of the First Intermediate period, there emerged, like the silver lining of a dark cloud, a graceful, poetic secular literature. With the decline of the divine authority of the pharaoh, this artistic expression appealed to emotions and minds of contemporary men and inspired Egyptian writers for centuries afterwards.

The reunification of Upper and Lower Egypt under the rule of Menthuhotep I marked the beginning of what is called the Middle Kingdom period which lasted four hundred and forty years (2080 B.C. *to* 1640 B.C.). A southerner, devoted to southern culture, Menthuhotep I reigned for fifty-one years, during which he made the city of Thebes the capital of Egypt and built many structures in Upper Egypt. His culture and manners were those of Nubia to the south. The women depicted in the art of this period were black and had tattoos on their bodies.

Ammenemes, first pharaoh of Twelfth Dynasty, moved the capital from Thebes to the fulcrum of Upper and Lower Egypt not far from Memphis near present-day el-Lisht. This did not indicate a lack of southern interests for his successor, Sesostris I, made a determined effort to conquer northern Nubia and parts of the Sudan, built several fortified towns in the region, and succeeded in extending the southern border of Egypt from above the first to the third cataract. Fortifications were also built on the northeastern frontier with Asia even though trade with all the neighboring countries continued. It was during this period that Joseph attracted the Jews to Egypt, and, later the pharaohs enslaved them until Moses led them to the Promised Land. The Middle Kingdom period ended during the Thirteenth Dynasty when the country came under the Hyksos.

There followed what is known as the Second Intermediate period during which the Fourteenth through the Seventeenth Dynasties ruled Egypt from 1640 B.C. to 1570 B.C. Who were the Hyksos?

Where did they come from? It was formerly thought that the Hyksos were "Shepherd Kings," a horde of invaders who suddently erupted into Egypt, conquering it by spreading death and destruction. Now it is believed that they were, in fact, the people known in the Middle Kingdom as "Rulers of Uplands." These people, Aldred tells us, "were no more than wandering Semites trading their products with Egypt, or going down there for sanctuary, or to buy corn, or water their flocks according to an age-old tradition. The story of Joseph reveals how some of these Asiatics may have arrived, sold into serfdom for corn in time of famine, or offering themselves as menials in return for food and shelter. . . . Famine or ethnic movements leading to large-scale infiltrations into the Delta of Semites, mixed perhaps with Hurrian elements, especially during the anarchy into which the Middle Kingdom lapsed, could have resulted in the founding of a Lower Egyptian State with an Asiatic king and officials taking over imperceptibly all the functions and machinery of Pharaonic government.

"This in fact seems to have happened. A Hyksos principality was established on the eastern borders of the Delta with Avaris as its capital, whence Asiatic influence spread over Lower Egypt until Memphis itself was wrested almost without a blow from the tired hands of the last feeble ruler of Dynasty XIII." [4]

The Hyksos formed Fifteenth and Sixteenth Dynasties, adopted Egyptian titles, costumes, and culture, and even worshiped Egyptian gods. They ruled over Lower Egypt and the territories in Sinai and Palestine. Upper Egypt remained independent under Theban princes, while further south Nubia and the Sudan were under the prince of Kush. Both the Theban princes and the prince of Kush were, however, in alliance with the Hyksos.

With the Hyksos, bronze, which was easier to work than copper and more effective for weapons and hardware generally, came into use. "More important than these weapons of destruction were certain abiding inventions of peace, such as improved methods of spinning and weaving, using an upright loom; new musical instruments, a lyre, the long-necked lute, the oboe, and tambourine. Humpbacked bulls were imported from an Asiatic source, probably brought by ship with the greatly increased trade that the Hyksos fostered. Other importations included the olive and pomegranate tree." [5]

Once more it was the southerners, Theban princes who spearheaded the fight against Hyksos rule and ultimately brought the whole of Egypt under one pharaoh in the time of Ahmosis, originator of the Eighteenth Dynasty. With Ahmosis' rule began the New Kingdom period, during which the Eighteenth through the Twentieth Dynasties, reigned over Egypt from 1570 B.C. to 1075 B.C. Ahmosis campaigned in Palestine and Syria and his successors extended Egyptian influence to the Euphrates.

In the south, Nubia and Kush were brought under effective Egyptian control and ruled by a viceroy titled, the "King's Son of Kush" appointed by, and solely responsible to, the pharaoh. Peace and efficient Egyptian government brought prosperity to this region as irrigation improved farming, cities and temples were built, gold and other precious stones mined, and ivory, ebony, cattle, gums, and similar products increased the wealth of Egypt. Trading expeditions were sent to Punt "where the inhabitants lived in grass huts built on piles," and the Egyptians offered "the trade-goods of all such African adventurers ever since—strings of beads, axes, and weapons" in exchange for their "gold, ivory, apes, and precious myrrh-trees, their root-balls carefully protected for transplanting in Thebes."[6]

It was during the New Kingdom period that pressure of populations from the Balkans and Black Sea areas caused great migrations on to the islands and coasts of the Mediterranean. Some of these landless people called simply, Sea-peoples, found their way to the African coast and allied themselves with the native tribes in what was then known as Libya. Increasing aridity in that area drove the Lybians and Sea-peoples to join forces and try to occupy the rich lands of the Delta. Consequently, generations of Egyptians were compelled to fight off invasions from Libya and their northeastern border with Asia. Aldred describes Rameses III as "the first great King of Dynasty XX and the last great Pharaoh of Egypt, [he] had to repulse with great slaughter two desperate invasions from Libya led by the Meshwesh, the classical Maxyes, and supported by such allies as the Philistines and Teucrians and accompanied by their families, cattle, and household goods. Even these disasters did not deter these land-hungry people from settling in Egypt and parties of Meshwesh filtered across the borders taking service as mercenaries in the Egyptian armies and forming an influential military caste. Their descendants became powerful enough to intervene in Egyptian affairs and form two dynasties of their own."[7] Egypt succeeded in keeping its borders inviolate even though its Asian possessions were lost.

The legacy of the New Kingdom period is impressive and varied, ranging from colossal statues in stone to little luxury items made of ivory and gold. There were also innovations, such as the manufacture of vessels in polychrome glass, the process of coloring gold in shades from palest rose to a deep red. The use of tapestry-weaving and needlework embroidery in clothing also came into fashion.

Towards the end of the New Kingdom period, Egyptians tended to rely on mercenaries from Nubia, Sudan, Canaan, Sardinia, Libya, and other places to fight in their army. Foreigners rose to high positions in the state while Egyptians turned more and more to the sedate professions of priest or scribe which could be passed on to their sons. As a result, Egyptian society stagnated. Meanwhile Philistines, with their iron weaponry, held a firm grip on former Egyptian territories in Palestine, and the Canaanites of Phoenicia took over mastery of the seas. Unemployment among Egyptian mercenaries increased lawlessness, and to make bad matters worse, there were famines caused by low tides of the Nile, dishonesty among officials, strikes and violence among people desperate with hunger, and a waning in the worship of the pharaoh as a god. This practice became more a superstition and less an article of faith, and the pharaoh was transformed into, and remained, from this time onward, a mere dictator dependent on mercenaries for his authority.

Early in the Late Kingdom period—from 1075 B.C. to 332 B.C.—the country split up. One dynasty ruled at Tanis in Lower Egypt, another at Thebes in Upper Egypt, while Nubia and Kush combined to become an independent, separate state with its capital in Napata. About 751 B.C. Pianky, a Kushite prince, marched from Napata at the head of Nubian and Kushite troops to conquer Egypt in the name of order and orthodoxy. He met no united resistance in Egypt. By this move he succeeded in bringing the country, once more, under the rule of a single pharaoh and originated the Twenty-fifth Dynasty. The Kushite pharaohs of this dynasty revived Egyptian arts and crafts, drawing their inspiration mainly from the Egyptian culture of the Middle Kingdom period. They erected many buildings, especially at Thebes, and encouraged a study of the past. The intrigues of Taharqa, fourth ruler of the dynasty, however, resulted in an invasion of Egypt by Assyrians about 670 B.C. The Assyrians used iron weapons, and although iron was not unknown in Egypt at this time, it was not yet in general use. With the Assyrian invasion, however, the Iron Age came to Egypt. Thebes was sacked and Taharqa's successor, Tanwetamani, was driven into his Kushite domains.

The Psammetichos, a Lower Egyptian family from Sais, mounted a successful resistance against the Assyrians, ultimately drove them out and originated the Twenty-sixth Dynasty. Their success also reduced the influence of the powerful Libyan military caste. This dynasty built a strong fleet, encouraged trade, and ruled as merchant princes. It was the second ruler of this line, Necho II, who to further trade commenced the cutting of a canal from the Nile to the Red Sea and sent sailors to circumnavigate Africa. Reporting this voyage, Herodotus, using the name Libya to mean Africa, as the Greeks did, says, "Libya is evidently surrounded by water (apart from its junction with Asia). The Egyptian ruler Necho was the first to prove this, so far as we know. After he [Necho] had abandoned the construction of the canal from the Nile to the Arabian Gulf [an undertaking completed by Darius about a century later], he despatched Phoenicians in ships with instructions to sail back to Egypt by way of the Pillars of Hercules [the Straits of Gibraltar]. They sailed southwards from the Erythraean Sea and when autumn came they disembarked on whatever coast of Libya they happened to have reached, sowed their seed and awaited the harvest. Then they reaped the corn and put to sea again. In the third year they rounded the Pillars of Hercules and reached Egypt with a report which may be credible to some but not to me, that as they sailed round Libya they had the sun to their right." [8]

About 525 B.C. however, the Persian Cambyses was able to invade and conquer Egypt. The Persians ruled the country for two centuries before being overthrown, with Greek aid, by Amyrteos of Sais in Lower Egypt. In 404 B.C. Amyrteos originated the Twenty-eighth Dynasty which, together with the Twenty-ninth and Thirtieth provided Ancient Egypt not only with a recrudescence of native arts but also with the last fifty years of rule by native pharoahs. After this from 341 B.C., Persian kings, Greek Ptolemies, and Roman emperors ruled Egypt.

In 332 B.C., Alexander the Great of Macedonia, seeking to conquer the world, climaxed his victories by taking Egypt and establishing his capital at Alexandria. Alexander's army had many black soldiers the most illustrious of whom was Clitus, son of his nurse, Dropsica. Alexander made Clitus king of Bactria and commander of his cavalry.

Ten years later, Alexander died and Ptolemy, one of his generals, established a dynasty that ruled Egypt until it was overthrown by Rome in 33 B.C. The earliest Ptolemies were white but as time went on, they intermarried with Egytians and became more and more Negroid, as Rogers observed, "The Negro strain in Alexander II is apparent and still more so in Ptolemy XIII, the flute-playing father of the most celebrated of the Cleopatras. Ptolemy's mother was a slave. Cleopatra herself is known through tradition as having been of tawny, or mulatto colour." [9]

The Ptolemies amassed wealth taxing the agricultural wealth of the Nile Valley and the luxury trade between Asia and Europe. Greeks migrated to Egypt and when they came, "Egypt was turned into a teacher of the world; its culture spread. Alexander and the Caesars sat at its feet." [10]

The Greeks delved into Egyptian literature and "when we speak of the literature of a nation, we are not thinking of inscriptions graven on obelisks and triumphal arches. We mean such literatures as may be stored in a library and possessed by individuals. In a word, we mean books—books, whether in the form of clay cylinders, of papyrus rolls, or any other portable material. The Egyptians were the first people of the ancient world who had a literature of this kind; who wrote books and read books; who possessed books, and loved them. And their literature, which grew, and flourished, and decayed with the language in which it was written, was of the most varied character, scientific, secular, and religious. It comprised moral and educational treasures; state-papers, works on geometry, medicine, astronomy, and magic; travel tales, fables, heroic poems, love-songs, and essays in the form of letters; hymns, dirges, rituals, and last, but not least, that extraordinary collection of prayers, invocations, and religious formulae known as the Book of the Dead. Some of these writings are older than the pyramids; some are as recent as the time when Egypt had fallen from her high estate and become a Roman province. Between these two extremes lie more than five thousand years." [11] Records indicate that by 240 B.C. the city of Alexandria had around four hundred and ninety thousand rolls of manuscript in its library.

From Africans in Egypt the Greeks learned mathematics. "The Mathematics," Rollin tells us, "hold the first place among the sciences, because they alone are founded upon infallible demonstrations. And this undoubtedly gave them their name. For *Mathesis* in Greek signifies science. . . . The Egyptians are said to have invented it on account of the innundations of the Nile. For that river carrying away the landmarks every year, and lessening some estates to enlarge others, the Egyptians were obliged to measure their country often, and for that purpose to contrive a method and art, which was the origin and beginning of geometry . . . it passed from Egypt to Greece, and Thales of Miletus is believed to have carried it thither at his return from his travels." [12]

Confirming the view that Africans taught the Greeks mathematics, Wilkinson says, "I have also shown that Herodotus and others ascribe the origin of geometry to the Egyptians, but the period when it commenced is uncertain. Anticlides pretends that Moeris was the first to lay down the elements of that science, which he says was perfected by Pythagoras; but the latter observation is merely the result of the vanity of the Greeks, which claimed for their countrymen (as in the case of Thales, and other instances) the credit of enlightening a people on the very subject which they had visited Egypt for the purpose of studying." [13] Thus even the Greeks were not above traveling to Egypt, kneeling at the feet of African masters, learning something, and then claiming to have invented it themselves.

When Greece came under the domination of Rome the greatest prize of the new empire was Africa: North Africa, from Ceuta on the Strait of Gibraltar, to the Red Sea, and the best part of this rich prize was Egypt. If Caesar conquered Egypt, Cleopatra VII, Queen of Egypt conquered Caesar. "Cleopatra VII, Queen of Egypt has come down to us through twenty centuries as the perfect example of the seductive art in women; with her beauty, learning, and culture she fascinated and held two masters of the world. The first, Julius Caesar, was debonair, elegant in manners and movement, a great swimmer, a swordsman, a beloved ruler, an orator. . . . In the arts of love, he was unique, excelling in licentiousness whether his amour was with women or young men. For any woman to hold him longer than a day was exceedingly difficult. . . . The second, Caesar's friend and successor, Mark Anthony, . . . Cleopatra held enslaved. She, on her side, was perhaps the most captivating, the most learned, and the most witty. It is said that she spoke Greek, Egyptian, Latin, Ethiopian, Hebrew, Arabic, Syrian, fluently as well as several African dialects.

". . . Caesar, who had arrived with a large army, ordered both Cleopatra and Ptolemy to yield. Ptolemy obeyed; Cleopatra thought the matter over. She had heard much of Caesar. . . . But to her people Rome was a land of barbarians. Still she could use him to further her ambitions. He had an army.

"She decided to call on him. . . . Then an idea occurred to her; calling a trusted slave, she bade him wrap her up in a silken covering, place a magnificent carpet over that . . . and take it as a present for Caesar.

"Caesar received her with his usual politeness. . . . Since his arrival he had been deluged with presents. . . . He made the slave undo the bundle. Then he gasped as the silken covering stirred and a laughing browned-skinned girl, with crinky hair, and a voluptuous figure, nude to the waist stood before him. In her eyes was a gleam that made him forget his fifty-four years. She addressed him in fluent Latin in a voice full of music; instinct told him that into his surfeited life had come at last the one woman. He ordered his attendants from the room and from then on began to lead the gayest of lives."[14] Yet we have been led to think of Cleopatra as an Elizabeth Taylor and not what she really was—"a soul sister."

In our cursory examination of four thousand years of Egyptian history, we have seen how Fayum and Khartoum received influences from an African dispersal center in the west, how Egypt and her neighbors on the African continent as well as in the Middle East, remained accessible to, and influenced by, one another in spite of the great barrier of desert conditions and the Sudd. We have seen the important role of southerners from Upper Egypt, the Ethiopia of biblical times. Nubia and Kush in the modern Sudan played an important part in the Egyptian state, as did Libya. We have seen that it was from the south, that Menes, the first king who united Upper and Lower Egypt came. Again and again it was a pharaoh from the south who reunited Egypt after the first Intermediate period of anarchy, after the Second Intermediate period caused by Hyksos rule, and in the Late period when the country had virtually split into three states. We have seen the trading and military contacts that Egypt maintained with her neighbors, the Nubians or Ethiopians in the south, Libyans in the west, and non-Africans in the northeast. In all this, we have seen nothing to justify the view, popular among white men, that Egyptian civilization was anything other than African, a view which has been responsible for the exclusion of the civilization of Egypt from African history and the use of that absurd phrase *Afrique Noir* ("Black Africa"), a phrase whose absurdity can only be equaled by talk of a "White France." While it cannot be denied that Egyptian civilization was refreshed and invigorated by new ideas, received from time to time, as a result of its contacts with the Middle East and Asia, there can be no doubt that its inspiration and character, remained rooted firmly in the dark fertile soil of Africa.

As W. E. B. DuBois wrote over a quarter of a century ago: "If we follow inherent probability, ancient testimony and legend, this would seem to have been the history of northeast Africa:

"In Ethiopia the sunrise of human culture took place spreading down into the Nile valley.

"Ethiopia, land of the blacks, was the cradle of Egyptian civilization.

"Beyond Ethiopia, in Central and South Africa, lay the gold of Ophir and the rich trade of Punt on which the prosperity of Egypt largely depended.

"Egypt brought slaves from black Africa as she did from Europe and Asia. But she also brought citizens and leaders from black Africa.

"When Egypt conquered Asia, she used black soldiers to a wide extent.

"When Asia overwhelmed Egypt, Egypt sought refuge in Ethiopia as a child returns to its mother, and Ethiopia then for centuries dominated Egypt and successfully invaded Asia.

"Neither Greece, Rome, nor Islam succeeded in conquering Ethiopia, although they pushed her back and shut her up in East and Central Africa, and hindered all contact between her people and the world until the day of imperialism." [15]

NOTES

1. Aldred, *Egyptians,* pp. 78-82.
2. Aldred, *Egyptians,* p. 83.
3. Earl Sweeting, *African History* (New York: Earl Sweeting, n.d.), pamphlet, n. fols.
4. Aldred, *Egyptians,* pp. 123-24.
5. Aldred, *Egyptians,* p. 127.
6. Aldred, *Egyptians,* p. 136.
7. Aldred, *Egyptians,* p. 138.
8. Herodotus as quoted by Zoe Marsh in *East Africa Through Contemporary Records,* 3rd ed. (New York: Cambridge University Press, 1961), p. 2.
9. Rogers as quoted by DuBois in *World and Africa,* p. 140.
10. DuBois, *World and Africa,* p. 126.
11. Sweeting, *African History.*
12. Charles Rollin, *Ancient History of the Egyptians,* Vol. II (Baltimore: Cushing and Jewett, 1820), p. 595.
13. J. G. Wilkinson, *A History of the Ancient Egyptians,* Vol. II (New York: Harper & Brothers, 1854), p. 319.
14. Rogers as cited by Sweeting in *African History.*
15. DuBois, *World and Africa,* p. 117.

CHAPTER 6
Nubia

The state of Egypt lay along the Nile, stretching from the delta on the Mediterranean coast to a point below the first cataract. The land south of this point was known as Nubia and consisted of two provinces, Wiwat in the north and Kush in the south. There were times when some areas of Nubia were part of, or ruled by, Egypt. Nubia was known as Ethiopia, "land of the blacks," to ancient Greeks and throughout biblical times.

"Of all the classical countries Ethiopia was the most romantic and the most remote," Winwood Reade tells us. "It was situated, according to the Greeks, on the extreme limits of the world; its inhabitants were the most just of men, and Jupiter dined with them twice a year. They bathed in the waters of a violet-scented spring, which endowed them with long life, noble bodies, and glossy skins. They chained their prisoners with golden fetters; they had bows which none but themselves could bend. It is certain that Ethiopia took its place among the powers of the ancient world. It is mentioned in Jewish records and in the Assyrian cuneiform inscriptions." [1]

After visiting Egypt about 450 B.C., Herodotus reported: "The furthest inhabited country towards the south west is Ethiopia. Here gold is found in great abundance, and huge elephants, and ebony and all sorts of trees growing wild. The men, too, are the tallest in the world, the best looking and the longest lived." [2]

Many black people figure prominently in classical Greek lore. Memmon, king of Ethiopia is remembered as leader of one of the great armies that besieged Troy. Another black man, "Eurybiates in whose large soul/Ulysses viewed an image of his own," is mentioned in Homeric legends. The illustrious Greek storyteller, Aesop, is described as an African slave, with a "flat nose, with lips thick and pendulous and a black skin from which he contracted his name Aesop, being the same as Ethiop." [3] Sappho the poetess was also black. The mythical Hercules was often represented as a black man with curly hair. "In the eyes of the Greeks a thousand years B.C. and even in the age of Pericles," says DuBois, "black Africans were considered equal to though different from Greeks, and superior to Europeans and Asiatic barbarians." [4] There was, thus, no idea of superiority based on skin color.

The population of Nubia, more than that of Egypt where there were some people of Caucasian stock, was Negroid and its civilization essentially African. Yet many white scholars who have written about these blackest of men and their brilliant civilization, have felt it necessary to warn their readers that these people were not Negroes and, as in the case of Egypt, to ascribe their achievements to Hamites. "Throughout its long period as an Egyptian colony, and also during the first two or three centuries of its independent existence," write Oliver and Fage in their widely used textbook, "Kush like Egypt, was basically a country of white Caucasians." [5]
In the following pages, Nubians are black people.

The earliest Nubians settled along the Nile, above the first cataract, practicing a culture not unlike that of Pre-Dynastic Egypt. They were joined, from time to time, by people the Sahara was discharging in its gradual desiccation. As we have seen, those in the northern province were, more often than not, involved in Egyptian trade and wars. As a matter of fact, the Nubians or Ethiopians, as they were called, considered themselves the ancestors of Egyptians and believed Egyptian laws and customs to be of Ethiopian origin, as one of the ancient writers, Diodorus Siculus, testified: "The Ethiopians say that Egyptians are one of their colonies brought under Egypt by Osiris. They even pretend that at the beginning of the world that country was only a sea, but that the Nile, carrying bits of soil in its floods from Ethiopia, finally filled it in and made it part of the continent. . . . They add that it is from them, as the authors and ancestors of Egypt, that the Egyptians received the greatest part of their laws. It is from them [the Ethiopians] that they [the Egyptians] learned to honor their kings as gods and to bury their dead with such pomp. Sculpture and writing were born in the land of the Ethiopians. . . . The Ethiopians also give other proof of their antiquity over Egyptians, but it is not necessary to repeat it all here." [6]

During the Middle Kingdom, Sesostris I subjugated Wiwat and parts of Kush and built a line of forts all the way to Semna and installed garrisons in the land beyond Kerma above the third cataract. His successors continued this policy of attention to Nubia, to such an extent that Sesostris III became so closely identified with the region that in later years he was worshiped as a god there.

In the Second Intermediate period during which Hyksos ruled Egypt, Nubians stormed and destroyed the formidable fortresses built by the pharaohs of the Twelfth Dynasty. In this task they may have been supported by the Hyksos because when an independent state of Nubia emerged, extending from Elephantine near the first cataract to the modern Sudan, it was under a prince of Kush in alliance with the Hyksos.

At the beginning of the New Kingdom, the expulsion of the Hyksos and the rise of Ahmosis in 1570 B.C., brought an end to Nubian independence. Both the provinces of Wiwat and Kush fell under Egyptian control and Nubia was once more ruled by an Egyptian viceroy titled the "King's Son of Kush," who resided at Napata. Thutmos I extended the southern boundary of Egypt as far as Kurgus, between the fourth and fifth cataracts and may have reached modern Khartoum. Irrigation works were improved, temples were built, and trading expeditions sent to Punt. The country prospered until the Late Kingdom period. When Egypt split into three states ruled from Tanis, Thebes, and Napata, about 1075 B.C. Nubia became independent once more.

Because its chiefs controlled the sources of Nubian gold in the south, the province of Kush became predominant in the country's affairs, and in 751 B.C., Pianky, a Kushite prince, succeeded in leading a Nubian force against Egypt and uniting the country under his rule as the pharaoh. Napata became the capital of Egypt. Nubia had thus become a world power ruling from the Mediterranean to the borders of modern Ethiopia or even Uganda. The Kushite dynasty lasted about a century. It revived Egyptian arts and crafts, encouraged a study of the past, and the worship of Amunre. It erected many buildings particularly at Thebes.

In Nubia, however, the people continued to live very much as they had done before their conquest of Egypt, although the court at Napata became very Egyptianized in its manners, style, architecture, literature, and rites. In spite of this, Nubian culture and people remained basically Nubian.

Kushite rule over Egypt was terminated by Assyrians who invaded the country in 666 B.C. using iron weapons. The Kushite pharaoh, Tanwetamani, was driven back to his domains in Kush. Prior to the Assyrian invasion, iron was not in general use in Egypt even though it had been known for centuries. Iron weapons, like daggers, were prized only as curiosities. With the Assyrian invasion of Egypt, however, the Iron Age dawned on Africa.

In the province of Kush, about a hundred miles north of Khartoum, lay Meroe, a center with large deposits of good iron ore, wood for fuel, plentiful rainfall, rich valleys for cultivating crops and pasturing animals. As the demand for iron spread throughout Africa, Meroe grew steadily until it became one of the largest iron-mining centers of the ancient world. Gradually, Napata yielded its political and economic importance to Meroe. By 590 B.C., the royal residence had been transferred there, though Napata continued to be an important religious center. In Meroe there developed a civilization that was nationalistic, self-conscious, and deliberately Kushite in character.

The people of Meroe worshiped gods and practiced rituals primarily indigenous to Kush. While they continued to use Egyptian hieroglyphs for inscriptions in their temples, they also wrote their own language in alphabetic script which, to this day, is not understood by anyone. They developed their own style of painting pottery, built palaces and temples, excelled in metal manufacture and organized trade, not only with neighbors on the African continent but also with countries as remote as India and China.

Perhaps Meroe's greatest contribution to African civilization was as the prime source of iron ore. To this day, a dozen huge slag heaps bear silent testimony to the immense mining operations that took place there five centuries before the birth of Christ. It was from Meroe that the knowledge of ironworking gradually diffused to other parts of Africa, spreading, perhaps, westward to Lake Chad and then southeastward towards East Africa, or diffusing directly to East Africa by a route east of the Sudd and along the foothills of present-day Ethiopia. By the first century of the present era, Africans as far afield as the Zambezi and Limpopo rivers were using iron tools and weapons.

Twenty-four kings are known to have reigned at Meroe between 593 B.C. and 220 B.C. They were not unknown to ancient writers for Herodotus reported how "Cambyses' spies went to the Ethiopian King with various gifts, a purple robe, a gold necklace, a jar of wine, and other things, but that the king of Meroe was not deceived. Instead, he stressed how powerful his country was, and gave the spies a bow which he said the Persian King could try to draw though he doubted if he would succeed. He told them of the long life of his people who were said to live for 120 years owing to their diet of boiled meat and milk. They were shown the 'Table of the Sun' [i.e,. a meadow on the outskirts of Meroe which was always full of meat, replenished at night, so that whoever came there might eat of it during the day] and other wonders and then returned to their Persian master. On their return, Cambyses set out with his army to invade Ethiopia but found the harshness of the country such that he turned back before he ever reached the capital." [7]

"There are legends of the visit of Alexander the Great to Candace, Queen of Meroe," DuBois tells us. "Fabulous perhaps, but they show her fame. It is said that Candace would not let Alexander enter Ethiopia. . . . She sent him gold, maidens, parrots, sphinxes, and a crown of emeralds and pearls. She ruled eighty tribes who were ready to punish those who attacked her." [8] Another reference to Candace is found in the book of Acts (8:27-39) which records that a eunuch of great authority under Candace, Queen of Ethiopia, returning from Jerusalem was sitting in a chariot and reading from the prophet Isaiah when Philip joined him. From the baptism of this man by Philip, it could be claimed that the Nubians were the first Christians in Africa even though the author of the Acts of the Apostles does not say the eunuch converted anyone else. Nubia, in fact, became Christian two centuries after Ethiopia had embraced the faith.

Because of several other such references by ancient writers, it was thought for a long time that Candace was the name of a queen, but as Shinnie tells us, "We now know from a study of the Meroitic sources that it was not a name but a title whose meaning is not absolutely clear, but is something like 'Queen Mother' or 'Queen.'" And he goes on to explain that in spite of the view, widely held in the Roman Empire, that Meroe, or Ethiopia, was ruled by a queen, "we know that the normal ruler was a man, but women played an important part and are frequently shown on the temple and funerary chapel reliefs. This story that Meroe was ruled by a queen must reflect the importance that attached to queens in Meroitic society," [9] which was, in fact, matrilineal and showed a great deal of respect for women.

Until the day scholars are able to read and understand the Meroitic script, our knowledge of Nubia will continue to be based, not on what Nubians wrote about themselves, but on what others said about them. Whatever may be hidden in their scrolls, there can be no doubt that Nubia bequeathed to the world an incomparable civilization. It gave to most of Africa the iron hoe and spear. The hoe revolutionized agriculture, increased both production and population. The spear facilitated the development of centralized authority and the growth of powerful states in the period known in Europe as the Middle Ages. As Shinnie says, "Whatever the role of Meroe may have been in the spread of culture among its neighbours, its own history stands as a major landmark of ancient Africa. Although much was owed to outside influences . . . Meroe was an African civilization, firmly based on African soil, and developed by an African population. That an urban, civilized, and literate state existed deep in the African continent and lasted nearly a thousand years in itself constitutes an achievement of outstanding importance." [10]

By A.D. 350 Meroe had become part of Axum, the forerunner of modern Ethiopia. Its contribution to African civilization, as Napata, or as Nubia, can be listed: first, the important part Nubians played in and through Egypt, for Nubians were not only the ancestors of Egyptians but continued to play a significant, and at times decisive, role in the affairs of Egypt; second, the contacts Nubians maintained through trade, with India, China, and other states in Africa. And third, the diffusion and dissemination of iron and the knowledge of ironworking to other parts of Africa.

NOTES

1. Reade as quoted by DuBois in *World and Africa,* pp. 120-21.
2. Quoted by Davidson in *Lost Cities of Africa* (Boston: Little, Brown, 1970), p. 29.
3. Rogers as quoted by DuBois in *World and Africa,* pp. 25-30.
4. DuBois, *World and Africa,* p. 119.
5. Roland Oliver and J. D. Fage, *A History of Africa* (New York: Penguin Books, 1966), p. 40.
6. As cited by Diop in "Negro Nations," p. 12.
7. P. L. Shinnie, *Meroe,* (New York: Praeger, 1966), p. 16.
8. DuBois, *World and Africa,* p. 140.
9. Shinnie, *Meroe,* pp. 19, 21.
10. Shinnie, *Meroe,* p. 169.

CHAPTER 7
Ethiopia

Ethiopia is among the oldest kingdoms in the world. It was in existence centuries before the birth of Christ. Its capital, originally at Axum, or Aksum, in Tigré, was gradually moved south; first to Gondar in Amhara north of Lake Tana, and then to Addis Ababa in Shoa, where it still stands. In the days when Axum was the center of the kingdom, the name Ethiopia designated Nubia. In the fourteenth century, when the Bible was translated from Greek into one of the country's native languages called Ge'ez, the translators used the name Ethiopia in place of Axum, and gradually the name Ethiopia was applied to the land of the descendants of Axum. The Arabs called the land Habashat, from which Abyssinia is derived. This was the name used in Anglo-Saxon countries, while the Latin countries called it Ethiopia. In 1941, however, Emperor Haile Selassie decreed that the country should, henceforth, be known only as Ethiopia.

About a hundred and seventy miles from Axum, on the coast of the Red Sea, lay the important port of Adulis through which Axum was in contact with countries of the Orient. Separated only by a narrow strip of water from the Yemen in Arabia, Africans from Axum crossed the Red Sea into Arabia, for social, economic, political, military, and other reasons; while Arabians came to Axum. There was consequently an intermingling of peoples and cultures. So, we find groups in Africa which claim to have come orignally from Arabia, just as there are people in Arabia whose ancestors can be traced to the African mainland. Among the earliest inhabitants of present-day Ethiopia, however, are the Watta, or Wayto, and the Sanye, or Ariangulo, on the coast.

An interesting feature of Ethiopian history is the wealth of strong, centuries-old tradition, some of which is recorded in the *Kebra Nagast,* or "Glory of the King," which Ethiopians treasure as history.

Ethiopian legend traces the origin of their royal house to King Solomon. An account of these events usually follows the same general pattern:

In the days when Solomon was building the temple at Jerusalem he sent messages to all the merchants in all parts of the world requesting them to bring him what he required and promised gold and silver in payment. Solomon's message reached Tamrin, the merchant of Makeda, Queen of Ethiopia. He set out for Jerusalem bringing gold and sapphires and wood of ebony so dark and strong worms could not harm it. The splendor and wealth of Solomon's kingdom and the wisdom of the king himself greatly impressed Tamrin, and he brought back a marvelous report to the queen. At once the queen determined to pay Solomon a visit. She set out on her journey accompanied by a great caravan of 797 camels and mules and asses all bearing rich gifts. After many days they arrived at Jerusalem, and Makeda presented herself to the king. Solomon made her welcome, arranging banquets and entertainments in her honor, and providing her with eleven changes of raiment each day. More than all this wealth and display, it was the wisdom with which Solomon directed the affairs of his kingdom and his knowledge in matters of religion which stirred the queen. Before long she turned away from the worship of the sun and the moon and the stars and began to worship the God of Israel. But at last the day came when she must return and look to her kingdom, and she made her intention known to the king. Then Solomon said in his heart, "A woman of such splendid beauty has come to me from the ends of the earth. Surely God will give me seed in her?"

So Solomon set about to achieve his purpose. He invited the queen to a farewell feast, but all the dishes set before the queen were full of pepper and spices to make her crave water. When the night was far spent, Solomon invited the queen to sleep in his palace. The queen hesitated for she was a virgin, but she finally consented after exacting the king's oath not to take her by force.

The king agreed and demanded that she also make a promise; not to take by force anything in the palace. She readily agreed to such a simple requirement only protesting at being thought a thief. Beds were prepared for the royal pair, and they retired. Presently the queen fell asleep but soon awoke with a burning thirst. King Solomon had instructed that a jar of water be placed in the center of the room, and when the queen saw it she longed to quench her thirst. She crept silently out of her bed so as not to awaken the king, but this was what Solomon had been waiting for. He leapt out and seized her arm, saying, "You have broken your oath not to take anything from my palace."

The queen stammered and protested that the oath could not possibly apply to water. To this King Solomon answered that nothing on earth was more precious than water. The queen admitted that she was wrong, but begged that she might drink. This released Solomon from his oath. He took the queen into his bed and worked his will on her.

Later the king had a dream in which the sun descended from heaven into the land of Judah, and presently it moved on to Ethiopia, shining brightly. It came again into Judah, but the Jews tried to destroy it and drive it away. So the sun left Judah and went to Ethiopia and Rome.

At the departure of the queen Solomon gave her a ring and said, "If a son is born to you, give him this ring and send him to me." Then the queen departed to her own land, and in due time she bore a son, and she named him Menelik.

When Menelik had grown to be a man, he wished to go to his father. So the queen summoned Tamrin the merchant, and sent him forth with a great retinue to accompany Menelik on his journey. Tamrin had instructions to ask that Solomon anoint Menelik and make a law providing that none but the male heirs of Menelik should sit on the throne of Ethiopia. So Menelik journeyed to the land of Judah, and as he passed through Gaza the people came to meet him hailing him with cries, "The King comes!" But some said, "This cannot be the king, he is in Jerusalem."

Then the messengers were sent to Jerusalem, and when they found King Solomon they said to him, "O king, one has come to our land who resembles thee in every feature." And Solomon asked where the stranger had come from. "We did not ask him, but from his followers we learned that they come from Ethiopia." At this King Solomon rejoiced in his heart, for though he had many wives, he had only one son, Rehoboam, a boy of seven years. So he summoned Menelik to Jerusalem, and received the ring from his hand, but Solomon said, "What need is there of the ring? Without a sign I know that you are my son."

Then Tamrin the merchant came forward to deliver the message from the queen. Solomon tried to persuade Menelik to stay and rule in Israel, but Menelik would not. Then King Solomon anointed Menelik with the holy oil of kingship and gave him the name of David. Also he made a law that henceforth only the male descendants of Menelik should reign in Ethiopia. And Zadok the high priest taught him all the law of Israel and pronounced on him the blessings if he should keep it and the curses if he should leave it. And Menelik begged Solomon to give him a piece of the fringe from the covering of the Ark of the Covenant, for the queen had requested such a relic that the Ethiopians might reverence it. Solomon promised to grant this wish. Next, Solomon summoned his counselors and chief officers and said, "My firstborn son goes to rule in Ethiopia. You also are to send your firstborn sons to be his counselors and officers." And they obeyed the king's command.

But when the time came to set forth, the sons of the nobles of Israel were sorrowful at leaving their native land, and they secretly reviled Solomon. Their greatest sorrow was that they must leave the Lady of Zion, which is, the Ark of the Covenant. Then Azariah, son of Zadok the high priest, thought of a plan, and binding the others to silence he revealed it to them. When they heard it they rejoiced greatly. Each man gave Azariah ten pieces of silver, and he went to a carpenter and instructed him to build a raft for their journey across the sea, one they could use if the ship should sink. And he gave to the carpenter the measurements which were the same as those of the Ark of the Covenant.

The night before they were to depart, Azariah took the raft, which was in every way like the Ark, and went to the temple and stole into the sanctuary, the angel of the Lord opening the doors for him. Once inside he took the Ark and put the raft in its place. Then he covered the raft with the three coverings belonging to the Ark so that none could see the change.

The next day Solomon sent Zadok to fetch the outer covering of the Ark and bring it as a present for Menelik. The young king rejoiced in the gift. Then Menelik and the sons of the nobles of Israel set out for Ethiopia with a great caravan of wagons. And the wagons were set up above the ground almost a cubit, so they could speed as quickly as eagles, and in one day they went a thirteen-days' journey.

When they came to the land of Egypt the sons of the nobles of Israel revealed to Menelik how they had brought the Ark with them. At this news Menelik was filled with joy, and he skipped and danced like a young ram before the Ark. Then the caravan moved on and came to Ethiopia. In Ethiopia Menelik ruled and his sons after him, and the sons of the nobles of Israel and their sons after them were the counselors and officers of the kingdom.

After Menelik departed Solomon's heart was heavy. He told Zadok of the dream that he had dreamed on the night that he lay with the Queen of Ethiopia. Zadok was smitten with fear and said, "O that you had told me of this dream before, for I fear that the Lady of Zion is gone from us." And he went into the sanctuary and took off the two under coverings, and he saw the raft which Azariah his son had caused to be made. Then Zadok wept and beat his breast and fell down in a swoon. Another priest who saw all came and brought word to Solomon. And Solomon arose with his host and marched into Egypt, and the king questioned the Egyptians about when the Ethiopians had passed that way. And they answered that it was many days since they had passed. So Solomon despaired of pursuing them and lamented greatly. But the king had a dream in which a spirit comforted him saying, "The Lady of Zion has not been given to strangers but to thine own firstborn son." So Solomon was comforted and returned to Jerusalem, but he charged his counselors and officers to tell no one that the Ark of the Covenant was missing. So the children of Israel knew nothing of this matter.

Now it chanced that Balthazar, king of Rome, had three daughters but no son. So he asked King Solomon to send one of his sons to marry one of the princesses and rule the Kingdom of Rome. And so the prophecy was fulfilled that the seed of David and Solomon should rule over all the world.

And there was also another prophecy that the king of Rome and the king of Ethiopia should rule the whole world, to the east and the west, the north and the south, and their kingdoms should meet in Jerusalem. This prophecy was fulfilled in the latter days, when the Jews lost their birthright by slaying the Son of God, and Justin, king of Rome, and Kaleb, king of Ethiopia, destroyed Judah. Next, the kings of Rome lost their birthright by following after the heresies of Arius and Nestorius, abandoning the true faith. And so it came about that the kings of Ethiopia, the descendants of the first-born son of Solomon, alone are the heirs of the promises of God.

The *Kebra Nagast,* in which the official version of this legend is recorded, is believed to have been written at the beginning of the fourteenth century. The royal copy came to be regarded with such reverence that when, in 1868, Sir Robert Napier carried it off to England, Emperor John IV wrote to Lord Grenville in 1872, "There is a book called *Kebra Nagast* which contains the law of the whole of Ethiopia and the names of the princes and churches and provinces are in the book. I pray you will find out who has this book and send it to me, for in my country my people will not obey my orders without it." [1] The British Museum returned the book to the king.

The legend itself is thought to have originated between the sixth century and the beginning of the second millennium of the Christian era. It had already taken root in the eleventh century when Ethiopia was ruled by the Zague dynasty. It was later translated into Ge'ez under the auspices of the restored Solomonian line.

The legend performs an important function in Ethiopian society and state, for it portrays Ethiopians as a chosen people of ancient origin, heirs to the promises God gave to Abraham, Isaac, and Jacob. Their royal house, with its kinship to Christ, has a divine right to the throne, and revolt against that throne is an act of sacrilege. This has given the kingdom three thousand years of stability and continuity. This confidence in themselves as a chosen people and custodians of the Ark of the Covenant has sustained the Ethiopians and enabled them to uphold the Christian faith and to face the armies of their enemies with the certainty that God is on their side.

In the hands of foreign writers Ethiopia's history loses some of its legendary quality. According to some sources, in the third century B.C., the Ptolemaic rulers of Egypt ordered some Greek sailors to explore the west coast of the Red Sea, with the object of opening up trade. It is in the *Periplus of the Erythrean Sea:* A Guide to Sailors of the Ocean, from the Coast of Africa to the Utmost Bounds of the East, however, that Axum is first mentioned. The *Periplus* was written between A.D. 50 and 60 by a Greek merchant whose name is unknown. It is an account of the commerce carried on along the Red Sea, along the coast of Africa, and on to the East Indies at a time when Egypt was a province of the Roman Empire.

The author of this travel guide describes the port of Adulis and says that the capital city of Axum lay eight-days' journey inland. He also tells us that the country was under King Zoscales whom he described as "a covetous and grasping man but otherwise noble and imbued with Greek education."[2] All the ivory, from as far afield as beyond the Nile, he reports, was carried to Adulis, from where it was exported to the Roman Empire. King Zoscales is the earliest king of Axum about whom we know anything.

Axum is also mentioned in the *Christian Cosmography* of Cosmas, a merchant who sailed the waters of the Red Sea and the Indian Ocean early in the sixth century. When retired, Cosmas entered a monastery and wrote this book. He relates how, while he was on a visit to Adulis, the king of Axum, whose name is not given, ordered the governor of Adulis to prepare copies of two ancient Greek inscriptions in the city. The governor requested Cosmas to do the work for him, and so Cosmas made two copies of each inscription. One was sent to the king, but the other he kept and subsequently published in his *Christian Cosmography*. One inscription recorded the activities of the Greek sailors sent to explore the coast by the Ptolemaic ruler of Egypt in the third century B.C. In the other, a king of Axum, after recounting his numerous victorious military campaigns, concluded:

"Of the kings that went before me I am the first and only one to have subdued all these peoples by the grace granted to me by my mighty Ares, who also begat me. It is through him that I have subdued all the peoples that border upon my empire, to the east as far as the land of perfumes, to the west as far as the land of

Ethiopia and Sasu. Some I fought myself, against others I sent my armies. When I established peace in the lands subject to me I came to Adulis to sacrifice on behalf of those who voyage on the sea to Zeus, Ares, and Poseidon. Having assembled all my armies I have set up here this throne and have consecrated it to Ares in the twenty-seventh year of my reign."[3]

It is believed this inscription recounts the exploits of Aphilas, a king of Axum who lived in the third century A.D. and whose coins are still extant. It is noteworthy that the king claims to have subdued all the people that border upon his empire. The "land of perfumes" was a reference to the Yemen in Arabia, parts of which were known as frankincense country. This is an example of the contacts between the regions which had already been going on for centuries. Noteworthy, also, is the fact that the king says he subdued people to the west as far as Ethiopia. Obviously, the people of Axum did not consider themselves Ethiopians because at this time the name referred to Nubia. It is also important to note that the king attributes his victories, not to the God of Abraham or to Christ but to a traditional god Ares. The ancestors of present-day Ethiopians were, at that time, neither Ethiopians nor Christians.

The next king of Axum about whom there is any information is Aezanes who reigned from about 325 to 375. Aezanes left a number of inscriptions in Greek, Ge'ez, and the Yemen language, Sabaean. The last of these inscriptions was once thought to be connected with the defeat of Meroe by an Axumite army. It is now believed that by this time Meroe had already succumbed to Axum and that the campaign the inscription records was to put down a revolt by the Noba, or Nubians, who were in possession of the island of Meroe. This inscription begins:

"Through the might of the Lord of Heaven, who is victorious in Heaven and on earth over all! Aezanes, the son of Ella-Amida, of the tribe Halen, the King of Aksum and Himyar and of Raidan and of Saba and of Salhen and of Siyamo and of Bega and of Kasu, the King of Kings, the son of Ella-Amida, who will not be defeated by the enemy. Through the might of the Lord of Heaven, who has created me, the Lord of All by whom the King is beloved, who will not be defeated by the enemy, no foe shall stand before me and behind me no foe shall follow."[4]

Aezanes, like his predecessor Aphilas, claims Himyar and Saba in the Yemen as part of his dominions, showing once more how this whole area was a cultural unit. The most significant thing about Aezanes' last inscription, however, is that his victories are no longer ascribed, as in the earlier ones, to Ares or any other god but to the "might of the Lord of Heaven," victorious in Heaven and on earth over all! Obviously, Aezanes had become a Christian toward the end of his reign, and his inscriptions are probably the earliest Christian documents of modern Ethiopia.

How did Aezanes become a Christian? On this issue, there is some difference between Ethiopian tradition and the writing of non-Ethiopians. According to Ethiopian tradition, the conversion of their country to Christianity began with the conversion of the eunuch by Philip recorded in the Acts of the Apostles.

Ethiopian tradition, recorded in 1520 by Father Francisco Alvarez, goes on to say that "here was fulfilled the prophecy which David spoke: 'Ethiopia shall arise and stretch forth her hands to God.' So they say they were the first Christians in the world. The eunuch at once set out very joyfully for Ethiopia, where was the house of his mistress, and converted her and all her household, and baptized them in consequence of what he related to them. And the queen caused all her kingdom, beginning with a kingdom which is now called the kingdom of Buno, to be baptized. This Buno is toward the east from the town of Aksum in the kingdom of the Barnagais, and it is now two lordships. In this town of Aksum, where she became Christian, she built a very noble church, the first there was in Ethiopia: It is named St. Mary of Zion. They say that it is so named because its altar stone came from Zion. In this country they have the custom always to name the churches by the altar stone, because on it is written the name of the patron saint. This stone which they have in this church, they say that the Apostles sent it from Mount Zion. This church is very large. . . ." [5]

As we have seen, Candace actually ruled in Meroe and was queen of Nubia, a country which became Christian long after Ethiopia, for, although the apostle Philip may have converted and baptized one of Candace's trusted servants, there is no reason to believe, and the author of the Acts of the Apostles certainly does not say, that the eunuch converted anyone else.

If Ethiopia was not converted to Christianity by Candace's eunuch, how, then, did it become the first country to embrace the Christian faith on the continent? According to Rufinus who lived in the latter part of the fourth century, "One Metrodorus, a philosopher, is said to have penetrated to further India in order to view places and see the world. Inspired by his example, one Meropius, a philosopher of Tyre, wished to visit India with a similar object, taking with him two small boys who were related to him and whom he was educating in humane studies. The younger of these was called Aedesius, the other Frumentius. When, having seen and taken note of what his soul fed upon, the philosopher had begun to return, the ship on which he travelled put in for water or some other necessaries at a certain port. It is the custom of the barbarians of these parts that, if ever the neighboring tribes report that their treaty with the Romans is broken, all Romans found among them should be massacred. The philosopher's ship was boarded; all with himself were put to the sword. The boys were found studying under a tree and preparing their lessons, and, preserved by the mercy of the barbarians, were taken to the king. He made one of them, Aedesius, his cupbearer. Frumentius, whom he had perceived to be sagacious and prudent, he made his treasurer and secretary. Thereafter they were held in great honour and affection by the king. The king died, leaving his wife with an infant son as heir of the bereaved kingdom. He gave the young men liberty to do what they pleased but the queen besought them with tears, since she had no more faithful subjects in the whole kingdom, to share with her the cares of governing the kingdom until her son should grow up, especially Frumentius, whose ability was equal to guiding the kingdom—for the other, though loyal and honest of heart, was simple. While they lived there and Frumentius held the reins of government in his hands, God stirred up his heart and he began to search out with care those of the Roman merchants who were Christians and to give them great influence and to urge them to establish in various places conventicles to which they might resort for prayer in the Roman manner. He himself, moreover, did the same and so encouraged the others, attracting them with his favour and his benefits, providing them with whatever was needed, supplying sites for buildings and other necessaries, and in every way promoting the growth of the seed of Christianity in the country. When the prince for whom they exercised the regency had grown up, they completed and faithfully delivered over their trust, and, though the queen and her son sought greatly to detain them and begged them to remain, returned to the Roman Empire. Aedesius hastened to Tyre to revisit his parents and relatives. Frumentius went to Alexandria, saying that it was not right to hide the work of God. He laid the whole affair before the bishop and urged him to look for some worthy man to send as bishop over the many Christians already congregated and the churches built on barbarian soil. Then Athanasius (for he had recently assumed the episcopate), having carefully weighed and considered Frumentius' words and deeds, declared in a council of the priests, 'What other man shall we find in whom the Spirit of God is as in thee, who can accomplish these things?' And he consecrated him and bade him return in the grace of God whence he had come. And when he had arrived in India as bishop, such grace is said to have been given to him by God that apostolic miracles were wrought by him and a countless number of barbarians were converted by him to the faith. From which time Christian peoples and churches have been created in the parts of India, and the priesthood has begun. These facts I know not from vulgar report but from the mouth of Aedesius himself, who had been Frumentius' companion and was later made a priest in Tyre." [6]

This story is believed to be authentic, and what Rufinus called India is in fact, Ethiopia. The king who made Aedesius his cup-bearer and Frumentius his treasurer was Ella-Amida, the father of Aezanes. It was Aezanes' mother who begged Aedesius and Frumentius to share with her the cares of governing the kingdom until her son was of age.

It is known that during the controversy over the Arian doctrine the Emperor Constantius addressed a letter to "his most precious brothers" Aezanes and Sazanas requesting them to have Frumentius examined in the faith by the new Arian patriarch of Alexandria since he had been consecrated as bishop by Athanasius, champion of the Nicene faith, who was out of favor at this time, and had been deposed. Constantius did not succeed in making Frumentius subscribe to the Arian faith, but his letter confirms that Aezanes was king of Ethiopia when Frumentius was bishop and enables us to date Ethiopian conversion to the fourth century.

Rufinus' account does not, however, say anything about King Aezanes' being a Christian. This is because Rufinus obtained his information from Aedesius who had become a priest in Tyre. Aedesius could not have known, in detail, what took place after he had left the country. Aezanes, then, must have become a Christian late, rather than early, in his reign as is shown by the fact that in his early inscriptions he ascribes his victories to Ares, but in the later ones to the Lord of Heaven. The coins of his reign also indicate the change. In the early years, these bore the non-Christian symbol of the crescent and the disk; in the latter years, however, they bore the Cross. Frumentius thus appears to have succeeded in converting Aezanes to Christianity only on his return from Alexandria after his consecration as Bishop.

But, does Ethiopian tradition refer, in any way, to Frumentius? Yes, it does. He is known as Abba Salama (the "father of peace"). The tradition is that when Ethiopia received Christianity from the eunuch of Queen Candace they did not have any priests, since the eunuch had not been consecrated a bishop. Frumentius' role was the introduction of the priesthood and sacrament to a people who were already Orthodox Christians. His consecration as bishop by the Patriach of Alexandria established a precedent whereby the head of the Ethiopian Church—from the fourth century until 1960—always had been a nominee of the Patriach of Alexandria. In 1960, however, Ethiopia received its own patriach, and no longer looks to Alexandria for the Catholicus, or *Abuna*. Centuries of association with Alexandria ensured that the Ethiopian Church remained Coptic i.e., Egyptian in its doctrine and monophysite in its faith.

We can argue, as long as we like, about the merits of traditional as opposed to the more factual view of the country's history. Does it matter? Our arguments will not alter the fact that for centuries Ethiopians have preserved their realm as an island bastion of Christianity in a hostile sea of infidels. "The Ethiopian people are ardent believers in their faith and will not be shaken by rumours and by empty words," proudly declared the Ethiopian Patriarch Basilios in 1960 and added, "The Ethiopian people are a faithful and a great people." [7] The revised 1955 Constitution of Ethiopia states in Article

2: "The Imperial Dignity shall remain perpetually attached to the line of Hailé Sellassie I, the descendant of King Sahle Sellassie, whose line descends without interruption from the dynasty of Menelik I, son of the Queen of Ethiopia, the Queen of Sheba, and King Solomon of Jerusalem, . . ." and in Article 4. "By virtue of his Imperial blood, as well as by the annointing which he had received, the Person of the Emperor is sacred, His dignity is inviolable and His power indisputable. . . ." [8] For centuries therefore, Ethiopians have believed, behaved, and acted in the light of their tradition. It has affected them much more than anything foreigners write about them. This is what matters. This is what is important.

There are other great names in Ethiopian history besides that of Aezanes. There are the twin brothers Atsbeha and Abraham, revered as champions of Christianity. Atsbeha, also known as Kaleb, was king of Ethiopia in the second quarter of the sixth century. During his reign, a Jewish king, who persecuted and massacred vast numbers of Christians, ruled over Himyar in the Yemen. Atsbeha decided to go to the aid of the Christians and to claim the rights of suzerainty for the kings of Axum. In 525, he sent a mighty army which was completely successful against the Jewish king, and for his victory, Atsbeha won great renown as a champion of Christianity.

Esimphaeus, a Christian, was installed as a tributary king of Himyar but, within a few years, the army of occupation revolted and replaced Esimphaeus with another Christian called Abraham. Atsbeha sent a punitive expedition against Abraham. On arriving in Himyar, however, Atsbeha's entire army went over to Abraham's side. He sent another army and was completely defeated by Abraham. Discouraged, Atsbeha recognized Abraham as king of Himyar in exchange for Abraham's consent to pay him tribute.

Abraham also made a reputation as the champion of Christianity. First, he gained fame for building a magnificent church at Sana'a, a church so beautiful that it not only excited the wonder of the Arab world but also bade fair to eclipse the Ka'aba at Mecca as a center of attraction. The Ka'aba is a Muslim shrine enclosing the sacred black stone said to have been given to the patriarch Abraham by the angel Gabriel. Muslim worshipers must face towards the Ka'aba when praying. Abraham also became famous for his expedition to destroy the Ka'aba. Tradition has it that he gathered a mighty army, and mounted on an elephant, led his host to Mecca. On the way, however, a flight of birds appeared and dropped tiny stones on his soldiers. Wounds developed wherever the soldiers had been struck by the stones, and the army sickened and died. In this way, Allah intervened to save the Ka'aba. In this very year, the Year of the Elephant, the Prophet Muhammad was born in Mecca.

His teaching has ripened into the Muslim religion now embraced by millions upon millions of people across several continents. Because an Ethiopian king gave refuge at his court to adherents of the Prophet in their early struggles with the aristocracy of Mecca and because, according to Muslim tradition, only the Ethiopian king, of all the kings of the earth to whom Muhammad announced his mission, received the Prophet's message with reverence, expressed approval of his teaching, and sent a reply; it is said Muslims have always declared that though the Ethiopians are Christian, there would be no *jihad,* or holy war, against them. This may account for the remarkable degree of tolerance and understanding which, in spite of some hostilities, has characterized relations between Ethiopians and Muslim Arabs since 642. In that year Arab armies occupied Egypt, cutting off Christian Ethiopia and Nubia from Alexandria and Rome. Again in the eighth century the Arabs occupied the Ethiopian coast.

In the sixth century Ethiopia's trading relations with the Orient and the interior of Africa continued to flourish. Cosmas has described how some of this trade was conducted by a method now known as dumb-barter.

"Every other year the king of the Axumities sends through the governor of Agau special agents to the land of Sasu, where gold is mined. These agents are accompanied by a large number of merchants, more than five hundred, and the caravan takes with it cattle and bars of salt and iron. When they reach the borders of Sasu they pitch a camp and fence it with a great hedge of thorns, and on the hedge they lay the bars of salt and iron and pieces of meat. Presently the natives arrive and lay nuggets of gold, the size of beans, on the objects which they want to buy, and then retire. If the merchant is satisfied with the price offered he removes the gold, and the purchaser then removes the meat or salt or iron. If the merchant is dissatisfied he leaves the gold and waits for the purchaser to add more, if he still wishes to buy, or to take away his gold if he thinks the price too high. The haggling generally takes about five days, the whole expedition about six months. The caravan travels well armed for fear of being robbed by the savage tribes through whose territory it passes. On its outward journey it has to move slowly on account of the cattle, on its homeward way it travels as fast as it can for fear of being caught by the rains." [9]

Herodotus has a similar description of trade between Phoenicians and Libyans.

We also have a description of the Ethiopian court, in the sixth century, from the pen of Julian, the Emperor Justinian's ambassador to Atsbeha: "The king was naked, wearing only a garment of linen embroidered with gold from his waist to his loins and straps set with pearls over his back and stomach. He wore golden bracelets on his arms, and on his head a turban of linen embroidered with gold from which hung four fillets on either side; around his neck was a golden collar. He stood on a four-wheeled chariot drawn by four elephants; the body of the chariot was high and covered with gold plates. The king stood on top carrying a small gilded shield and holding in his hands two small gilded spears. His council stood around similarly armed and flutes played." [10]

On being introduced Julian knelt and made obeisance, but the king bade him rise. As soon as he was brought forward, he presented the emperor's letter. When the king had the letter in his hand he kissed the seal and expressed great pleasure at the gifts which were produced. Then he opened the letter and it was read to him by an interpreter. The gigantic, granite, monoliths of Axum even today bear silent testimony to that splendor.

A thousand years after the visit of Julian to Atsbeha, Alvarez, the Portuguese priest, visited the emperor and left an eyewitness account.

"When he moved in state he rode on a mule led by six pages within a moving enclosure of red curtains held up on poles. In front marched twenty pages, headed by six saddled mules and six saddled horses, each led by four men. With him always went the four lions led each by two chains, and a hundred men each carrying a jar of meat and a hundred men each carrying a basket of bread. The portable altars of the churches were also carried in great state on trestles covered with precious cloths. Each altar was carried by four priests with four other priests in attendance and was preceded by two deacons, one with thurible and cross, the other with a bell to warn people off the road.

"The king normally lived in sacred seclusion within his enclosure, seen only by his pages and the high officials of state. He displayed himself to his people on a high platform three times a year, on Christmas Day, Easter, and Holy Cross Day." [11]

Such a manner of life was not unlike that of medieval monarchs in Europe. There is, therefore, no justification for the view that until the beginning of the colonial era, Africa was a land of darkness.

Medieval Europe treasured the tale that somewhere in the remote East, ruled an emperor who was both king and priest, called Prester John. He was said to rule over dominions so vast that he had seventy-two tributary kings, a patriarch, twelve archbishops, twenty bishops, a protopope, and an archprotopope under him. There were also said to be all manner of animals in his dominion. One of these fabulous animals was supposed to be the salamander which lived in fire and from whose incombustible skin Prester John's robes were made. These robes, the story went, were washed, not with water but with fire. Also, in this empire of Prester John, Europeans heard, were Amazons and evil races of strange men whom Alexander the Great had imprisoned in walled cities, to be released only on judgment day.

Prester John's palace was said to have been designed by St. Thomas, and it was reported to have a marvelous mirror in which he could see into any part of his dominions. Whenever he went to war, the emperor was preceded by thirteen golden crosses, each cross being followed by ten thousand horsemen and a hundred thousand footmen. The emperor's greatest ambition was to march to Jerusalem and wipe out the infidels who held it. But in spite of his greatness and might, the emperor was so humble that he chose for himself the title "prester," which is no higher than that of a priest.[12]

Gradually, the bits of information accumulated and grew over centuries, and the people of Europe came to identify the legendary

Prester John, with the king of Ethiopia. This resulted in contact between Europe and Ethiopia, contact which brought new ideas and new problems. Eventually, it culminated in the subjection of the country to colonialism and finally its emergence as a modern, independent, nationalist state.

To fellow Africans on the continent, as indeed to black men everywhere throughout the ages, Ethiopia has symbolized African dignity and self-respect. For here was a black state whose grandeur no white man could disdain. Throughout the colonial era, the Ethiopian Emperor Menelik's crushing victory over Italy's invading force at Adowa in 1896, remained an inspiration to other Africans; and when, in 1936, the Italians drove Emperor Haile Selassie into exile, it was as much an African as an Ethiopian tragedy. Today His Imperial Majesty, Haile Selassie, Conquering Lion of Judah, King of Kings, often wines and dines anti-imperialist African heads of state who, nevertheless, raise their glasses and drink to his Imperial Majesty's health.

NOTES

1. A. H. Jones and Elizabeth Monroe, *A History of Ethiopia* (New York: Oxford University Press [1935] 1955), p. 20.
2. Quoted by Jones and Monroe in *Ethiopia,* p. 22.
3. Quoted by Jones and Monroe in *Ethiopia,* pp. 23-24.
4. From the inscription [tr. Kirwan, *Kush* 8 (1960), 163-65] as quoted by Shinnie in *Meroe,* pp. 52-53.
5. Quotations from Francisco Alvarez, *A True Relation of the Lands of Prester John,* from *The Prester John of the Indies,* ed. C. F. Beckingham and G. W. B. Huntingford (published 1961 by Cambridge University Press on behalf of the Hakluyt Society). Used by permission.

6. Quoted by Jones and Monroe in *Ethiopia,* pp. 26-27.
7. Richard Greenfield, *Ethiopia* (New York: Praeger, 1965), p. 411.
8. Greenfield, *Ethiopia,* p. 41.
9. Quoted by Jones and Monroe in *Ethiopia,* pp. 30-31.
10. Quoted by Jones and Monroe in *Ethiopia,* pp. 31-33.
11. Quoted by Jones and Monroe in *Ethiopia,* pp. 68-69.
12. Jones and Monroe, *Ethiopia,* p. 59.

CHAPTER 8
Libya

In earliest times Egyptians called the land to the west of their country Libya. It is mentioned in the book of Genesis (10:13) as Lehabim, and in the *Odyssey* Homer refers to the Libyans. Herodotus says the name originally belonged to a local slave woman, but in Arabic legend, Libya is a great Egyptian queen and granddaughter of the founder of Memphis. Later, with the exception of Egypt, the whole of North Africa above the Sahara—what the Arabs call the Maghreb—was known as Libya. After this, ancient writers applied the name Libya to the whole continent. Today, Libya is composed of what was once known as Tripolitania and Cyrenaica, together with the adjoining desert of the Fezzan. Not until Roman times was the name Africa used. Even as late as the seventeenth century, the name Libya was still being used as an alternate name for the entire continent.[1]

What does the name Africa mean? What is its derivation? Frankly, we do not know. Some say it came from one Afer, a son of Hercules. Others say it is derived from a legendary son of Abraham whose name was Africos or Ifricos. There are those who attribute its origin to another Afer, a descendant of the giant Goliath, whose family is supposed to have fled from Asia to the continent after that disastrous encounter with David.[2] One suggestion is that the name was originally applied to that part of the sea between Africa and Sicily while another is that it means "ungirded," that is, not girded for war as Roman soldiers always were. Take your pick!

While the Egyptians were, as Herodotus said, "the best skilled in history of any men I ever met," and left much material that tells us about their past; the men who lived between the Nile and the Atlantic Ocean showed no such interest in their past. Unfortunately, they did not write any. Consequently, it is through their neighbors, and often their enemies that we know anything definite about them.

Libya, like Ethiopia, figures prominently in Greek mythology. It was in ancient Libya, at Cape Bon near modern Tunis, that Hercules is supposed to have struggled with the 105-foot giant, Antaeus, whose body was subsequently dug up by a Roman general who quickly but prudently offered sacrifices and reverently closed the giant's tomb. This is said to have happened at Tangier, the city named after the legendary lady who was Antaeus' widow and Hercules' sweetheart and from which the tangerine orange derives its name.[3]

According to the stories, it was Hercules who opened the strait, the "Pillars of Hercules," between Africa and Europe and made the passage so narrow that great whales could not pass into the Mediterranean. He set hills, one of which is Gibraltar, on either side of the strait as a lasting monument to his expedition. The Garden of Hesperides where Hercules performed his twelfth and last labor, killing the dragon on guard and fetching the golden apples, was believed to be in ancient Libya.

It was also in Libya that Hercules exterminated Queen Merina's thirty thousand female soldiers who wore war dress made from the skins of great serpents. After serving in the army as youthful virgin soldiers, Merina's warriors took mates and had children. Afterward the matrons conducted affairs of state while their husbands were made to do the housework. Hearing of this unusual society, Hercules was seized with rage and immediately wiped out the entire army because, as Diodorus says, "it was a thing intolerable to him to suffer any nation to be governed by women."[4]

The climate along the Mediterranean has changed. We know this from the fact that well into historic times, some areas of the Maghreb were semi-jungles with giant trees so large that Romans could carve "panther tables" four feet wide from a single piece of wood, and they enjoyed bunches of grapes almost two feet long.

The prehistoric art works, the rock paintings in the Tassili Range of the Hoggar Mountains in the central Sahara between Algeria and present-day Libya, indicate luxurious vegetation and forest animals.

From hundreds of wall paintings depicting "innumerable domestic cattle as well as sheep and goats and brilliantly executed sketches of wild beasts including elephants, giraffes, several varieties of deer, hippopotami and many others,"[5] including horse-drawn chariots, found in caves and grottoes of these sandstone mountains, scholars have been able to deduce a number of facts. Many of them estimate that some of these paintings were made about 8000 B.C. while others are dated to about 3500 B.C. The Fezzan has also yielded some dated to 1500 B.C. According to Henri Lhote, leader of an expedition that studied these ancient works of art in 1956, the Sahara paintings were done by people of Negroid stock. The older ones are symbolic, while those that have been dated to about 2500 B.C. show evidence of Egyptian influence and occasionally portray people with Caucasoid features. Those that have been found in the Fezzan are, however, believed to be the work of the Garamantes known to the Romans in the fifth century of the present era. Even today, in inaccessible areas of North Africa like the Ramla el Dawada, there are tribes of Negroid people known as the Dawada, or "Worm Eaters."[6] So, there is much evidence to show that the population of North Africa in ancient times was predominantly black; in spite of the assertion by Oliver and Fage that these peoples were not Negroes, but rather the fair-skinned Caucasians called Libyans by the ancient Greeks and distinguished by them from the "Ethiopians" (the "men with burnt faces") as they called Negroes.[7] That many groups of Caucasoid stock from time to time entered North Africa in the same way that Negroids migrated to Europe and other parts of the world is beyond dispute. But that Caucasoids found the region uninhabited and became the dominant racial group in North Africa is a myth, born of the white man's desire to deprive black men of their heritage and credit the achievements of Africans in this region to the white race.

It is obvious from these rock drawings that the Sahara must have, at this time, supported a luxuriant vegetation for the pictures portray domestic and wild animals that require ample grazing grounds and an abundant supply of water. Clearly, the climate of Libya has changed, for desert sand has now replaced vegetation in most parts of the Sahara.

When desert conditions eventuated in the Sahara, oases became extremely important to travelers in Libya. Oases have natural springs or wells whose water is replenished from underground rivers. There were several oases in Libya which were known and used by ancient Egyptians. Caravans used them as rest stops to refill their bags and water their camels. Egyptian rulers were quick to realize the strategic importance of oases, and they constructed reservoirs at some of them for use by detachments of troops operating over the vast stretches of waterless desert. "A modern desert expedition discovered in 1917 an ancient storage depot of hundreds of pottery jars at Abu Ballas far to the south-west of Dakhlah." Kees tells us, "It was situated on the old caravan route that by-passed the Sahara to the south and went north by way of Gilf Kebir to Kufra. Stories were still current at Dekhlah that in primer times the oasis had frequently been attacked by bands of Negroes for whom this water depot had served as a springboard for assault."[8] Moving troops through the desert could be dangerous, as the destruction of Cambyses' army, which lost its way while marching to Siwa, clearly shows.

The supervision of oases under Egyptian influence was entrusted to the highest royal official, the grand vizier. Egypt received tribute in oasis products such as, minerals, dates, natron used in the process of mummification, and wine. Frequently, fugitives took refuge in remote oases where they were often tracked down by detachments of troops. These desert outposts were also used to exile important political or other prisoners. In the Christian era, recalcitrant bishops, like Athanasius and Nestorius fled to the desert, and the early monks often built their monasteries there.

As we have seen, during the New Kingdom period, the Sea-people allied themselves with Libyan native tribes and invaded Egypt, seeking to occupy its rich lands of the Delta. As Welch says, "Once started on the drive to Egypt, starvation chased them. They struggled across North Africa's stretches of arid sands. They must take over North Egypt or perish. They had brought along their women and children and herds. It was—or it sought to be—an immigration. Along the road babies were born and women died dreaming of Egypt's green comfort—water, corn. Thirsty cattle smelt the Nile."[9]

Egypt's Pharaoh Merneptah met the invaders on April 15, 1221 B.C., about fifty miles southeast of present-day Alexandria. "Merneptah had planned well. His bowmen slew the enemy for six hours from a distance, possessed evidently of superior weapons and technique, then they closed in on them with the sword. The enemy chief, King Meryey, fled so fast that arrows remained behind him."[10] In spite of this victory, groups of Libyans inobtrusively filtered into Egypt. Unopposed and unnoticed, these infiltrations gradually turned into incursions, and incursions became full scale invasions, climaxed by the conquest of Egypt and the setting up of the first of two Libyan dynasties that ruled over Egypt.

In the second millennium B.C. some Canaanites, probably from the Persian Gulf, settled along the strip of land between the mountains of Lebanon and the sea. The Greeks called these people Phoenicians, which means "dark-skinned," and the land they settled, Phoenicia. The Romans called them *Poeni,* from which is derived the word Punic.

Phoenicians were seafarers who made their living by maritime trade. The famous cedars of Lebanon provided them with the finest timber for building their ships while their location, between the empires of the Hittites in the north and the Egyptians in the south, was along caravan routes to and from all points. So, along caravan routes and shipping lanes, Phoenicians organized their trade, carrying from "Arabia incense, myrrh, and onyx; from India precious stones, spices, ivory, and perfumed wood; from Egypt horses, linen, and cotton; from Spain wheat and silver; from the Greek islands copper, tin, marble, and the shell-fish that provided purple dyes; from Assyria precious stuffs, carpets perfumes and dates; from the Caucasus metals and slaves. Their slave markets provided servants for all the palaces in the Middle East and Egypt. In addition to these imports and exports, the Phoenicians manufactured consumer goods by mass-production in factories, particularly vases, jewels, necklaces, bracelets, broaches, earrings, images of gods, and textiles. Their great speciality was transparent glass made from the white sand of their coastline, and Tyrian purple, the dye from the mollusc Murex of which the Phoenician species provided a royal purple colour. (A more violet colour is derived from the molluscs of Greek waters, and from the Atlantic variety an almost black tint)." [11]

Phoenicians also did work on contract. They built Solomon's temple in Jerusalem and the port of Ezion-Geber on the Red Sea. For Sennacherib, they built a fleet of ships on the Euphrates and the Persian Gulf. To aid them in their commercial enterprises, the Phoenicians developed, in the tenth century B.C., an alphabet of twenty-two letters which is the basis of other letter systems, including Hebrew, Greek, Etruscan, and Latin. Phoenicians can, therefore, be regarded as having made a significant contribution to literacy in the world. At Byblos, they conducted such a brisk trade in papyrus that the port gave its name to *biblos,* the Greek word for book. Unfortunately, except for a few inscriptions, Phoenician literature is lost; a tragic state of affairs. With one exception, there is no known account of Phoenician history by Phoenicians.

The exception is the *Periplus of Hanno,* an account of his voyage in search of gold from the Mediterranean Sea southward along the Atlantic coast of Africa, the first such voyage of which there is any record. Sometime between 600 and 500 B.C., with sixty vessels carrying considerable goods, men and women, Hanno sailed from Carthage through Gibraltar, along the Moroccan coast to Mehdia, north of Casablanca. From here the fleet sailed southward, stopping here and there to trade perfumes and crockery for lion and panther skins until they reached what was probably the island of Fernando Po, and from there they obtained the skins of three female gorillas, under the impression that they had captured and skinned three fierce women of that place. Hanno caused his adventure to be carved on a bronze tablet and set into a wall of a temple in Carthage.[12]

As early as the eleventh century B.C. Phoenicians increased their business by establishing agencies or concessions in cities of other countries, such as Memphis, in Egypt. Where there were no suitable cities, they founded their own trading stations. Some of the ports which began as trading stations soon grew in size. In the course of time, they colonized their hinterlands, exploiting them and the native people for their own profit. The Phoenician's famous Libyan cities of Utica, Hippo Zarytus, Carthage, Tangier, and Leptis Magna, Hadrumetum were founded in this way.

According to tradition, Carthage was founded by the sister of King Pygmalion of Tyre, Dido-Elissa, who secretly left Tyre with a band of friends after her brother had caused her husband, who was also her uncle, to be murdered. Dido-Elissa and her friends sailed westward and stopped at Cyprus while the islanders were observing one of their old and honored festivals during which maidens gave themselves for the night in a form of ritual or religious sexual intercourse. Dido-Elissa ordered the kidnaping of eighty of these young women, insuring that children would be born in her city. The fleet sailed on to the coast of North Africa, where, near Utica, a local king named Hiarbas promised to grant her only as much land as can be covered with an ox-hide. However, by slicing the hide into many thin strips and spreading them out as far as possible, Dido-Elissa and her people obtained a substantial piece of land.

On this land the city of Carthage was built. Gradually, its influence increased until it covered half the state of present-day Tunisia, parts of modern Libya, Tripolitania, Algeria, and Morocco. Carthage owned rich farm lands on which she used people of Negroid and mixed stock to work the fields. She became the richest and most powerful Phoenician city. Although she did not own or control all the Phoenician cities on African soil, she dominated them with the strength of her fleet, army, and commerce. Other cities looked to her for defense since they had no military forces of their own. It was because of this preeminent position that Carthage was in the forefront of the struggle against Rome, a struggle that did not end until the Cartheginian forces led by Hannibal had been defeated at the battle of Zama by Roman legions under Scipio Africanus.

Because Carthage had become a dangerous rival Rome destroyed it and, by senatorial decree, annexed a small portion of present-day northeastern Tunisia as a Roman province. Gradually, this territory was extended until it stretched from the Gulf of Sirte to the Atlantic coast. It was bounded on the south by a fortified frontier line, a ditch now known as the Roman Limes. This territory included all the fertile agricultural land in parts of modern Libya, Tunisia, Algeria, and Morocco. Beyond the Limes the Romans built observation ports at oases like Cydamus, the modern Ghadames on the Libyan-Algerian frontier.

Although Rome sent a small number of Italian immigrants as colonists, the administration of her African possessions was based on an army of about five thousand men and auxiliaries recruited from the native population. Originally of European stock the regular Roman army was recruited, as time went on, more and more from the local population. As Jane Nickerson says, "Soldier's sons born on African soil of African mothers took their father's places in the ranks, and by the second century of our era the army of Africa was wholly African-born. It formed an invaluable colonial school. By the time of the Emperor Augustus the twenty years' service was instituted, the troops automatically acquiring Roman citizenship, and after the better part of a lifetime spent in the ranks, whether native or foreign, they had learned Roman methods and science and had no thought of leaving the country. On retirement they were given grants of land, very often near their barracks and could be counted upon for invaluable loyalty and support in case of barbarian incursions, and still more of forming an element in society of purely Roman sympathies. Modern European armies do not attempt to mix native and white troops in the same corps; but the Third Augustan Legion did not recognize racial differences, and became composed of Roman citizens who had acquired much Roman science and at all events a veneer of Roman culture, but were of African race." [13]

The colony was divided into four provinces: Africa Proconsularis, which included the original colony in parts of Tunisia and Tripolitania; Numidia in eastern Algeria; Mauritania Caesariensis, west of Algiers; and Mauritania Tingitana in Morocco. It was run for the profit derived from agricultural products, cultivated by laborers from the native population. Wheat, corn, wine, olive oil, wood for heating public baths of Rome, marble, ivory, horses, and fruits, were some of the popular products. There was also a large demand for wild beasts: elephants, lions, leopards, boars, bears, hyenas, ostriches, antelopes, and others for the circus and gladiatorial combats. All these made the African colony a valuable possession. During the reign of Augustus "no less than 3,500 wild beasts from Africa were put to death for the delectation of the Roman populace in the course of one single series of celebrations lasting twenty-six days." [14] That, of all this wild life, only a few leopards and boars have survived, is hardly surprising. Among the animals exterminated in North Africa was the elephant which, no longer used in war, was hunted for its ivory. Imported into the area, however, was the ship of the desert, the camel whose ability to live and work in extremely arid conditions facilitated travel and commerce across the Sahara.

As Roman rule extended, the native population was gradually pushed out of the best land and into the less fertile mountainous areas south of the Limes. The camel carried them deep into the desert and from there they constantly harassed, raided, pillaged, and plundered Roman provinces and outposts.

There were native Africans, however, who remained in the provinces and became so Romanized as to be the intellectual equals of the upper classes of European-born Roman citizens. Many rose to the highest positions in the Empire, including the position of emperor, a position which often called for the qualities of a soldier, statesman, and intellectual. "One of the best and most successful of these later soldier emperors was of African birth, a loyal son of his native land, who by the accident of his accession to the highest position in the State did much to further the interests of Africa Romana." [15]

Septimius Severus was born at Leptis Magna in Tripolitania in 146, a member of the Romanized ruling class. He received a good education in his native province and set out on an official career as a civil magistrate and as a soldier. This path finally led him to Rome. After the murder of Commodus, the weakling son of Marcus Aurelius, Septimius won the support of the provincial legions and rose to the imperial throne. He became emperor by virtue of military force, but his exceptional ability enabled him to maintain his position, and his reign from 193 to 211 marks the summit of Africa's importance under Rome. The triumphal arch commemorating one of his eastern campaigns still stands in the city. He also left several magnificent monuments in his native Leptis.

To the end of his life, Septimius Severus wore his African birth and education with pride. He was bilingual, having learned Punic from his mother, and the Latin he spoke was pronounced with the provincial accent. It is reported that after his accession to the throne, he was visited by a sister from Africa. When her lack of manners and language made her appear ridiculous, Septimius sent her home. The emperor was reputed to be as much an expert in Roman literature as he was in military science.

But for all the grandeur of his position, he never lost his taste for African cuisine; and fruits and vegetables grown in North Africa were brought to Rome and specially prepared for his table.

This was the first and last time that African interests were of first importance to the head of the empire. However, it was not the lower classes among the Berbers who interested the emperor, but the Romanized upper class to which he himself belonged.

Since Septimius had risen to his imperial rank from the army, his policy was aimed at ensuring its loyalty to himself. He increased the material rewards and the distinctions and honors of the service. He did this so lavishly that some accused him of corrupting the troops. However, the army he left was a much more efficient instrument than the one he had found in the beginning. Three legions were added, and the Praetorian Guard was reformed chiefly by opening its ranks to promotions from all the legions. Also recruitment was extended beyond Italy into the neighboring provinces. Many retired officers were appointed to posts formerly filled by civilians of equestrian rank, until the whole administration took on a martial flavor.

The interests of Roman Africa were promoted enthusiastically. Septimius Severus realized the enormous value of the camel, and the number of these animals in Africa increased markedly during his reign.

The African emperor's career came to an end in Great Britain. Basically a soldier to the last, Septimius Severus spent his last three years in reorganizing and strengthening this northern frontier. Accompanied by his son Caracalla, he stayed in one of the most distant and barbarous of the provinces partly because he wanted his son to be removed from the corrupting atmosphere of the court. In York in February, 211, Septimius Severus died, and there were dark rumors that Caracalla may have had something to do with his father's demise. However, Yorkshire is a harsh and chilling place at that time of year, especially for a son of the south who had sixty-five winters behind him.

It would be interesting to know how long the news of his death took to reach his hometown of Leptis Magna. "It is a far cry from the hot sea-plain of Tripolitania, its olive groves and fig trees which the emperor so much loved, and the blue waters of the Mediterranean, to the short pale light and great wood fires of a Yorkshire winter. . . ." [16]

Septimius Severus was not the only illustrious African of the Roman era. St. Augustine of Hippo, born in Numidia, educated at Carthage, was one of the greatest Christian theologians of all time.

In 429 the Roman Colony, constantly under pressure from raids by Africans from desert sanctuaries in the south, was threatened from the sea by the appearance of a Vandal fleet under King Genseric. Before long Genseric was ruler of ancient Libya. The Vandals ruled for a hundred years, though always under pressure from raids by Africans from the recesses of the desert, before they succumbed to an invasion by the Emperor Justinian's Byzantine forces under the command of Belisarius. But Justinian, like other foreign rulers before him, exploited his subjects and failed to secure the good will of the native population.

Byzantine rule was terminated in the seventh century by the invasions of the followers of the Prophet Muhammad who were strongly resisted only by the subjects of La Kahina, a Libyan queen. The Muslims swept across Egypt, ancient Libya, and on to Spain and France before they were halted by Charles Martel, at the battle of Poitiers near Tours in 732. The Muslims were, however, gradually driven out of Europe onto African soil. In course of time, North Africa, itself, was colonized by Europeans: a colonization that has only ended in recent times.

NOTES

1. Galbraith Welch, *North African Prelude* (New York: Morrow, 1949), p. 39.
2. Welch, *Prelude,* p. 46.
3. Welch, *Prelude,* pp. 16-17.
4. Quoted by Welch in *Prelude,* p. 18.
5. Jane G. Nickerson, *A Short History of North Africa* (New York: Biblo and Tannen, 1961), p. 7.
6. James Wellard, *Lost Worlds of Africa* (New York: Dutton, 1967), pp. 13-36.
7. Oliver and Fage, *History,* p. 53.
8. Herman Kees, in *Ancient Egypt,* ed. T. G. James (University of Chicago Press, 1961), p. 129.
9. Welch, *Prelude,* p. 37.
10. Welch, *Prelude,* p. 37.
11. Sir Garvin de Beer, *Hannibal* (New York: Viking Press, 1969), p. 23.
12. Welch, *Prelude,* p. 68.
13. Nickerson, *Short History,* p. 17.
14. Nickerson, *Short History,* p. 26.
16. Nickerson, *Short History,* pp. 26-29.

CHAPTER 9
Ancient Ghana

We have seen that the Sahara was a fertile land before it became a desert barrier—a porous barrier to be sure—but a barrier to communication between the northern and southern parts of Africa, all the same. How and why did people cross the Sahara once its expanse became so forbidding? Rock paintings, depicting horse-drawn chariots in the Sahara, reveal one mode of transportation, and Herodotus also reports seeing chariots in this part of Africa. This is not surprising because this form of transport was common in the Mediterranean area in biblical times. It is certain, then, that horse chariots were used in the Sahara as late as 500 B.C.

One of the reasons for crossing the Sahara or for sailing along the coast of West Africa as the Phoenicians occasionally did was the quest for metals, the most important and valuable of which was gold. West Africa has, from time immemorial, been famous as a source of gold where it is found in alluvial deposits and is easily mined. We have seen how West Africa may well be one of the areas of the world where agriculture developed independently. The early development of agriculture was conducive to the growth of villages, towns and a settled population. These factors facilitated the development of trans-Saharan trade. There were stable settlements to serve as marketplaces and two valuable products. Gold, always in great demand, was known to exist across the Sahara to the south. The West African settlements, on the other hand, needed salt, mined in the north and as essential as water to man, for our bodies need two to five grams a day to function normally. So trans-Saharan trade, mainly gold and ivory in exchange for salt, developed. As desert conditions became more severe, horse-drawn chariots were replaced by the camel. To this day camel caravans, navigating their way across the Sahara by means of the sun, stars, and wind patterns, carry salt to the south as they have done for hundreds of years.

To organize and take advantage of this trade, cities and rulers arose. These grew into kingdoms and kings, empires and emperors. One such empire was Ghana whose grandeur inspired present-day west Africans to name their country Ghana, at the independence of the Gold Coast, even though the center of ancient Ghana lay more than two thousand miles to the northwest. The then-prime minister, later to become the first president of the new republic, Dr. Kwame Nkrumah told the young nation: "The Government proposes that when the Gold Coast attains independence, the name of the country should be changed from 'Gold Coast' to the new name of 'Ghana.' The name Ghana is rooted deeply in ancient African history, especially in the history of the western portion of Africa known as the Western Sudan. It kindles in the imagination of modern African youth the grandeur and the achievements of a great medieval civilisation which our ancestors developed many centuries before European penetration and subsequent domination of Africa began. According to tradition the various peoples or tribal groups in the Gold Coast were originally members of the great Ghana Empire that developed in the Western Sudan during the medieval period.

For the one thousand years that the Ghana Empire existed, it spread over a wide expanse of territory in the Western Sudan. Its influence stretched across the Sudan from Lake Chad in the east to the Futa Jalon Mountains in the west and from the southern fringes of the Sahara Desert in the north to the Bights of Benin and Biafra in the south. Thus the Ghana Empire was known to have covered what is now the greater part of West Africa—namely, from Nigeria in the east to Senegambia in the west. While it existed, the Ghana Empire carried on extensive commercial relations with the outside world—extending as far as Spain and Portugal. Gold, animal skins, ivory, kola-nuts, gums, honey, corn and cotton were among the articles that writers had most frequently named. It is reported that Egyptian, European and Asiatic attended the great and famous universities and other institutions of higher learning that flourished in Ghana during the medieval period to learn philosophy, mathematics, medicine and law.

It is from this rich historical background that the name Ghana has been proposed as the new name of the Gold Coast upon the attainment of independence; we take pride in the name, not out of romanticism, but as an inspiration for the future." [1]

Most of our information about the ancient empire of Ghana comes from Arab writers. Arabic history is based on what is known as *isnad* or *silsila.* This is the chain of the transmission of information, containing actual names, from the earliest teacher to the latest student. Thus a writer may state that his source of information is D, who was taught by C, the student of B, who heard it from A. Several generations may separate D from A. One of our main informants about ancient Ghana is Al Bakri, author of *Roads and Kingdoms,* a book on international trade written about 1067-68 and based on the writings and narratives of people who had traveled in these areas. Al Bakri was the fourth link in the chain of transmission which began about A.D. 900. This makes the main source of the information a contemporary of the empire.

Although some people believe Ghana to have been in existence at the beginning of the Christian era, the earliest written reference to it appears in the work of an astronomer, Al Fazari, who wrote between A.D. 788 and 793 on the main kingdoms of the world and referred to the kingdom of Ghana as a land of gold, two hundred miles long and a hundred miles wide. The second reference is given by the geographer, Al Kharazani, who indicated Ghana's location on his map. Al Yaqubi, another geographer, in his *Book of Countries,* described an important trans-Saharan caravan route from the city of Sijilmassa, as being under the domination of the veiled Sanhaja Berbers. In his second book, *The History,* written in 904 or 905, Al Yaqubi describes different countries and says that Ghana has many gold mines and a powerful king who has other kings under him.

The next reference to Ghana is that of Al Masudi of Baghdad who died in 956. Al Masudi wrote *The Golden Savannas,* or the *Golden Prairies,* in which he described Ghana as a kingdom of great importance adjoining the land of the gold mines where silent trade, or dumb-barter, was practiced. He also said that in this land gold was visible in the ground and was minted at Sijilmassa. Another writer from Baghdad who visited Ghana in 901 or 902 was Ibn Kawoala. In his *Book of Ways and Provinces,* Ibn Kawoala said that the king of Ghana was the richest in the world because of his gold. He described the town of Awdoghast as one of the ports of call between Sijilmassa and Ghana and was impressed by the magnitude of the business on the trans-Saharan route. Ibn Hawqal reported seeing a merchant sign a check for forty dinars (about $250,000). Obviously, the gold trade was big business. The ancient Empire of Ghana was, therefore, not only known far and near it was also known as a land of gold. A popular traveler's tale of the time was that the king of Ghana had a gold nugget weighing over thirty pounds to which he tied his horse.

But, what kind of a country was Ghana? What sort of administration and towns did it have? For answers to these questions, we turn to Al Bakri. The historian speaks of the city of Sijilmassa in the north as the starting point for some caravans making their journey across the desert. He also tells of another city: Awdoghast, which was fifteen-days' journey from Ghana. What is believed to have been the site of Awdoghast was discovered in 1939.

Al Bakri reports that *ghana* was a title given to the kings in the region of Awkar. At the time he wrote, Tankamanin was the powerful ruler over an enormous kingdom. He possessed great authority, and "led a praiseworthy life on account of his love of justice and his friendship for the Muslims." * Tankamanin had succeeded Basi on the throne. However, Basi was a maternal uncle rather than the father to Tankamanin. One unusual feature of this society was the custom of uterine descent, i.e., the kingdom was inherited not by the son of the king, but the son of his sister. Working on the assumption that only a wise man knows his father, ancient Ghanaians accepted the obvious corollary that one does not have to be a genius to know one's mother. In that way they were certain

* Quotations from Al Bakri, *Roads and Kingdoms,* translated by Dr. W. W. Rajkowski. From "Ancient Ghana: A Review of the Evidence," by J. D. Fage, in *Transactions of the Historical Society of Ghana,* Vol. III (Anchimota, 1952), pp. 80-82.

of having, at least, fifty percent royal blood in the veins of their king.

Ghana was, as we have noted, a title that later became the name of the empire. It was also once used to designate a city, for Al Bakri speaks of the city of Ghana consisting of two towns lying in a plain, one inhabited by Muslims.

"It is large and possesses twelve mosques in one of which the people assemble for the Friday prayer. There are imams, muezzins, and assistants as well as jurists and learned men. Around the town are wells of sweet water from which they drink and near which they grow vegetables." This was obviously a caravansary occupied mostly by immigrants. It is just possible this town is Kumbi Saleh excavated by Raymond Mauny about two hundred miles north of Bamako in modern Mali. The excavations reveal a large town. Two houses were excavated completely. One had seven rooms on the ground floor and the other nine. Both were double-story buildings constructed in stone with plastered walls, staircases, weapons, farming implements, pottery, glassware, and stones with Koranic inscriptions.

According to Al Bakri, six miles from the Muslim town was Al Ghaba, the town in which the king lived. "The land between the two towns is covered with houses. The houses of the inhabitants are made of stone and acacia wood. The king has a palace and a number of dome-shaped dwellings, the whole surrounded by an enclosure like the defensive wall of a city. In the town where the king lives, and not far from the hall where he holds his court of justice, is a mosque where pray the Muslims who come on visiting diplomatic missions. Around the king's town are domed buildings, woods, and copses where live the sorcerers of these people, the men in charge of the religious cult. In these also are idols and the tombs of their kings. These woods are guarded and no unauthorized person can enter them, so that it is not known what is within them. In them also are the prisons of the king, and if anyone is imprisoned there, no more is ever heard of him. The king's interpreters, his treasurer, and the majority of his ministers, are Muslims." As long as traders paid their taxes, they were welcome in ancient Ghana.

The description of the king's town is interesting. It was essentially traditional in its religion. There were guarded sacred groves containing idols, royal tombs, and prisons. It is clear, nevertheless, that in government Muslims dominated, for most ministers were Muslims. It was a society in a state of transition. In religion, for instance, ancient gods persisted but Muslims were welcomed and were moving into positions of power. This is understandable. Ghana depended on long-distance trade with the Muslim north, so it was politic for her to use Muslim advisors, scribes and record-keepers. Furthermore, it was prudent for a ruler to rely on strangers because these were not likely to act as a source of revolution while enjoying his patronage. These may be the reasons why Muslims moved into most positions of authority.

Of the Mande people populating the Ghana Empire and adhering to their traditional religion, Al Bakri says, only the King and "his heir presumptive, who is the son of his sister, may wear sewn clothes. All other people wear cloths of cotton, silk, or brocade, according to their means. All men shave their beards and women shave their heads. The king adorns himself like a woman, wearing necklaces and bracelets, and when he sits before the people he puts on a high cap decorated with gold and wrapped in turbans of fine cotton. The court of appeal is held in a domed pavillion around which stand ten horses with gold embroidered trappings. Behind the king stand ten pages holding shields and swords decorated with gold, and on his right are the sons of the subordinate kings of his country, all wearing splendid garments and with their hair mixed with gold. The governor of the city sits on the ground before the king, and around him are ministers seated likewise. At the door of the pavilion are dogs, of excellent pedigree which, guarding the king, hardly ever leave the place where he is. Round their necks they wear collars of gold and silver, studded with a number of balls of the same metals. The audience is announced by the beating of a drum which they call *daba,* made from a long hollow log. When the people who profess the same religion as the king approach him, they fall on their knees and sprinkle their heads with dust, for this is their way of showing him their respect. As for the Muslims, they greet him only by clapping their hands." The wearing of clothes of cotton, silk or brocade was not, as is sometimes claimed, introduced in West Africa by white men.

The religion of the people of Ghana particularly impressed Al Bakri, even though he considered them pagans and worshipers of idols. "When their king dies they build, over the place where his tomb will be, an enormous dome of *saj* wood. Then they bring him on a bed covered with a few carpets and cushions and put him inside the dome. At his side they place his ornaments, his weapons, and the vessels from which he used to eat and drink, filled with various kinds of food and beverages. They also place there the men who have served his meals. They close the door of the dome and cover it with mats and materials, and then they assemble the people, who heap earth upon it until it becomes like a large mound. Then they dig a ditch around the mound so that it can be reached only at one place. They sacrifice victims for their dead and make offerings of intoxicating drinks." Ancient Ghanaians, like the Ancient Egyptians, obviously believed in life after death.

As regards trade Al Bakri wrote, "For every donkey loaded with salt that enters the country, the king takes a duty of one golden *dinar,* and two *dinars* from every one that leaves. From a load of copper the duty due to the king is five *mithqals,* and from a load of merchandise ten *mithqals.* The best gold found in this land comes from the town of Ghiyaru, which is eighteen days traveling from the city of the king, over a country inhabited by tribes of the Negroes, their dwelling places being contiguous. The nuggets found in all the mines of this country are reserved for the king, only gold dust being left for the people. Without this precaution, the people would accumulate gold until it had lost its value. The nuggets may be of any weight from an ounce to a pound. It is said that the king owns a nugget as large as a big stone. The town of Ghiyaru is twelve miles from the Nile (i.e., the Niger) and contains many Muslims." Apparently gold was mined in remote areas and brought by middle men to the towns. There was a production and an export tax. The supply of gold on the market was controlled.

Of its military strength we are told, "When the king of Ghana calls up his army, he can put 200,000 men in the field, more than 40,000 of whom are bowmen. The horses in Ghana are very small." This army, which used iron weapons ensured the power and authority of the emperor as well as the peace and security of the realm.

There were other important towns in the empire, such as Gao in the Songhai region along the Niger River. Yaqubi considered it stronger than Ghana while another writer, Al Muhallabi described it as consisting of two towns, a caravansary and a king's town. Al Muhallabi says, however, that by the year 1000 the king of Gao was already a Muslim, a fact borne out by the recent discovery of marble tombstones of Spanish origin bearing Muslim inscriptions.

Such towns as Ghana and Gao functioned as "ports." Like ports they grew at points where one form of transportation changed to another. For instance, salt came on camels from the north and at these points was transferred to donkeys, bullocks, or human carriers for transportation into the interior. These ports were thus collecting and breaking points where gold and ivory were collected, bulked, and transported on camels to the north, while salt was debulked for distribution in the interior.

Because of the economic dependence of the empire on trade, Muslim mercantile interests were gradually being entrenched in the towns, and at the same time, there was mounting pressure for the rulers in predominantly non-Muslim societies to accept Islam. Trade was, therefore, a very important factor in the spread of the Muslim faith in West Africa.

Thus, after the early neolithic revolution in West Africa, there was a steady growth of villages and towns: an advanced urban revolution which facilitated trans-Saharan trade in the gold and ivory of West Africa and the salt, copper, blue pearls, hides, dates, and textiles from the north. Based on the organization and control of this trade, the Empire of Ghana arose and flourished for centuries, extending westward as far as Tekrur in modern Senegal, northward into the Sahara, eastward beyond the Niger bend, and southward past the Futa Jalon. It was an empire based on allegiance to the supreme emperor. Below him were lesser rulers and kings who were allowed to govern in accordance with their own traditions and customs. It is, therefore, almost impossible to determine its precise boundaries. There can be no doubt, however, that its sphere of influence extended over a very wide area indeed.

Ghana, like other great empires of the world, did not fall; it crumbled. Its decline from a position of preeminence was gradual and extended over a hundred years. It was, however, precipitated by a band of people known in history as the Almoravids. Their story begins among the various Berber tribes; the Goddala, Masipa, Lemtuna, and others in and around the Sahara. During the ninth century, these tribes formed a political alliance, the Sanhaja Confederacy with Awdoghast as its capital. The confederacy controlled the trans-Saharan route from Sijilmassa to Ghana. Probably founded in the sixth century, Awdoghast had become an important link on that route. In about 918, however, the confederacy broke up enabling Ghana to take Awdoghast, install a governor, and exact tribute. The loss of Awdoghast and the threat of Ghanaian domination brought the Sanhaja together. In 1020 one of the Goddala chiefs, Yahya, son of Ibralim, went to Mecca. Returning through Sijilmassa in 1035, he met Wajjajibn Zalwi, a Muslim holy man from whom he requested a teacher for his people. Zalwi recommended one of his students, Ibn Yasin, who, with his brothers Ibn Umar and Abu Bakr, went to live among the Goddala tribesmen. Yasin was unsuccessful in his mission, and at the death of his sponsor and protector, he fled to Tekrur with eight followers, including his two brothers.

The ruler of Tekrur welcomed him, and there Ibn Yasin built a *ribat,* a religious and military training center. By 1042 his followers numbered a thousand, and he was ready to launch a jihad, a religious war, against the people who had received him coldly. The opportunity to acquire booty ensured the success of the jihad. The Goddala were offered Islam or death, and they chose Allah and the Muslim faith. Tribe after tribe succumbed to the persuasive powers of Yasin's followers who were given the anme the Almoravids even though they called themselves the al Murabeitun.

After this success, Yasin's teacher encouraged the Almoravids to attack Sijilmassa because he disapproved certain practices of the Zanata Berbers who controlled the city. The Almoravids went north and took Sijilmassa in 1054-55, turned south and took Awdoghast from Ghana the same year. There were, however, constant rebellions among the conquered tribes, and in quelling one of these rebellions Ibn Umar was killed in 1057.

The Almoravids conquered Morocco in a campaign during which Ibn Yasin was killed. Their victory laid the foundation for Almoravid rule in that area which lasted till 1147. They changed the capital from Sijilmassa to Marrakesh. Crossing the Mediterranean, they conquered Spain and threatened Europe where they are remembered as the Moors.

While part of the Almoravids army was conquering Spain and advancing towards France, another part under Abu Bakr was giving its attention to the Empire of Ghana. After many battles, the capital of Ghana was sacked and occupied by the Almoravids in 1076. But the empire had by no means come to an end with this occupation. It continued to offer strong resistance to the Almoravids who were busy quelling revolts in the areas under their occupation. In one of the revolts, Abu Bakr was killed in 1087.

All the same, the blows the empire received, from the Almoravids affected it: a number of the subordinate kings seized the opportunity to withdraw their allegiance and became, virtually, sovereign in their own kingdoms. This, nevertheless, happened gradually.

Among the kingdoms that threw off allegiance to Ghana was Tekrur. Tekrur not only reasserted its independence but embarked on a path of conquest of its own. Under Sumanguru, it conquered several other kingdoms, and seized Kumbi Saleh, the capital of Ghana, in 1203. Sumanguru's attempt to make Tekrur the successor of Ghana was, nevertheless, opposed and frustrated, first, by the Muslim merchants of Kumbi Saleh who, for religious and commercial reasons, rejected Sumanguru's overlordship, quit Kumbi Saleh, and traveled northward to Walata where they formed a new trading center beyond his reach.

Next, the people of Kangaba, who were middlemen in the gold trade about 1230, accused Sumanguru of harsh taxation and of bad government which resulted in insecurity and such a break down of law and order that it was impossible to prevent the seizure of Kangaba girls. But Sumanguru had acquired a wide reputation as a magician, and, fearing reprisals, the king of Kangaba fled. The king's flight gave his exiled half-brother, Sundiata, an opportunity to return to his country, save the kingdom, win renown, and build an empire for himself. Sundiata was the son of Maghan, king of Kangaba. His mother, Sogolon, was a hunchback. When Sundiata was only seven years old, Maghan died and was succeeded by Dankaran, a son by another wife. One day, the new king fell ill.

His mother blamed Sundiata and Sogolon for the illness of the king and wished them put to death. The pair was exiled from Kangaba.

"Returning from exile with an army which he had raised with the help of the ruler of the Mema, who lived near Lake Faguibine on the middle reaches of the Niger, Sundiata gathered friends and allies, increased his forces, gave them fresh heart and courage, and marched boldly against the dreaded Sumanguru.*

" 'As Sundiata advanced with his army to meet Sumanguru,' say the old legends, 'he learned that Sumanguru was also coming against him with an army prepared for battle. They met in a place called Kirina [not far from the modern Kulikoro]. When Sundiata turned his eyes on the army of Sumanguru, he believed they were a cloud and he said: 'What is this cloud on the eastern side?' They told him it was the army of Sumanguru. As for Sumanguru, when he saw the army of Sundiata, he exclaimed: 'What is that mountain of stone?' For he thought it was a mountain. And they told him: 'It is the army of Sundiata, which lies to the west of us.

" 'Then the two columns came together and fought a terrible battle. In the thick of the fight, Sundiata uttered a great shout in the face of the warriors of Sumanguru, and at once these ran to get behind Sumanguru. The latter, in his turn, uttered a great shout in the face of the warriors of Sundiata, all of whom fled to get behind Sundiata. Usually, when Sumanguru shouted, eight heads would rise above his own head.'

"But Sumanguru's witchcraft, the legends say, proved less powerful than the witchcraft of Sundiata. Thanks to this, Sundiata prevailed. Sumanguru was struck with an arrow bearing the spur of a white cock, fatal to his power, and 'Sumanguru vanished and was seen no more . . . [but] as for Sundiata, he defeated the army of Sumanguru, ravaged the land of the Susu [allies and subjects of Sumanguru], and subjugated its people. Afterward Sundiata became the ruler of an immense empire.' "[2]

* Quotations from Basil Davidson, *A History of West Africa to the Nineteenth Century*. Copyright © 1966 by Basil Davidson, © 1965 by Longman's Green and Co., Ltd. Reprinted by permission of Doubleday & Company, Inc.

At this time, the capital of Kangaba was a city called Niani, along the Niger River. The name Mali, which means "where the king resides," began to be used instead of Kangaba and so the medieval Empire of Mali came into existence. Thus, about 1240, the crumbling Empire of Ghana eventually fell apart, disappeared, and was effectively superceded by Mali, one hundred and seventy years after it had sustained the crippling blows of the Almoravids. Thus, an ancient empire passed into history and, in its place, arose a medieval one.

NOTES

1. Kwame Nkrumah, *I Speak of Freedom* (New York: Praeger, 1961), pp. 67-68.
2. Davidson, *West Africa*, pp. 54-55.

CHAPTER 10
Medieval Mali

As we saw in the last chapter, the Mande people of Kangaba were dissatisfied with Sumanguru's rule and eventually took up arms against him because of his high taxes and the insecurity throughout the land, resulting from a breakdown of law and order. Both these reasons were of vital importance to the people of Kangaba since they were middle men in the trade in such things as gold, salt, kola nuts, ivory. High taxes reduce profits, and insecurity in the land stultifies trade. So, it is not surprising that under Sundiata, Mali took over Ghana's role of maintaining order and the development and control of trade. To achieve this, it was necessary for Sundiata's authority to penetrate not only the far-flung agricultural areas where gold was mined, but also the ports and caravan routes across the Sahara to North Africa. A political and military machine, to ensure conditions in which producers and traders could work in peace and security over the widest area, was built up. New territories were conquered, and Mali grew into an empire, with Sundiata at its head. At the zenith of its power in the fourteenth century, the Mali Empire extended as far as the Atlantic in the west, beyond Gao towards the borders of Hausaland in the east and to the Sahara in the north, encompassing such famous cities as Gao, Timbuktu, Jenne, Walata, and Tekedda.

There were many *mansas*, or kings, who sat on the Mali throne after Sundiata and it is not necessary to mention them all. One we must not overlook is Mansa, Kankan Musa, who reigned from 1312 to 1337 and became the most famous of Mali's emperors.

Once, when Mansa Musa was asked how he became emperor of Mali he replied that his predecessor, who was his uncle, had often looked at the sea and wondered what lay beyond it. One day, he decided to find out. He called his councilors and informed them of his intention to fit out ships with men and sufficient provisions to last a long time and sail across the Atlantic to see what lay beyond it adding, "If I do not return, you, my sister's son, Kankan Musa, will take my place as king, in accordance with our custom." He never returned.[1] On the basis of this and other evidence, Sweeting concludes that "the Mandingoes of Mali and Songhay Empires, and possibly other Africans, crossed the Atlantic to carry on trade with the Western Hemisphere Indians and further succeeded in establishing colonies throughout the Americas. . . . This daring Monarch, Abubakari II (1305-1307), did not believe that it was impossible to conquer the limits of the neighboring ocean. Employing Arab navigators who had a knowledge of longitude and latitude, the compass, quadrant, sextant, he equipped 400 ships with men, food, water, and gold, in sufficient quantity for an extended duration, and sent them sailing across the Atlantic. His Captains were informed not to return until they had discovered land, or had exhausted their supplies."[2]

It is not this story, or his acknowledged administrative ability, however, which made Mansa Musa famous, but his fabulous pilgrimage to Mecca in 1324-25. Why did this journey attract such great attention? After all, other people of Mali, including emperors, had gone on pilgrimage to Mecca and become *alhajis*. Why did Mansa Musa's pilgrimage literally put him and his country on the map? It was his splendid standard of living, his manner and style of traveling, his display of immense wealth in gold and boundless generosity that flabbergasted those who saw him and set tongues wagging about him all over the world.

Mounted on a beautiful horse with gold trappings, Mansa Musa traveled with five hundred men, each bearing a staff of gold before him, a retinue of eight thousand people, and trains of camels laden with gold and gifts. On his way, he passed through Walata, Tuat, and Cairo giving generous presents and gifts of gold. In the holy cities, his gifts were particularly large. Mansa Musa gave away so much gold, according to Al-Omari, a North African scholar who lived in Cairo a few years after the fabulous visit, that "the people of Cairo earned incalculable sums." [3] So generous, in fact, was Mansa Musa with his gold that the value of goods on the Cairo market was upset, and the price of gold itself fell by about twelve percent. The pomp and glittering glory of Mansa Musa's caravan, his immense wealth and generosity, the well-mannered behavior of his retinue created a good impression wherever he went and excited wonder and gossip for many years. Al-Omari declared Mansa Musa to be, of all the Muslim rulers of West Africa, "the most powerful, the richest, the most fortunate, the most feared by his enemies and the most able to do good to those around him." [4]

News of Mansa Musa and his fantastic wealth filtered through the Arab world to Europe and Asia. In 1339 Jewish cartographers at Majorca drew a map in which Mali and a picture of Mansa Musa appeared. Mediterranean and European map makers also began to put Mali on their maps and even tried to show travelers how to get there. On one of these maps it is stated, "This Negro lord is called Musa Mali, Lord of the Negroes of Guinea. So abundant is the gold which is found in his land that he is the richest and most noble king in all the land." [5] These maps not only showed Mali but cities, like Timbuktu and Gao, also. As Davidson points out, "Mali was now a world power and recognised as such." [6]

While on pilgrimage to Mecca, Mansa Musa attracted and took many learned men into his service. Among these men was As-Sahili, a poet and architect. During this time, also, Mansa Musa's army at home conquered new territory adding to the Mali Empire lands along the Niger bend, including Gao, the capital of Songhai, and Timbuktu. So, on his way home from Mecca, Mansa Musa visited his newly acquired lands and received the submission of the Songhai king himself. As was the custom, Mansa Musa took two sons of the Songahai king, ostensibly to be trained in court etiquette and ways, but really to be held at his court as hostages to ensure the good behavior of their father. In these lands, As-Sahili was able to show his skill and great ability as an architect by constructing magnificent mosques at Gao and the University of Sankore at Timbuktu as well as palaces for the emperor to live in. It was As-Sahili who introduced the use of burnt bricks in Mali and inaugurated a new style of architecture. Just as one can talk of Gothic or Romanesque architecture, so can one talk of a Malian style originated by As-Sahili. So we see the Malian state enjoyed many attributes of a civilized state: law and order, a language that could be written (Arabic), and a distinct form of architecture.

European maps advertized Mali as a land with plenty of gold at a time when gold was in short supply. Europeans became interested in West Africa, or, Guinea, as they called it. They even believed Guinea gold to be better than gold mined in other places, consequently, a gold sovereign struck from West African metal was called a "guinea" and was worth a shilling more than a sovereign struck from other gold. To this day, a guinea is one pound, one shilling.

Extensive trade brought prosperity to Mali. There was an increase in culture and learning. Scholarship flourished. Congregating at Timbuktu were lawyers, doctors, and Muslim theologians. Men of letters found honor in the land at a time when Arab scholarship was second to none. By 1337 when Mansa Musa died, the Mali Empire stretched far and wide, was wealthy, prosperous, and well organized while its cities were renowned for their learning and culture.

How did the people of Mali live? We are very fortunate in having an excellent contemporary description of life in the Empire of Mali bequeathed to us by the experienced traveler, Muslim theologian and scholar, Ibn Battuta. He was a Berber tribesman born and educated at Tangier. At the age of twenty-one, he went to study at Mecca and became a renowned scholar. He traveled extensively in the Middle East, India, Ceylon, Assam, and many other places, including Peking in China. He was, therefore, not only an outstanding man of letters, but also an experienced observer. From the things he said about "Negroes," it is reasonable to assume that he was a white Berber. Although he thought the Niger was the Nile and on many occasions evinces the prejudices of a Muslim among non-Muslims, a man in one culture passing judgment on people of another culture, the description of Mali he left us is as fascinating as it is valuable.*

* Quotations from Ibn Battuta translated by H. A. R. Gibb from *Travels of Ibn Battuta in Asia and Africa* (London: Routlege & Kegan Paul, 1927), pp. 317-331. Used with permission of Routledge & Kegan Paul, and Augustus M. Kelley Publisher.

Starting from Sijilmasa, Ibn Battuta went first to Taghaza, as he tells us: "At Sijilmasa I bought camels and a four months' supply of forage for them. Thereupon I set out on the 1st Muharram of the year seven hundred and fifty-three [18th February 1352] with a caravan including, amongst others, a number of the merchants of Sijilmasa. After twenty-five days we reached Taghaza, an unattractive village, with the curious feature that its houses and mosques are built of blocks of salt, roofed with camel skins. There are no trees there, nothing but sand. In the sand is a salt mine; they dig for the salt, and find it in thick slabs, lying one on top of the other, as though they had been tool-squared and laid under the surface of the earth. A camel will carry two of these slabs. No one lives at Taghaza except the slaves of the Masufa tribe, who dig for the salt; they subsist on dates imported from Dara and Sijilmasa, camel's flesh, and millet imported from the Negrolands. The Negroes come up from their country and take away the salt from there. At Walata a load of salt brings eight to ten *mithqals;* in the town of Mali it sells for twenty to thirty, and sometimes as much as forty. The Negroes use salt as medium of exchange, just as gold and silver is used elsewhere; they cut it up into pieces, and buy and sell with it. The business done at Taghaza, for all its meanness, amounts to an enormous figure in terms of hundredweights of gold dust. . . ."

It is interesting to note that today salt is still being mined in the Sahara and transported to the south by camel caravans very much as in the days of Ibn Battuta's visit in 1352.

Ibn Battuta's next port of call was the city of Walata, to which Muslim businessmen had repaired, in opposition to Sumanguru's rule.

"Thus we reached the town of Walata after a journey of two months to a day. Walata is the northernmost province of the Negroes, and the sultan's representative there was one Farba Husayn, *farba* meaning deputy [in their language]. When we arrived there, the merchants deposited their goods in an open square, where the blacks undertook to guard them, and went to the *farba.* He was sitting on a carpet under an archway, with his guards before him carrying lances and bows in their hands, and the headman of the Masufa behind him. The merchants remained standing in front of him while he spoke to them through an interpreter, although they were close to him, to show his contempt for them. It was then that I repented of having come to their country, because of their lack of manners and their contempt for the whites. . . ."

Here, we see the control exercised on merchants by the *farba.* By speaking to merchants through an interpreter, the *farba* was not necessarily showing contempt for the whites. In many African societies, the king or chief, speaks through an official called the "king's mouth."

"Later on," Ibn Battuta continues, "the *mushrif* [inspector] of Walata, whose name was Mansa Ju, invited all those who had come with the caravan to partake of his hospitality. At first I refused to attend, but my companions urged me very strongly, so I went with the rest. The repast was served—some pounded millet mixed with a little honey and milk, put in a half calabash shaped like a large bowl. The guests drank and retired. I said to them, 'Was it for this that the black invited us?' They answered, 'Yes, and it is in their opinion the highest form of hospitality.' This convinced me that there was no good to be hoped for from these people, and I made up my mind to travel back to Morocco at once with the pilgrim caravan from Walata. Afterwards, however, I thought it best to go see the capital of their king [at Mali]."

Somebody, obviously, did a good public relations job because Ibn Battuta stayed on at Walata and tells us something about the city and its inhabitants. "My stay at Walata lasted about fifty days; and I was shown honor and entertained by its inhabitants. It is an excessively hot place, and boasts a few small date-palms, in the shade of which they sow watermelons. Its water comes from underground water beds at that point, and there is plenty of mutton to be had. The garments of the inhabitants, most of whom belong to the Masufa tribe, are of fine Egyptian fabrics. Their women are of surpassing beauty, and are shown more respect than the men. The state of affairs amongst these people is indeed extraordinary. Their men show no sign of jealousy whatever; no one claims descent from his father, but on the contrary from his mother's brother. A person's heirs are his sister's sons, not his own sons. This is a thing which I have seen nowhere in the world except among the Indians of Malabar. But those are heathens; *these* people are Muslims, punctilious in observing the hours of prayer, studying books of law, and memorizing the Koran. Yet their women show no bashfulness before men and do not veil themselves, though they are assiduous in attending prayers. Any man who wishes to marry one of them may do so, but they do not travel with their husbands, and, even if one desired to do so, her family would not allow her to go.

"The women have their 'friends' and 'companions' amongst the men outside their own families, and the men in the same way have 'companions' amongst the women of other families. A man may go into his house and find his wife entertaining her 'companion' but he takes no objection to it. One day at Walata I went into the qadi's house, after asking his permission to enter, and found with him a young woman of remarkable beauty. When I saw her I was shocked and turned to go out, but she laughed at me, instead of being overcome by shame, and the qadi said to me, 'Why are you going out? She is my companion.' I was amazed at their conduct, for he was a theologian and a pilgrim to boot. I was told that he had asked the sultan's permission to make the pilgrimage that year with his 'companion' (whether this one or not I cannot say) but the sultan would not grant it."

After touring Walata, Ibn Battuta traveled to the capital city, Mali: "When I decided to make the journey to Mali, which is reached in twenty-four days from Walata if the traveler pushes on rapidly, I hired a guide from the Masufa (for there is no necessity to travel in company on account of the safety of that road), and set out with three of my companions. On the way there are many trees, and these trees are of great age and girth; a whole caravan may shelter in the shade of one of them. There are trees which have neither branches nor leaves, yet the shade cast by their trunks is sufficient to shelter a man. Some of these trees are rotted in the interior and the rain water collects in them, so that they serve as wells, and the people drink of the water inside them. In others there are bees and honey, which is collected by the people. I was surprised to find inside one tree, by which I passed, a man, a weaver, who had set up his loom in it and actually weaving."

It is interesting to note what Battuta says about the safety of the road, for a traveler in Europe at this time would not have been able to say the same thing because brigands and highway robbers were common along the roads there. The baobab trees that fascinated Battuta are still a spectacular feature of the African landscape today.

"A traveler in this country carries no provisions, whether plain food or seasonings, and neither gold nor silver. He takes nothing but pieces of salt and glass ornaments, which the people call beads, and some aromatic goods. When he comes to a village the womenfolk of the blacks bring out millet, milk, chickens, pulped lotus fruit, rice, *funi* (a grain resembling mustard seed, from which *kuskusu* and gruel are made), and pounded haricot beans. The traveler buys what of these he wants, but their rice causes sickness to whites when it is eaten, and the *funi* is preferable to it. . . .

"Ten days after leaving Walata we came to the village of Zaghari, a large village, inhabitated by Negro traders called *wanjarati,* along with whom lived a community of whites of the Ibadite sect. It is from this village that the millet is carried to Walata. After leaving Zaghari we came to the great river, that is the Nile, on which stands the town of Karsakhu. The Nile flows from there down to Kabara, and thence to Zagha. In both Kabara and Zagha there are sultans who owe allegiance to the king of Mali. The inhabitants of Zagha are of old standing in Islam; they show a great devotion and zeal for study. Thence the Nile descends to Timbuktu and Gao, both of which will be described later; then to the town of Muli in the land of the Limis, which is the frontier province of [the kingdom of] Mali; thence to Nupe, one of the largest towns of the Negroes, whose ruler is one of the most considerable of the Negro rulers. It cannot be visited by any white man because they would kill him before he got there. . . .

"I saw a crocodile in this part of the Nile, close to the bank; it looked just like a small boat. One day I went down to the river to satisfy a need, and lo, one of the blacks came and stood between me and the river. I was amazed at such lack of manners and decency on his part, and spoke of it to someone or other. He answered, 'His purpose in doing that was solely to protect you from the crocodile, by placing himself between you and it.'"

To enter Mali Battuta needed a visa of some sort: "We set out thereafter from Karsakhu and came to the river of Sansara, which is about ten miles from Mali. It is their custom that no persons except those who have obtained permission are allowed to enter the city. I had already written to the white community [there] requesting them to hire a house for me, so when I arrived at the river, I crossed by the ferry without interference. Thus I reached the city of Mali, the capital of the king of blacks. . . .

"The sultan of Mali is Mansa Sulayman, *mansa* meaning [in Mande] sultan, and Sulayman being his proper name. He is a miserly king, not a man from whom one might hope for a rich present. . . .

"On certain days the sultan holds audiences in the palace yard, where is a platform under a tree, with three steps; this they call the *pempi.* It is carpeted with silk, and has cushions placed on it. [Over it] is raised the umbrella, which is a sort of pavilion made of silk, surmounted by a bird of gold, about the size of a falcon. The sultan comes out of a door in a corner of the palace, carrying a bow in his hand and a quiver on his back. On his head he has a golden skull-cap, bound with a gold band which has narrow ends shaped like knives, more than a span in length. His usual dress is a velvety red tunic, made of the European fabrics called *mutanfas.* The sultan is preceded by his musicians, who carry gold and silver *guimbris* [two-stringed guitars], and behind him come three hundred armed slaves. He walks in a leisurely fashion, affecting a very slow movement, and even stops from time to time. On reaching the *pempi* he stops and looks round the assembly, then ascends it in the sedate manner of a preacher ascending a mosque pulpit. As he takes his seat the drums, trumpets, and bugles are sounded. Three slaves go out at a run to summon the sovereign's deputy and the military commanders, who enter and sit down. Two saddled and bridled horses are brought, along with two goats, which they hold to serve as a protection against the evil eye. Dugha stands at the gate, and the rest of the people remain in the street under the trees.

"The Negroes are, of all people, the most submissive to their king and the most abject in their behavior before him. They swear by his name, saying, '*Mansa Sulayman ki.*' If he summons any of them while he is holding an audience in the pavilion, the person summoned takes off his clothes and puts on worn garments, removes his turban and dons a dirty skullcap, and enters with his garments and trousers raised knee-high. He goes forward in an attitude of humility and dejection, and knocks the ground hard with his elbows, then stands with bowed head and bent back listening to what he says. If anyone addresses the king and receives a reply from him, he uncovers his back and throws dust over his head and back, for all the world like a bather splashing himself with water. I used to wonder how it was they did not blind themselves. If the sultan delivers any remarks during his audience, those present take off their turbans and put them down, and listen to what he says. Sometimes one of them stands up before him and recalls his deeds in the sultan's service, saying, 'I did so-and-so on such a day,' or, 'I killed so-and-so on such a day.' Those who have knowledge of this confirm his words, which they do by plucking the cord of the bow and releasing it with a twang, just as an archer does when shooting an arrow. If the sultan says, 'Truly spoken,' or thanks him, he removes his clothes and 'dusts.' That is their idea of good manners. . . ."

It is interesting to note that Europeans would perhaps have understood better what Ibn Battuta described as submissive and abject behavior towards a king. This was nothing more than the expression of loyalty to one's sovereign. The more abject and submissive it seems, the greater the honor, credit, and nobility it reflects in the subject. An Englishman would certainly have understood this better than Ibn Battuta.

Battuta goes on to describe some festivals, "I was at Mali during the two festivals of the sacrifice and the fastbreaking. On these days the sultan takes his seat on the *pempi* after the mid-afternoon prayer. The armor-bearers bring in magnificent arms—quivers of gold and silver, swords ornamented with gold and with golden scabbards, gold and silver lances, and crystal maces. At his head stand four *amirs* driving off the flies, having in their hands silver ornaments resembling saddle stirrups. The commanders, qadi, and preacher sit in their usual places. The interpreter Dugha comes with his four wives and his slave-girls, who are about a hundred in number. They are wearing beautiful robes, and on their heads they have gold and silver fillets, with gold and silver balls attached. A chair is placed for Dugha to sit on. He plays on an instrument made of reeds, with some small calabashes at its lower end, and chants a poem in praise of the sultan, recalling his battles and deeds of valor. The women and girls sing along with him and play with bows. Accompanying them are about thirty youths, wearing red woollen tunics and white skullcaps; each of them has a drum slung from his shoulder and beats it. Afterward come his boy pupils who play and turn wheels in the air, like the natives of Sind. They show a marvelous nimbleness and agility in these exercises, and play most cleverly with swords. Dugha makes a fine play with the sword. Thereupon the sultan orders a gift to be presented to Dugha and he is given a purse containing two hundred *mithqals* of gold dust, and is informed of the contents of the purse before all the people. The commanders rise and twang their bows in thanks to the sultan. The next day each one of them gives Dugha a gift, every man according to his rank. Every Friday after the *'asr* prayer, Dugha carries out a similar ceremony to this that we have described.

"On the feast-days, after Dugha has finished his display, the poets come in. Each of them is inside a figure resembling a thrush, made of feathers, and provided with a wooden head with a red beak, to look like a thrush's head. They stand in front of the sultan in this ridiculous make-up and recite their poems. I was told that their poetry is a kind of sermonizing in which they say to the sultan: 'This *pempi* which you occupy was that whereon sat this king and that king, and such were this one's noble actions and such and such the other's. So do you too do good deeds whose memory will outlive you.' After that the chief of the poets mounts the steps of the *pempi* and lays his head first on the sultan's right shoulder and then on his left, speaking all the while in their tongue and finally he comes down again. I was told that this practice is a very old custom amongst them, prior to the introduction of Islam, and that they have kept it up.

"The Negroes disliked Mansa Sulayman because of his avarice. His predecessor was Mansa Mabha, and before him reigned Mansa Musa, a generous and virtuous prince, who loved the whites and made gifts to them. It was he who gave Ibn Ishaq as-Sahili four thousand *mithqals* in the course of a single day. I heard from a trustworthy source that he gave three thousand *mithqals* on one day to Mudrik ibn Faqqus, by whose grandfather his own grandfather, Saraq Jata, had been converted to Islam."

Battuta emphasizes the avarice and miserly nature of Mansa Sulayman as a man from whom one might have little hope for a rich present, because generosity is the hallmark of an African king or chief. No one should go hungry in his presence. He receives gifts but bestows richer and greater ones to those who come to pay their respects to him. He must give gifts worthy of a king.

"The Negroes possess some admirable qualities. They are seldom unjust, and have a greater abhorrence of injustice that any other people. The sultan shows no mercy to anyone who is guilty of the least act of it. There is complete security in their country. Neither traveler nor inhabitant in it has anything to fear from robbers or men of violence. They do not confiscate the property of any white man who dies in their country, even if it be accounted wealth. On the contrary, they give it into the charge of some trustworthy person among the whites, until the rightful heir takes possession of it. They are careful to observe the hours of prayer, and assiduous in attending them in congregations, and in bringing up their children to them. On Fridays, if a man does not go early to the mosque, he cannot find a corner to pray in, on account of the crowd. It is the custom of theirs to send each man his boy [to the mosque] with his prayer-mat; the boy spreads it out for his master in a place befitting him and remains on it [until his master comes to the mosque]. The prayer-mats are made of the leaves of a tree resembling a date-palm, but without fruit.

"Another of their good qualities is their habit of wearing clean white garments on Fridays. Even if a man has nothing but an old worn shirt, he washes it and cleans it, and wears it at the Friday service. Yet another is their zeal for learning the Koran by heart. They put their children in chains if they show any backwardness in memorizing it, and they are not set free until they have it by heart. I visited the qadi in his house on the day of the festival. His children were chained up, so I said to him, 'Will you not let them loose?' He replied, 'I shall not do so until they learn the Koran by heart.'"

Fairness and justice, security and safety of life and property, even the property of strangers; assiduous attention to religious duties; personal cleanliness and zeal in the learning of the Koran were some of the good qualities of the people of Mali, Battuta observed.

He also recorded what he thought were their bad qualities.

"Among their bad qualities are the following. The women servants, slave-girls, and young girls go about in front of everyone naked, without a stitch of clothing on them. Women go into the sultan's presence naked and without coverings, and his daughters also go about naked. Then there is the custom of their putting dust and ashes on their heads as a mark of respect, and the grotesque ceremonies we have described when the poets recite verses. Another reprehensible practice among many of them is the eating of carrion, dogs, and asses."

This is a good example of looking at one culture or society through spectacles colored by the tastes, prejudices, mores, and outlook of another. Battuta talks of slave-girls, were they really slaves? He disliked seeing servants (women) going about naked. Even the qadi's daughters went about naked, so it was not a matter of being able to afford clothes.

No doubt, he was embarrassed as all of us would be today. The putting of dust and ashes on the heads might not be too surprising to people who donned sackcloth and ashes as a sign of repentance; nor would the ceremonies during which poets recited their verses, to people familiar with the role and functions of poets laureate in other societies. Even carrion—dogs, asses, and horses—is eaten in various parts of the world today. So, whether or not one is shocked by something may depend on the cultural spectacles through which one is looking. There is no doubt, however, that Ibn Battuta, carefully recorded his honest reactions and observations to the things and life of the people he saw in Mali.

As we have seen, the Empire of Mali stretched to its farthest limits at the time of Mansa Musa's death. To administer and keep together such a large empire required great skill and wisdom, and Mansa Musa had these qualities. As long as he was alive the empire remained intact, but after his death less gifted emperors sat on the throne, and the large empire began to disintegrate. There were also rival claimants to the throne and even usurpers. The Muslim religion embraced by the emperors was not accepted by the vast majority of the people who remained content to practice their traditional religion. This created problems and brought disunity in the empire.

The Mossi people from the upper Volta attacked and took Timbuktu burning the city to the ground. The two Songhai princes escaped and returned to Gao where they drove out Mali rulers from their kingdom. One of the brothers, Ali Kholeni, established himself as king in his father's old capital of Gao. The Tuareg of the southern Sahara seized Walata. Tekrur and other kingdoms also broke away. Clearly, Mali had long outgrown its political and military strength. By about 1550, the Mali Empire no longer existed. Another, that of Songhai, had risen in its place.

NOTES

1. This story is from Prof. Ivor Wilks in a lecture at Indiana University in 1965.
2. Sweeting, *African History.*
3. Al Omari as quoted by Davidson, *West Africa,* p. 51.
4. Al Omari as quoted by Davidson, *West Africa,* p. 51.
5. Margaret Shinnie, *Ancient African Kingdoms* (New York: St. Martin's, 1965), p. 55.
6. Davidson, *West Africa,* p. 51.

CHAPTER 11
Songhai

As we have seen, Songhai became a tributary of Mali about 1325 when Mansa Musa, returning from his memorable pilgrimage to Mecca, personally received the submission of its king.

Songhai kings remained vassals of the emperors of Mali until Ali Kholeni and his brother escaped from the Mali court and restored the independence of their country. To maintain this independence, Songhai had to fight not only the people of Mali but also the Tuareg and the Mossi who wished to conquer it. Because of the necessity to defend itself against enemies around it, Songhai built an army that soon became an effective offensive instrument for the conquest of other people.

The Songhai army reached the zenith of its power under the command of one of its kings, Sonni Ali, otherwise known as Ali Ber, or simply as the Shi. He is still remembered as the great wizard who ascended to the Songhai throne in 1464. Sonni Ali was a man of indomitable spirit, monumental courage, great foresight, and irresistible power. He was a military genius, ambitious and ruthless. Always moving swiftly from one campaign to another, always changing his place of residence, always reorganizing his army, always refashioning his plans, always restless, Sonni Ali was invincible. In thirty-five years of waging war, he was never once defeated. As Mahmud el Kati recorded, "He was always victorious. He directed himself against no country without destroying it. No army led by him in person was put to rout. Always conqueror, never conquered, he left no region, town, or village . . . without throwing his cavalry against it, warring against its inhabitants and ravaging them." [1]

He drove out the Mossi from Songhai lands, and hearing of quarrels among Tuareg rulers of Timbuktu, set out with an army and captured the city in 1468, putting many of its citizens to the sword because, he alleged, they had cooperated with his enemies, the Tuaregs. For this slaughter of its citizens, some learned men of Timbuktu afterwards described Sonni Ali as a ruthless tyrant and oppressor.

After the capture of Timbuktu, Sonni Ali laid siege to Jenne which had become a great center of learning and an important market for the gold and kola-nut trade. Jenne held out for seven years before capitulating to the Songhai emperor, enabling him to complete the establishment of his power in all the major trading cities of the region—Gao, Timbuktu, and Jenne. Sonni Ali's army fought the Mossi, Tuareg, and many other people, including the Dogon, Koromba, and Fulani of Gurma.

In November 1492, Sonni Ali died while returning from an expedition against the Fulani of Gurma. He was succeeded by his son, Sonni Baru. Sonni Baru was neither a great enough soldier nor a shrewd enough politician to remain long on the Songhai throne. Unlike his father, who based his power on the loyalty of the non-Muslim majority of his subjects in the countryside while cultivating the support of Muslims in the cities by making important concessions to Islam, Sonni Baru refused to declare himself a Muslim and made it quite clear he was going to side entirely with non-Muslims. Muslims were too powerful, particularly in the cities, to be treated in this manner. One of his father's ablest generals, Muhammad Turé, organized a rebellion against him less than fourteen months after he had become emperor. Civil war broke out. Sonni Baru was defeated in battle and deposed. So in 1493, at the age of fifty, Muhammad Turé became emperor of Songhai and, before long, was known as Askia the Great. He reigned for thirty-five years as an avowed Muslim. Even though many traditional customs and practices were observed at his court, his power was based on the cities and his laws were largely in accord with Islamic ideas. While on a pilgrimage to Mecca in 1495-97, he was appointed *Caliph,* i.e., spiritual leader of Muslims in West Africa.

It was, indeed, fortunate for the people of the Empire of Songhai that such a man as Askia the Great had taken over the reigns of power, for he was a man of vision, a great political and military strategist, an able organizer and an inspiring administrator. He built on the solid foundations laid by Sonni Ali.

Like his predecessor he consolidated the empire and extended its boundaries. He waged war and conquered people as far as the Futa Toro in the west, past the Hausa states to the borders of Bornu in the east, and into the ancient market towns of Air and Agades, in the north. He developed the administrative innovations initiated by Sonni Ali to a point where the Songhai Empire's machinery of central government was among the strongest and most effective in existence. It had many modern features, as Margaret Shinnie points out, "He divided his kingdom into provinces and put a governor, often a member of his own family or a trusted friend, in charge of each province. He created a number of central offices, almost like the Ministries of a modern government, to look after justice, finance, agriculture, and other matters of importance in the running of a state. He instituted a system of taxation whereby each town or district had its own tax collector, and he made some improvements which were designed to benefit trade, as for example putting an inspector in charge of each important market, and making weights and measures the same all over the kingdom. Apart from this kind of administrative reform, as a Muslim, he was sympathetic to the work of Muslims within his state, and encouraged them—the traders, and especially the learned men. Timbuktu, Jenne, and Walata flourished as centers of religion and learning, and as always when the Muslim population was settled and at peace trade flourished also and brought added wealth to Gao and Timbuktu. Sudan gold continued to flow northward, together with slaves, ivory, ebony and ostrich feathers, and in exchange came manufactured goods of copper and iron, brassware, sword blades from Spain and Germany, cloth, and of course salt. Timbuktu became a great centre, and its University, one of the first in Africa, was so famous that scholars came to it all over the Muslim world."[2] These are modern ideas of administration which, all too often, Africans are not given credit for initiating and developing.

What kind of life did the people of the Songhai Empire live? There is a firsthand description of the Empire of Songhai, in the days of Askia the Great, by Al Hassan Ibn Muhammad, better known as Leo Africanus, who accompanied his uncle on a mission to Timbuktu from the Sultan of Fez to Askia the Great in 1513.* Leo Africanus was a Moor born in Granada, Spain about 1495. After the fall of Granada to Ferdinand and Isabella, his family crossed the Mediterranean and settled at Fez where he received a very good Muslim education. He traveled extensively in West Africa and other parts of the world. While returning from Constantinople in 1520, he was captured by Christian pirates and taken to Rome where Pope Leo X gave him his freedom and a pension which enabled him to lead a scholarly life in Rome reading Italian, Latin, Greek, and also writing. On his conversion to Christianity, he was christened Giovanni Leo. It is believed, however, that he again embraced Islam in later years when he returned to Africa. While in Rome he wrote of his visit to West Africa during the reign of Askia the Great.

"Here are many shops of artificers and merchants, and especially of such as weave linen and cotton cloth. And hither do the Barbary merchants bring cloth of Europe. All the women of this region, except the maid-servants, go with their faces covered, and sell all necessary victuals. The inhabitants, and especially strangers there residing, are exceeding rich, insomuch that the king that now is, married both his daughters to rich merchants. Here are many wells containing most sweet water; and so often as the river Niger overfloweth, they convey the water thereof by certain sluices into the town. Corn, cattle, milk, and butter this region yieldeth in great abundance: but salt is very scarce here; for it is brought hither by land from Taghaza which is 500 miles distant. When I myself was here, I saw one camel's load of salt sold for 80 ducats. The rich king of Timbuktu hath many plates and sceptres of gold, some weigh 1300 pounds: and he keeps a magnificent and well-furnished court. When he travelleth any whither he rideth upon a

* Quotations from Leo Africanus, *The History and Description of Africa done into English by John Pory*, pp. 824-26, from Roland Oliver and Caroline Oliver, ed., *Africa in the Days of Exploration*, © 1965, pp. 22-23. Reprinted by permission of Prentice-Hall, Inc., Englewood Cliffs, New Jersey.

camel which is led by some of his noblemen; and so he doth likewise when he goeth forth to warfare, and all his soldiers ride upon horses. Whoever will speak unto this king must first fall down before his feet, and then taking up earth must sprinkle it upon his own head and shoulders: which custom is ordinarily observed by . . . ambassadors from other princes. He hath always 3000 horsemen, and a number of footmen that shoot poisoned arrows, attending upon him. They have often skirmishes with those that refuse to pay tribute, and so many as they take, they sell unto the merchants of Timbuktu. Here are very few horses bred, and the merchants and courtiers keep certain little nags which they use to travel upon: but their best horses are brought out of Barbary. . . . Here are great store of doctors, judges, priests, and other learned men, that are bountifully maintained at the king's cost and charges, and hither are brought divers manuscripts or written books out of Barbary, which are sold for more money than any other merchandise. The coin of Timbuktu is of gold without any stamp or superscription: but in matters of small value they use certain shells brought hither out of the kingdom of Persia, 400 of which are worth a ducat: and 6 2/3 pieces of their gold coin weigh an ounce. The inhabitants are people of gentle and cheerful disposition, and spend a great part of the night singing and dancing through all the streets of the city. . . ."

It is interesting to note that the people wove linen and cloth even though cloth was also imported from Europe. Unlike Ibn Battuta, Leo Africanus does not say anything about some women being naked, only that they were veiled and engaged in the sale of victuals. The people, especially foreign merchants, were rich, so rich in fact that merchants could marry into the royal family.

Notice also that at that time Africans already knew how to sink wells and divert water in sluices, how to grow crops and look after cattle, and they were engaged in long-distance trade. Notice that the aristocracy had many plates and scepters of gold, and the Askia's palace was one that a well-educated and widely traveled man like Leo, who had seen the best in Rome, could describe as "a magnificent and well-furnished court." Notice the use of camels and horses and the fact that the king had the men and means to back his authority and power.

It is not sufficiently appreciated that there were doctors, judges, priests, and learned men in the cosmopolitan African city enjoying the patronage of the emperor. Notice that "divers manuscripts" or books were written in the country and exported, presumably to Europe and other parts of the world, and that books sold for more money than any other merchandise. Only an intellectually oriented society places that kind of value on books. The society had gone beyond the mere exchange or barter of goods, for there was money, gold coins and cowrie shells. And, finally, notice the peaceful and happy disposition of the people who delighted the traveler with singing and dancing through the streets at night.

It is necessary to draw particular attention to all these things because Africans have been described as "savages," "barbarians," and uncivilized people who are emerging from darkness only because of the efforts of white men. Is what we have seen in Ancient Ghana, Medieval Mali, and Songhai the history of an uncivilized and barbaric people? Was Europe any better at the time? Do not let anyone brainwash you with that kind of nonsense anymore.

Long before Europeans dominated Africa, Africans had organized large empires with a high civilization, great cities, and a flourishing economy based on agriculture, mining, and trade. Among the great cities of Africa in the precolonial period was Timbuktu. This city was not only an important administrative center in which was one of the palaces of the emperors of Songhai, it was, also, a great commercial, religious, and educational center. It had business houses, mosques, and also the famous University of Sankore, which attracted learned professors and students from all parts of the world. According to Basil Davidson, "Timbuktu and Jenne had well-known scholars of their own. The most renowned of the sixteenth century was probably Ahmad Baba. Born in Timbuktu in 1556, Ahmad Baba composed many works on Islamic law as well as a biographical dictionary of Muslim scholars. At least thirteen of his works are still in use by the 'ulama' of West Africa. His library was so good that it was held in high esteem for many years after his death. His bravery and independence of mind were also much respected. It is easy to see why.

"When the Moroccan invaders seized Timbuktu, Ahmad Baba

refused to serve them. Fearing his influence and accusing him of fomenting a rebellion, the Moroccans took him in chains across the Sahara to Marrakesh. There they detained him for many years before allowing him to come home again. So it may be said that Ahmad Baba, who never ceased to protest against the invasion of his native land, was not only an outstanding scholar but also in his daily life one of the forerunners of West African nationalism.

"Two important histories of the Western Sudan were also written by scholars of Timbuktu. They are the *Tarikh al-Fattash*. the Chronicle of the Seeker after Knowledge, and the *Tarikh as-Sudan*, the Chronicle of the [Western] Sudan. Both were composed in Arabic, for this was the literary language of these learned men, just as Latin was the literary language of their contemporaries in Europe. Both were the work of West Africans born in Timbuktu. The first of these was Mahmud Kati, who was born in about 1468 and is said to have lived to the age of 125; and the second was Abd al-Rahman as-Sadi, who was born in 1569 and lived until about 1655.

"Both had fine careers. Kati was only twenty-five when the famous Songhay ruler, Askia Muhammad the Great, took over power from Sunni Baru; Kati became a member of the Askia's personal staff. He went to Mecca with the emperor and was thus well placed to observe and understand the events of his time. He began his great book in about 1519, but his sons and grandsons, who were also scholars, continued to work on it and brought the story of Songhay and Timbuktu down to about 1665.

"Abd al-Rahman as-Sadi was born only a few years before the Moroocan invasion, which he suffered as a child. He tells us in the *Tarikh as-Sudan* that it was because of all the sad events he had witnessed in youth that he decided to write his book. In a moving preface he recalls how he saw 'the ruin of learning and its utter collapse' under the hammer-blows of Moroccan onslaught. 'And because learning is rich in beauty,' he explains, 'and fertile in its teaching, since it instructs men about their fatherland, their ancestors, their history, the names of their heroes and what lives they lived, I asked God's help and decided to set down all that I myself could learn on the subject of the Songhay princes of the Sudan, their adventures, their story, their achievements, and their wars. Then I added the history of Timbuktu from the time of its foundation, of the princes who ruled there and the scholars and saints who lived there, and of other things as well.' For some of these 'other things' we can be very thankful: they include, for example, many of the early stories of Ancient Ghana and Mali.

"This capacious activity of Muslim scholarship and writing never ceased in West Africa, but has grown and spread with the passing of years. Today there are many *ulama* ("teachers") with many pupils, whether in the northern country of the plains or the southern country of the forests. In the little town of Wa in northern Ghana, for example, the present writer was told in 1964 that its Koranic school was teaching a regular two-year course and producing about one hundred *talibe,* or qualified students, every two years. Often these *ulama* have considerable libraries of their own with works ranging from ancient manuscripts to the newest books and periodicals. It was from libraries such as these that Europeans first learned of such works of historical scholarship as the Tarikhs of Timbuktu. Only in the last few years has there been any systematic effort at publishing the more interesting contents of these libraries, and much in this respect still remains to be done." [3] But it is obvious that West Africa's history began to be written long before the white man came.

Es-Sadi, author of the *Tarikh es Sudan* who was born of an aristocratic Timbuktu family and became the *imam,* i.e. the spiritual and secular authority, of both Timbuktu and Jenne, tells us more of Timbuktu's history.* "The town was founded by the Maghsharen Tuareg at the end of the fifth century of the Hegira [c. 1200 A.D.]. They came to the region to graze their herds. In the summer season they used to camp on the banks of the Niger in the village of Amazagha. In the autumn they returned to Aruan where they lived. It was their extreme limit in the highland regions. They actually chose the site which is occupied by this exquisite, pure, charming, celebrated, blessed, rich, and gay city, which is my birthplace, and that which I hold dearest in all the world.

"Never has Timbuktu been profaned by the worship of idols.

* Quotations from Es Sadi, *Tarikh es Sudan,* translated from the French (tr. O. Houdas, Paris, 1900) by Caroline Oliver. From Oliver and Oliver, eds. *Africa in the Days of Exploration,* © 1965, pp. 20-21. Reprinted by permission of Prentice-Hall, Inc., Englewood Cliffs, New Jersey.

On its soil no one has ever knelt but to the Merciful. It is the refuge of the learned and the devout, the habitual dwelling of saints and pious men.

"At first it was the meeting place of travelers coming by land or water. They made there a warehouse for their tackle and grain. Soon the place became a crossroads for travelers who passed through going to and fro. They entrusted the care of their effects to a female slave called Timbuktu, a word which in the vernacular means 'the ancient one.' It is from her that the blessed spot has taken its name.

"Later on, the place where by God's will people went to cross the river began to be residential. They came from all parts, and soon it became a center of commerce. To begin with it was the people of Wagadu who came to trade in the greatest numbers. Later traders came from all the neighboring regions.

"Formerly, the center of commerce was at Biru. The caravans of all nations flowed there, and great scholars and pious persons and rich men of all races and all countries settled there. They came from Egypt, Awdjela, Fezzan, Ghadames, Tuat, Dana, Tafilelt, Fez, Sus, Bitu, etc.

"All this transferred itself little by little to Timbuktu, and ended by being concentrated there entirely. The tribes of the Sanhadja added themselves to the population as well. The prosperity of Timbuktu was the ruin of Biru. Its civilization came to it entirely from the Maghrib, both as regards religion and commerce.

"At first the dwelling of the inhabitants consisted of straw huts in thorn enclosures, and then changed to mud huts. Eventually the town was enclosed with very low mud walls, of a kind which enabled you to see from outside what was going on inside. They built a big mosque, sufficient to their needs, and then the Sankore mosque. Anyone standing at the city gate at that time could see those who were entering the big mosque, as then the town had few walls and buildings. It was only at the end of the ninth century [of the Hegira] that the prosperity of the town finally sprang to life. The dense medley of buildings was not completed till the middle of the tenth century [of the Hegira] in the reign of Askia Daud, son of the Amir Askia-el-Hajji-Muhammad. As has already been said, the first dynasty to reign in Timbuktu was that of the people of Mali. It lasted a hundred years starting from 737 [1336-1337 A.D.]. Following that, the Maghsharen Tuareg ruled for forty years from 837 [1433-1434]. After them came Sonni Ali, whose reign, starting in 873 [1468-1469], lasted twenty-four years. It was replaced by the Prince of Believers, Askia-el-Hajji-Muhammad, whose reign, and that of his successors, lasted a hundred-and-one years, from the 14th Djumada II of the year 898, to the 17th Djumada II of the year 999 (2nd April 1493–12th April 1591). Finally the power fell to the Hashimite ruler, the Sultan Mulay Ahmad adh Dhahabi [of Morocco] whose domination began with the fall of the Songhai dynasty, that is to say, on the 17th Djumada II 999 (12th April 1591). Today it is sixty-five years since the reign of this prince and his successors began."

When Askia the Great was eighty-five years old, blind and almost out of his mind, his eldest son took over the throne in 1528, ten years before the father died. Askia Musa did not treat his aged father well. He let the former emperor suffer much misery and, like Sonni Baru, turned against Islam. He was assassinated after reigning only three years.

From 1531 to 1588 there were several askias, the most notable and ablest of whom was Daud (1549-82). During the reign of Issihak II, who ascended to the throne in 1582, however, Songhai military supremacy was shattered by a Moroccan army.

Moroccans had long been aware and envious of Songhai wealth and power across the desert. In 1578 Portugal invaded Morocco with twenty-five thousand men and was thoroughly defeated, her huge army being almost totally wiped out at Al-Ksar al-Kabir. Morocco was ruled after this by Mansur the Victorious, a twenty-nine-year-old prince who succeeded his brother, killed in the hour of victory. Mansur was compelled to secure his place on the Moroccan throne by making so many and such generous gifts that his financial resources were soon exhausted. So he turned his attention to Songhai across the desert.

In 1582 Mansur sent a force of two hundred men to seize the Songhai salt mines at Taghaza which he claimed were in his dominions. His soldiers were armed with the arquebus, a form of musket totally unknown in the Songhai Empire. The skirmish which ensued marked the introduction of firearms in West Africa. It was also the beginning of a war between Morocco and Songhai which ended in the ruin of the Songhai Empire.

Mansur's assault on Taghaza was successful. The salt mines were seized, but he soon found that he could not hold them. It was impossible to keep an army permanently in that dry, thirsty region. Mansur, therefore, decided to invade the Songhai homeland hoping thereby to get quickly the gold and wealth he needed to improve his own financial position.

In 1591, he sent an army against Songhai led by a Spaniard named Judar, who had become a Muslim. Judar had four thousand men under his command. Most of these men were Europeans; Christian, Portuguese, and Spaniards captured at Al-Kabir; who had turned Muslim and accepted service in the Moroccan army rather than suffer death or long imprisonment. Some were European slaves bought from pirates along the coast and European mercenaries willing to fight anyone, anywhere, for money. There were also with these men, regular Moroccan troops. Judar's two thousand infantry were armed with muskets, as were his five hundred horsemen. The fifteen hundred light cavalry were equipped with long spears. In addition they had six small cannons and nine thousand transport animals with them.

Judar's men took about six months to cross the desert and, not unnaturally, Issihak II, Emperor of Songhai, heard about them. His scouts filled up most of the wells along the route causing many of Judar's men to die of thirst. When the Moroccan army finally entered the Songhai homeland, thirst and the perils of crossing the desert had reduced its four thousand soldiers to a thousand men.

Issihak II decided to meet the invaders at Tondibi, thirty-five miles from Gao. He put into the field against them an army of eighteen thousand cavalry and nine thousand infantry armed with spears, axes, bows and arrows. But the advantages of gunpowder and firearms over spears, bows, and arrows was too much for them, and the Songhai army was soon routed, despite its heroic bravery. The Moroccans made for the towns which, one after another, fell to them. They found and took some wealth, but not as much as they expected. Mansur was not satisfied with what he received.

The Songhai Emperor changed his tactics. He avoided pitched

battles and resorted to guerilla warfare. The Moroccans were never complete masters of the land in spite of several bodies of reinforcements being sent.

They were too few to subdue completely the whole empire. Trade was interrupted and gold ceased to flow to the cities. The Moroccans were unable to penetrate deep into the rural areas where gold was mined. They lingered on in the cities, married local girls, and created a new ruling class—the *arma.* The arma was soon torn by rivalry and dissention which resulted in several competing governments arising where there had been but one.

In spite of this, the Songhai Empire never recovered from the blow struck by the Moroccan army. It disintegrated and, once more, a great West African empire passed into history.

NOTES

1. M. Shinnie, *Ancient Kingdoms,* p. 58.
2. Shinnie, *Ancient Kingdoms,* p. 58.
3. Davidson, *West Africa,* pp. 167-69.

CHAPTER 12
Other Empires of West Africa

The West African empires of Ghana, Mali, and Songhai are not the only great empires Africa can boast of. There were others just as noteworthy. Unfortunately, we do not have space in this book to scrutinize them all in detail. We shall, therefore, only take a glance at a few.

Kanem-Bornu

Eastward in the region of Lake Chad but west of the Nile, flourished the states of Kanem and Bornu. The fertile lands of the lake shores and the absence of such natural barriers as deserts, mountains, and tropical forests, attracted nomadic herdsmen as well as communities of farmers. Among the early inhabitants of this region were the dark-skinned Zaghawa.

Several Arab chroniclers took note of them, and from the writings of such men as El Yakubi and El Muhallabi many interesting facts may be learned. The Zaghawa were skilled in agriculture, raising millet, beans, and wheat. They also kept herds of cattle, camels, horses, and goats. These people held their king in special reverence. They worshiped him as divine, and he was believed to be the source of life and death, health and sickness. One of the restrictions placed on the king himself was that he never eat in public.

As Kanem became powerful and conquered territory after territory, it adopted a form of government similar to that of the great empires of the Sudan. The king became an emperor, enjoying the allegiance of weaker kings who were forced to pay tribute but were left to rule very much according to their own laws and customs. During the reign of Emperor Salma (1194-1221), Islam was established in Kanem. Mosques were built, and the Koran and other books in Arabic were introduced. There was contact with Arab traders and scholars, and Kanem became part of the Arab world.

Perpetual fighting, revolts, and fratricidal strife, nevertheless, weakened the empire to a point where it could no longer prevent the invasion of its territory by Bulala tribesmen. About 1386, the *mai*, or king, Omar of the Kanuri, decided to move to a more secure region west of Lake Chad. Here his people settled amidst a native population whose rulers were left undisturbed. In these lands, his kingdom became known as Bornu. It was a kingdom divided into provinces and estates whose administration was entrusted to individuals on whom the mai relied for soldiers in time of war. The mai continued to be a godlike figure, completely secluded from his subjects. He was never seen by them, and he spoke to them from behind a curtain or screen.

One of the great kings of Bornu was Mai Ali (1476-1507) builder of the capital city of Birni Gazargamo on the river Tobe, along the boundary of the present-day republics of Nigeria and Niger. Ruins of this city include an earth wall twenty feet high, which surrounds an area 1 3/4 miles in diameter, in which the remains of a red brick palace and other buildings can still be seen today. Another famous mai was Idris Aloma, who became king of Bornu in 1570. His military exploits were carefully recorded by his religious leaders. Most of his soldiers wore chain mail, quilted armor, and iron helmets. They fought mounted on horses and used firearms a few years before guns were generally known in West Africa. Although Idris Aloma did not extend the boundaries of Bornu very widely, he cleared former Kanuri territory of Bulala tribesmen. He made Islam the state religion and law, and exercised effective control over tribes paying tribute to Bornu.

The splendor of Bornu was still very much in evidence during the nineteenth century when some Europeans visited the country. Although, at this time, real power had passed from the ancient dynasty of Bornu to a military adventurer from the eastern Sudan, the Shaikh, Al-Amin ibn Muhammad al-Kanemi, who had refused to be sultan and maintained a member of the hereditary family as a puppet sultan, the essential character of the state had not changed.

In 1823 three Englishmen Major Dixon Denham, Captain Hugh Clapperton, and Dr. Oudney visited Bornu. They wrote a valuable account of their arrival at Kukawa the capital, of their meeting with Shaikh Al-Amin ibn Muhammad al-Kanemi and their audience with the sultan. They also observed Bornu soldiers on the march and on review.*

"Our accounts had been so contradictory of the state of this country, that no opinion could be formed as to the real condition or the numbers of its inhabitants. We had been told that the Shaikh's soldiers were a few ragged Negroes armed with spears, who lived upon the plunder of the black Kaffir countries, by which he was surrounded, and which he was enabled to subdue by the assistance of a few Arabs who were in his service; and, again, we had been assured that his forces were not only numerous, but to a certain degree well trained. The degree of credit which might be attached to these reports was nearly balanced in the scales of probability; and we advanced toward the town of Kukawa in a most interesting state of uncertainty, whether we should find its chief at the head of thousands, or be received by him under a tree, surrounded by a few naked slaves.

"These doubts however were quickly removed. I had ridden on, a short distance in front of Boo-Khaloom, with his train of Arabs, all mounted, and dressed out in their best apparel; and from the thickness of the trees, soon lost sight of them, fancying that the road could not be mistaken. I rode still onward, and on approaching a spot less thickly planted, was not a little surprised to see in front of me a body of several thousand cavalry drawn up in a line, and extending right and left quite as far as I could see; and, checking my horse, I awaited the arrival of my party, under the shade of a wide-spreading acacia. The Bornu troops remained quite steady, without noise or confusion; and a few horsemen, who were moving about in front giving directions, were the only persons out of the ranks. On the Arabs appearing in sight, a shout, or yell, was given by the Shaikh's people, which rent the air: a blast was blown from

* Quotations from Dixon Denham and Hugh Clapperton, *Narrative of Travels and Discoveries in Northern and Central Africa* in Roland Oliver and Caroline Oliver, eds., *Africa in the Days of Exploration*, © 1965, pp. 26-33. Reprinted by permission of Prentice-Hall, Inc., Englewood Cliffs, New Jersey.

their rude instruments of music equally loud, and they moved on to meet Boo-Khaloom and his Arabs. There was an appearance of tact and management in their movements which astonished me. Three separate small bodies, from the center of each flank, kept charging rapidly towards us, to within a few feet of our horses' heads, without checking the speed of their own until the moment of their halt, while the whole body moved onward. These parties were mounted on small but perfect horses, who stopped, and wheeled from their utmost speed with great precision and expertness, shaking their spears over their heads, exclaiming, 'Barca! barca! Allah hiakkum cha, alla cheraga!—Blessing! blessing! Sons of your country! Sons of your country!' and returning quickly to the front of the body, in order to repeat the charge. While all this was going on, they closed in their right and left flanks, and surrounded the little body of Arab warriors so completely, as to give the compliment of welcoming them very much the appearance of a declaration of their contempt for their weakness. I am quite sure this was premeditated. We were all so closely pressed as to be nearly smothered, and in some danger from the crowding of the horses and clashing of the spears. Moving on was impossible; and we therefore came to a full stop. Our chief was much enraged, but it was all to no purpose; he was only answered by shrieks of 'Welcome!' and spears most unplesantly rattled over our heads expressive of the same feeling. This annoyance was not however of long duration. Barca Gana, the shaikh's first general, a Negro of noble aspect, clothed in a figured silk robe, and mounted on a beautiful Mandara horse, made his appearance; and after a little delay, the rear was cleared of those who had pressed in upon us, and we moved on, although but very slowly, from the frequent impediment thrown in our way . . . .

"The shaikh's Negroes, as they were called, meaning the black chiefs and favorites, all raised to that rank by some deed of bravery, were habited in coats of mail composed of iron chain, which covered them from the throat to the knees, dividing behind and coming on each side of the horse. Some of them had helmets, or rather skull-caps, of the same metal, with chin-pieces, all sufficiently strong to ward off the shock of a spear. Their horses' heads were also defended by plates of iron, brass, and silver, just leaving sufficient room for the eyes of the animal.

"At length, on arriving at the gate of the town, ourselves, Boo-Khaloom, and about a dozen of his followers, were alone allowed to enter the gates; and we proceeded along a wide street completely lined with spearmen on foot, with cavalry in front of them, to the door of the shaikh's residence. Here the horsemen were formed up three deep, and we came to a stand. Some of the chief attendants came out, and after a great many 'Barca's! Barca's!' retired, when others performed the same ceremony. We were now again left sitting on our horses in the sun. Boo-Khaloom began to lose all patience, and swore by the bashaw's head that he would return to the tents if he was not immediately admitted. He got, however, no satisfaction but a motion of the hand from one of the chiefs, meaning 'wait patiently': and I whispered to him the necessity of obeying, as we were hemmed in on all sides, and to retire without permission would have been as difficult as to advance. Barca Gana now appeared, and made a sign that Boo-Khaloom should dismount. We were about to follow his example, when an intimation that Boo-Khaloom was alone to be admitted again fixed us to our saddles. Another half hour at least passed without any news from the interior of the building; when the gates opened, and the four Englishmen only were called for, and we advanced to the *skiffa* (entrance). Here we were stopped most unceremoniously by the black guards in waiting, and were allowed, one by one only, to ascend a staircase; at the top of which we were again brought to a stand by crossed spears, and the open flat hand of a Negro laid upon our breast. Boo-Khaloom came from the inner chamber, and asked, 'If we were prepared to salute the shaikh as we did the bashaw?' We replied, 'Certainly': which was merely an inclination of the head, and laying the right hand on the heart. He advised our laying our hands also on our heads, but we replied, 'The thing is impossible! We had but one manner of salutation for any body, except our own sovereign.'

"Another parley now took place, but in a minute or two he returned, and we were ushered into the presence of this Shaikh of Spears. We found him in a small dark room, sitting on a carpet, plainly dressed in a blue *tobe* [robe] of Sudan and a shawl turban. Two Negroes were on each side of him, armed with pistols, and on his carpet lay a brace of these instruments. Firearms were hanging in different parts of the room, presents from the bashaw and Mustapha al-Ahmar, the sultan of Fezzan, which are here considered as invaluable. His personal appearance was prepossessing, apparently not more than forty-five or forty-six, with an expressive countenance, and a benevolent smile.

Reception by the Sultan of Bornu

"Soon after daylight we were summoned to attend the sultan of Bornu. He received us in an open space in front of the royal residence. We were kept at a considerable distance while his people approached to within about 100 yards, passing first on horse-back; and after dismounting and prostrating themselves before him, they took their places on the ground in front, but with their backs to the royal person, which is the custom of the country. He was seated in a sort of cage of cane or wood, near the door of his garden, on a seat which at the distance appeared to be covered with silk or satin, and through the railing looked upon the assembly before him, who formed a sort of semi-circle extending from his seat to nearly where we were waiting. Nothing could be more absurd and grotesque than some, nay all, of the figures who formed this court. Here was all the outward show of pomp and grandeur, without one particle of the staple commodity, power, to plead its excuse. He reigns and governs by the sufferance of the shaikh: and the better to answer his views, by making him more popular with all parties, the sultan is amused by indulging in all the folly and bigotry of the ancient Negro sovereigns. Large bellies and large heads are indispensable for those who serve the court of Bornu; and those who unfortunately possess not the former by nature, or on whom lustiness will not be forced by cramming, make up the deficiency of protuberance by a wadding, which, as they sit on the horse, gives the belly the curious appearance of hanging over the pummel of the saddle. The eight, ten, and twelve shirts, of different colors, that they wear one over the other, help a little to increase this greatness of person. The head is enveloped in folds of muslim or linen of various colors, though mostly white, so as to deform it as much as possible; and those whose turban seemed to be most studied had the effect of making the head appear completely on one side. Besides this they are hung all over with charms, enclosed in little red leather parcels, strung together. . . .

"When these courtiers, to the number of about two hundred and sixty or three hundred, had taken their seats in front of the sultan, we were allowed to approach to within about pistol-shot of the spot where he was sitting, and desired to sit down ourselves. The ugliest black that can be imagined, his chief eunuch, the only person who approached the sultan's seat, asked for the presents. Boo-Khaloom's were produced, enclosed in a large shawl, and were carried unopened to the presence. Our glimpse was but a faint one of the sultan, through the lattice work of his pavilion, sufficient however to see that his turban was larger than any of his subjects' and that his face, from the nose downward, was completely covered. A little to our left, and nearly in front of the sultan, was an extempore declaimer shouting forth praises of his master, with his pedigree; and near him one who bore the long wooden *frumfrum,* on which he ever and anon blew a blast, loud and unmusical. Nothing could be more ridiculous that the appearance of these people squatting down in their places, tottering under the weight and magnitude of their turbans and their bellies, while the thin legs that appeared underneath but ill accorded with the bulk of the other parts.

The Bornu Army on the March

"We now commenced our march with the Bornu army, in which but little order is preserved previous to coming near the enemy. Everyone seems to know that at a certain point the assembly is to take place; and the general instructions seem to be to everyone to make the best of his own way. The shaikh takes the lead, and close after him comes the sultan of Bornu, who always attends him on these occasions, although he never fights. The former is preceeded by five flags, two green, two striped, and one red, with extracts from the Koran written on them in letters of gold, and attended by about a hundred of his chiefs and favorite slaves. A Negro, high in confidence, rides close behind him, bearing his shield, jacket of mail, and wearing his skullcap of steel; he also bears his arms. Another mounted on a swift *maherhy,* and fantastically dressed with a straw hat and ostrich feathers, carries his timbral or drum, which it is the greatest misfortune to lose in action. On the expedition which cost the Sultan Denhamah, the late sultan of Bornu, his life, the timbrel and the shaikh were supposed to have fallen in a sudden rush of Baghirmis. Almost everyone near him suffered. The people, however, firmly believe that he was saved by a miracle. They say, 'He became invisible; that the Baghirmi chiefs scoured the field, calling out for the shaikh; that his drum sounded at intervals, but could not be seen, any more than their leader.' Close in the rear of the maherhies follow the eunuchs and the harem. The shaikh takes but three wives, who are mounted, astride, on small trained horses, each led by a boy slave, or eunuch—their heads and figures completely enveloped in brown silk burnooses, and a eunuch riding by the side of each. The sultan of Bornu has five times as many attendants, and his harem is three times as numerous: he is attended, also, by men bearing trumpets (frumfrum) of hollow wood, ten and twelve feet long. With these a kind of music is constantly kept up. As this instrument is considered an appendage of royalty alone, the shaikh has no *frumfrums*. The *kaigamma* or standard-bearer, rides in front of him, carrying a very long pole, hung round, at the top, with strips of leather and silk of various colors, in imitation probably, of the bashaw's *tigue*, or tails. And two ride on each side of him, called *meestrumha dundelmah*, carrying immense spears, with which they are supposed to defend their sultan in action, whose dignity would be infringed upon by defending himself. But the spears are so hung round with charms, and the bearers so abominably unwieldy, that the idea of such weapons being of any use in the hands of such warriors is absurd. Indeed the grotesque appearance of the whole of this prince's train, with heads hung round with charms, and resembling the size and shape of a hogshead—their protruding stomachs and wadded doublets—is ridiculous in the extreme.

The Shaikh of Bornu Reviews His Troops

"The sun had scarcely risen this morning when the shaikh was on horseback inspecting his favorite troops, the Kanembu infantry. A hollow space under some sandhills, called Gornamaree, was chosen, about a quarter of a mile from the camp, and the whole was conducted with a good deal of order and system. He was attended to the ground by the four sultans who accompanied the expedition under his orders, and a circle was formed by the Arabs and the Bornu horse. The Shaikh's principal slaves and commanders were dispensed in different parts, habited by their scarlet burnooses with gold lace, and surrounded also by their followers. His own dress was, as usual, neat and simple. Two white figured muslin *tobes,* very large, with a burnoose of the same color, and a cashmere shawl for a turban, composed his dress. Over the whole across his shoulders, hung the sword which, as he repeatedly said, 'The Sultan Inglese had sent him.' He was mounted on a very beautiful bright bay horse from Mandara, and took his station on the right side of the circle; while the Kanembus were drawn up on the opposite extremity in close column, to the number of nine thousand. On the signal being made for them to advance, they uttered a yell, or shriek, exceeding anything in shrillness I ever heard; then advanced, by tribes of from eight hundred to one thousand each. They were perfectly naked, with the exception of a rather fantastical belt of the goat or sheepskin, with the hair outward, round their middles, and a few *gubkas* (narrow strips of cloth, the money of the country) round their heads, and brought under the nose. Their arms are a spear and a shield, with a dagger on the left arm reserved, secured by a ring which goes on the wrist, the point running up the arm, and the handle downward. The shields are made of the wood of the fogo, a tree which grows in the shallow waters of the great lake, and are so extremely light as to weigh only a few pounds. The pieces of wood of which it is formed are bound together by thongs of the hides of bullocks with the hair on, which is also carried along the edge of the outside of the shield, in vandykes, and forms an ornament. They are something the shape of a gothic window, and most of them slightly convex. Under cover of these, the Kanembu attack the bowmen with great order, and at a slow pace. Their leaders are mounted, and are distinguished merely by a *tobe* of dark blue, and a turban of the same color.

"On nearing the spot where the shaikh had placed himself, they quickened their pace, and, after striking their spears against their shields for some seconds, which had an extremely grand and stunning effect, they filed off to the outside of the circle, where they again formed, and awaited their companions, who succeeded them in the same order. There appeared to be a great deal of affection between these troops and the shaikh. He spurred his horse onward into the midst of some tribes as they came up, and spoke to them, while the men crowded round him, kissing his feet, and the stirrups of his saddle. It was a most pleasing sight. He seemed to feel how much his present elevation was owing to their exertions, while they displayed a devotion and attachment deserving and denoting the greatest confidence. I confess I was considerably disappointed at not seeing these troops engage, though more than compensated by the reflection of the slaughter that had been prevented by that disappointment."

The Englishmen were, of course, entitled to their views concerning "the folly and bigotry" of "large bellies and large heads" being "indispensable for those who serve the court." Needless to say, Africans saw nothing ridiculous in the appearance of the courtiers. As a matter of fact, even today, in some parts of Africa, portliness and a big belly are still considered prestigious and a sign of opulence.

Hausa States

In the land between Songhai and Kanem-Bornu, lay the Hausa states of Gobir, Daura, Katsina, Zaria, Kano, Rano, and Biram. About eight or nine hundred years ago, these Hausa settlements, each dominated by its main city, came into existence as centers of internal and external trade, government, and a place of refuge when there was a threat of war. The states remained separate; often at loggerheads with one another, even though, they sometimes banded together for their common good. The Hausa states never became a Hausa empire. They developed into strong commercial centers and, when most Hausa kings embraced Islam about 1400, they became an important area of Islamic culture and religion.

Oyo

According to their oral tradition, the Yoruba people are descended from the children of Oduduwa, a prince who came from the east and settled in Ife. Ife is, therefore, regarded by some Yorubas as their spiritual ancestral home. Situated at the edge of the forest, Ife became the great center of Yoruba culture famous for its magnificent art, bronze and brass statuettes which rank with the great art of the world.

Oranmiyan, one of the descendants of Oduduwa, is credited with being the founder of the Empire of Oyo which, at the zenith of its power in the eighteenth century, was bounded by the Niger in the north, Benin in the east, the sea on the south, and included most of the present day Dahomey in the west. At the head of the empire was the *alafin*, or ruler, who was considered sacred. To obviate autocracy and tyranny, the emperor's power was circumscribed by palace, state, and provincial officials; as well as secret political and religious societies. In these groups were those who selected and appointed the alafin. They could condemn him to death by suicide and could review or repudiate his decisions.

Like other African empires, Oyo was based on the allegiance of lesser rulers to the emperor. There was an orderly system of taxation and tribute collection. The practice of executing generals who lost battles in war made the Oyo army formidable. In the nineteenth century, however, the Oyo Empire disintegrated as a result of civil war, brought on in a large measure, by the activities of European slave traders who undermined imperial authority and upset the delicate checks and balance of power by introducing firearms in the empire.

Benin

The Yoruba Empire of Benin, in the forest region east of Oyo, also claimed Oduduwa as ancestor. It is said that the people of Benin, being in need of a good king, asked Oduduwa to send them a prince to rule over them. The choice fell on Oranmiyan who decided that only a prince with Benin blood in his veins could rule successfully in that land. So, he took to wife the daughter of a Bini chief, and they had a son, Eweka, who grew up to be the founder of the Benin Empire. Ewuare, one of its kings who ruled in the middle of the fifteenth century, extended Benin's influence as far as Lagos in the west and the Niger in the east. Like Ife, Benin is famous for its works of art, cast bronzes and carved ivories. The most famous ivory is a mask still used on ceremonial occasions.

European observers of Benin in the seventeenth century were impressed by the efficiency of its government. "The king might be considered just and equitable, as desiring continually his officers to administer justice exactly, and to discharge their duties conscientiously . . . ," John Barbot wrote. "He seldom passes one day, without holding a cabinet council with his chief ministers, for dispatching of the many affairs brought before him . . . appeals from inferior courts of judicature in all parts of the kingdom, and audiences to strangers, or concerning the affairs of war and other emergencies."[1]

Another account, written by a Hollander in 1602, says of the principal city of Benin: "The Towne seemeth to be very great, when you enter it. You goe into a great broad street, not paved, which seemeth to be seven or eight times broader than the Warmoes Street in Amsterdam; which goeth right out, and never crooketh, and where I was lodged with Mattheus Cornelison it was at least a quarter of an hour from the gate, and yet I could not see to the end of the street. . . .

"At the gate where I entered on horsebacke, I saw a very high Bulwarke, very thick of earth, with a very deepe broad ditch, but it was drie, and full of high trees. . . . The gate is a reasonable good Gate, made of wood after their manner, which is to be shut, and there always there is watch holden. . . .

"When you are in the great Street aforesaid, you see many great streets on the sides thereof, which also goe right forth, but you cannot see the end of them, by reason of their great length. A man might write more of the situation of this Towne, if he might see it as you may see the Townes of Holland, which is not permitted there, by one that alwaies goes with you–some men say, that he goeth with you, because you should have no harme done unto you, but yet you goe not further than he will let you.

"The Houses in this Towne stand in good order, one close and even with the other, as the Houses in Holland stand." The houses of the wealthier citizens had steps leading to the entryway, and there were porches "where a man may sit drie; which Gallerie every morning is made cleane by their Slaves, and in it there is a Mat spread for men to sit on . . . but they have other places besides, as Kitchins and other roomes. . . .

"The King's Court is very great, within it having many great four-square Plaines, which round about them have Galleries, wherein there is alwaies watch kept; I was so far within the Court, that I passed over four such great Plaines, and wheresoever I looked, still I saw Gates upon Gates, to goe into other places, and in that sort I went as far as any Netherlander was, which was to the Stable where his best Horses stood. . . ."[2]

Unfortunately, the Empire of Benin, like that of Oyo, eventually disintegrated, primarily as a result of wars consequent upon the importation of firearms. These were often brought in by European slave traders to bolster the power of vassal states against the imperial government. By 1700 Europeans reporting on the principal city of Benin told a different story. The city which had been so impressive and so close-built now had only scattered buildings.

Ashanti

A great African empire of comparatively recent times is the Ashanti Empire. It arose, towards the end of the seventeenth century, in the Akan forest lands between the coast and the Volta River. For centuries past these lands had supplied salt, gold, kola nuts, and other items to trade routes leading to Saharan entrepots. At the close of the seventeenth century, however, Europeans—Dutch, British, Danish, Portuguese, and French—were opening trading station to the south along the coast. The Akan people, being at the junction of northern and southern trade routes, found themselves in a most advantageous position to capture this trade. Through the outstanding leadership of their kings, one of the Akan peoples, the Ashanti, threw off the overlordship of their Denkyira ruler and started on a path of conquest of their own.

Under Osei Tutu, the Ashanti were spiritually united by a sacred symbol, the Golden Stool. According to their sacred lore it had come from Nyame, the supreme god, and had been obtained through the magic powers of Anotchi Okomfo Anokye, the greatest doctor in the land. He had caused it to descend through thick black clouds roaring with thunder, and when the Golden Stool came to rest on Osei Tutu's knees, he became the *asantehene,* the head of the Ashanti nation.

According to Parrinder, Anotchi told the king and people that this Golden Stool contained the soul of all the people of the Ashanti nation and that their health and welfare were in it. From the king, queens and chiefs he took hairs of their bodies and nails from their forefingers. These were made into magical powder, some of which was drunk and some poured on the stool. Anotchi said that the stool must not be sat upon, though on great occasions the king might pretend to sit on it three times and rest his arm on it. Once a year it was taken out in procession, carried under umbrellas and attended with royal state.[3] The king had four bells made and hung on each side of the stool.

When Osei Tutu died on the battlefield in 1717, he had considerably extended the boundaries of Ashanti through conquest. He was succeeded by his nephew Opuku Ware who continued the policy of expansion until Ashanti controlled an empire that stretched from Cape Mount, in present-day Liberia to Dahomey, and from the southern coast to Dagomba and Manprussi in the north.

The administration of this empire was eventually placed in the hands of appointed officials instead of hereditary rulers. Ministers and proconsuls responsible solely to the emperor and under his surveillance took charge of the financial, military, political, and administrative affairs of the empire. The member states, while enjoying a measure of autonomy, were bound together in a federal form of government in which the authority of the central government steadily grew until there was a complex bureaucratic structure uncommon among African nations. Because people of low birth often rose to important positions in the government it was forbidden to enquire of a man's antecedents. Like other African empires of recent times, the Ashanti became involved in eighteenth-century wars for the acquisition of European firearms and in the slave trade, and it was eventually overthrown by the British in 1825.

Fante

Fante people say their ancestors came from Tekyiman in the savanna and migrated to Mankessim along the coast in five groups under the leadership of three priests: Obunumankoma, Odapagyan, and Oson. When the old priests died, they were all buried in a grave at Nananom Mpoon. Because of an increase in the population, wealth, the need to control surrounding territory and political rivalry, groups of Fante left Mankessim to form new kingdoms. The states of Abora, Ekumfi, Nkusukum, Ayan Abasa, Ayan Denkyira, Ayan Maim, etc., were formed in this way. The new states appear, nevertheless, to have recognized the king of Mankessim as supreme head. Unfortunately, this did not prevent them from acting as if they were separate and independent rivals. Disunity prevented the Fante from further expansion at this time.

When the Ashanti emerged as a potential political and economic threat, it was clear that any further Ashanti advance southward would result in the occupation of Fante territory and the loss of their role as middemen in the coastal trade with Europeans. To meet this challenge the Fante rallied together under the leadership of Abora. They realized the importance of preventing the Ashanti from acquiring guns and powder. So, seeking to incorporate neighboring lands in their union, the Fante once more began to expand their territory.

In the face of the Ashanti threat, the Fante stood together and formed a union with a parliament composed of delegates from various states. Unfortunately, they did not have the same unity of spirit and the sense of cohesion that strengthened the Ashanti. They were bound together only by the fear of the Ashanti threat, and whenever this force was removed, they fell into dissension. When the threat was strong during the first thirty years or so of the eighteenth century, the Fante union was stable. Abora was the capital city and center of the union. But after 1720 the Ashanti turned their attention to the north, and the threat of an invasion by them faded. When this happened the union disintegrated. By 1750 each section —the western Fante, or Boroboro, and the eastern Fante, or Ekumfi —had come to consider itself separate and independent.[4]

NOTES

1. Quoted by Basil Davidson in *Black Mother: The Years of the African Slave Trade* (Boston: Little Brown, 1961), p. 232.
2. Quoted by Davidson in *Black Mother*, pp. 230-31.
3. Geoffrey Parrinder, *Religion in Africa* (London: Pall Mall Press, 1969), p. 93.
4. Boahen, *Topics in History*, pp. 181-82.

CHAPTER 13

Empires of Southern and Central Africa

The Bantu People

Among the peoples of southern, central, and eastern Africa linguists have discovered as many as three hundred languages similar to one another. For instance, in all of these, the word for "person" has *ntu,* or a variation, while the plural has *ba,* or a variation. A comparison of the word in several of these languages will illustrate the similarity:

LANGUAGE	SINGULAR	PLURAL
Shona	*munhu*	*vanhu*
Zulu, Xosa, Isindebele	*umuntu*	*abantu*
Sotho, Tswana	*muthu*	*bathu*

Members of one of these language groups do not generally understand members of another, despite the common forms. Linguists call this large group of related languages "Bantu," and its speakers are usually referred to as "Bantu people."

On the basis of the more than two thousand roots these languages have in common it has been concluded that Bantu people originated from a single source, and have since achieved a wide geographical dispersion with only a small linguistic divergence; their linguistic family is regarded as distinctly new.

Various other evidence has led to the deduction that the central

Cameroons and east central Nigeria were the original homelands of the Bantu people. According to linguistic evidence gathered by Professor Joseph Greenberg, the people in eastern Nigeria simply moved straight on southwards and eastwards into the Congo basin and from there fanned out to occupy the whole of what is now Bantu Africa. Professor Malcolm Guthrie studied the concentration of Bantu word roots according to area, and on the basis of the heaviest concentrations, he asserted that wherever Bantu people originally came from, the area in which their descendants multiplied profusely and gradually dispersed over the rest of Bantu Africa is an elliptical area at the heart of which lies the woodland region of the Kantanga. This theory is supported by the oral tradition of several Bantu tribes who say their ancestors came from the north. The Mashona, for instance, say they came from Guruwuskwa, which means "big grass," somewhere in the north.

The evidence also indicates that the Bantu dispersal produced a dynamic population explosion as they pushed southward. This in turn produced a cultural revolution introducing the use of iron tools for agriculture and weapons for hunting and military purposes. The food crops included not only the sorghums, millets, and dry rice, native to the sub Saharan savanna, but also southeast Asian food plants—bananas and yams, which were being grown in Africa at the beginning of the Christian era.*

In the areas where the Bantu spread, they found the land inhabited by hunter-gatherers like Pygmies, Bushmen, and Dorobo; pastoralists like the Hottentots and the Tatog; and cultivators like the Iraqw. Numerous rock paintings and other archaeological evidence testify to the occupation of these areas prior to the arrival of the Bantu.

The stories of some Bantu tribes also indicate the existence of a mysterious short people: *Vana wandi wonerepi,* meaning "from where did you see me." Children are warned that if they ever meet a strange, short man who asks, "From where did you see me?" they are to reply, "I saw you when you were far away, beyond those hills over there." The short man will then leave them alone and go

* See Roland Oliver ,"The Problem of Bantu Expansion," *Journal of African History* 3 (1966), 361-76. Oliver's treatment of this problem provides the point of departure for this chapter.

on his way, pleased that he is a big man visible from a long distance away. But if they reply, "I saw you just now when you were right here," the short man would be displeased and might cause them harm.

Because of their superior skill as hunters and as food growers, the Bantu subdued and absorbed most of the people they found in these lands and, as a result, exhibit a very wide variety of physical types and social customs. In some areas, absorption of the indigenous older culture was only partial, and some representatives of these older types, like the Pgymies and Bushmen, are now found only in the most inhospitable parts of the land—thick forests and the Kalahari desert.

Luba Kingdoms

During the eighth and ninth centuries, A.D., in the region of the elliptical zone described by Guthrie as the area of Bantu population explosion, there was a concentration of people in the vicinity of Lake Kisal. About A.D. 1500 there lived in this area a man named Kongolo who subdued villages and chiefdoms and built his capital at Mwibele, near Lake Boya. According to tradition it is this man who was the founder of the Luba people.

At his capital, Kongolo was visited by Ilunga Mbili, a hunter from east of the Lualaba River. In time, Ilunga Mbili married Kongolo's two sisters, Bulanda and Mabele. A quarrel broke out between Ilunga Mbili and Kongolo, when the former tried to teach the chieftain ways befitting his position, and in the end Ilunga Mbili left Mwibele. After his departure his two wives both bore sons. Bulanda's son was named Kalala Ilunga while Mabele's was called Kisulu Mabele.

Kalala Ilunga grew up to be a brave warrior. He helped Kongolo in the wars of conquest which extended the southern boundary of his kingdom. But Kongolo became jealous of the young man's popularity and grew suspicious of him. He finally made an attempt to kill Kalala Ilunga, but the youth escaped and fled to the land of his father. He returned some time later with a large army and so terrified Kongolo that the old chief did not make a stand, but fled and hid himself in the caves of the Lwembe River near Kai. But the hiding place was betrayed by his own sisters, and he was captured and executed. Kalala Ilunga became king and extended the Luba Kingdom's boundaries still farther.

The conquests of Kongolo and Kalala Ilunga had an important result for they brought about political unification in the area. This was a federation of villages preserved by a system of headmen, called "owners of the land," who were the link between the king and the villages. The descendants of Kongolo and Kalala Ilunga were called *balopwe,* and only one of that royal line could be king. Their positions as "owners of the land" were hereditary.

The Luba kings ruled by divine right and were considered to have supernatural powers. Even after his death, a king's influence dominated the village that had been his capital, for when he died a *mwadi,* a woman in contact with the dead king's spirit, together with his former chief minister, a *twite,* took charge of the *kitena,* as his old capital was called. Meanwhile, the new king appointed a new chief minister and established a new capital for himself in another place. This unusual hierarchy of the mwadi and the twite was also passed down to their heirs who took over their functions. The old kitenas were considered sacred places and were never interferred with by anyone.

There were other Luba kingdoms. One was in the Kikonja area between the Luvuma and Lualaba rivers. Kaludwe lay between the Lwembe and Lubilashi rivers, while a third, the Kaniok, lay between the Lubilashi and Bushimai rivers. These kingdoms were, however, independent states.

The Lunda Empire

The Lunda people appear to have inhabited, from time immemorial, the valley of the Nkalaany near Sekapemb. Their folklore claims that the first men were put into the world in this valley. From time to time, groups left the Nkalaany Valley under the leadership of men who became known as the "chiefs of the land" to settle on plains in the west. These chiefs of the land contracted a perpetual kinship which had the effect of binding together, in a loose but single political entity, all the groups and chiefdoms of the Lunda.

According to Lunda lore, their rulers are descendants of a male twin, Mwaakw, who himself came from a long line of twins descended from the first men. Mwaakw had a son, Nkond, who had two good-for-nothing twin sons, Kinguri and Chinyama. One day, Kinguri and Chinyama beat their father and would have killed him if their sister, Lueji, had not intervened to save his life. Because of this, Nkond decided that his daughter rather than his sons would succeed him. In this way, Lueji became queen and a matrilineal succession was established.

A *balopwe* of the Luba people, Cibinda Ilunga, came and married Queen Lueji. At this development, Kinguri and Chinyama left the land to found kingdoms of their own: a Lunda kingdom of Kasanje was founded on the Kwango River in Angola, and another along the Lwena River. Soon after this, the Chokwe and Bemba peoples left the Lunda land to impose their rule in neighboring areas. In this way Lunda institutions and influence were extended to other parts of the continent.

Queen Lueji had no children; so, Luseeng, her husband's son by another wife, succeeded her. Luseeng was a good administrator. Under him, a stable political structure was created in Lunda kingdoms, which has lasted to the present. He was succeeded by his son Yaav Naweej, also a good administrator, whose name has become the generic name for Lunda kingship. The *yaav,* or ruler, of the Lunda was considered to be divine.

The king administered a centralized government, and presided over a national council and court. He ruled with the assistance of titled officials, who held both religious and perpetual kinship ties, and of tributary chiefs, who were allowed to follow their own laws and customs so long as they paid tribute once a year. As Jan Vansina says, "The whole political structure rested on the twin mechanisms of positional succession and perpetual kinship. A successor inherited not only an office but also the personal status of the deceased, including his name and kinship relationships. Thus, ancient kinship relations were re-enacted every generation and new links were created only after all the old 'positions' in the system had been filled. In practice, these mechanisms proved to be extremely useful; they divorced the political structure from the real descent structure since they were not bound to any principle of descent in particular.

For example, the northern Lunda are bilateral, but matrilineal with regard to succession for the mwaantaangaand; elsewhere in the empire matrilineality would prevail or it might be, as in Kazembe or with the Yaka, that the people would be matrilineal but the chiefs patrilineal. All this did not matter, however, for the principles of positional succession and perpetual kinship could be applied everywhere. Therefore the mechanisms could be diffused without necessitating any changes in the existing social structures, which explains why so many Central African cultures could take over the system with little or no cultural resistance even when, as with the Lwena, there are already segmentary lineages with political functions.

"Other basic aspects which enabled the system to be adapted anywhere were its 'indirect rule' features. Local chieftains could be assimilated to *mwaataangaand* and the newcomers would be *cilool*. They would settle and found a Lunda colony [*iyanga*] which would become a neutral place from the point of view of the non-Lunda residents in an area, a place where one could go for arbitration, a place to which one was ultimately subjected without the use of force.

"When the Luba and the Lunda political systems are compared, it can be understood why the Luba kingdom did not expand far beyond its homeland while the Lunda did so successfully. The Luba did not practice positional succession or perpetual kinship. They did not exploit the division which existed between 'owner of the land' and 'political chief' and they never did assimilate foreign chiefs into their own system even though they would put Luba villages near tributary chiefs to supervise payments. From the point of view of the tributary chief, the Lunda system was better since he became an honored and respected 'owner of the land', while in the Luba system he was but a defeated chief who was usually overtaxed." [1] Thus, Lunda culture, with a strong strain of Luba influence, was able to be widely diffused and its kingdoms widely dispersed throughout the Congo-Zambezi watershed.

Empire of the Manikongo

At its peak the Empire of the Manikongo was bordered roughly by the lower Congo River in the north, the Atlantic Ocean in the west, the Stanley Pool on the Congo in the east, and the Kwamp River in the south. The Kongo state originated from the adventures of Ntinu Wene, sometimes known as Nimi, who, with a band of followers, came from the Lukeni lands north of the river and conquered the Ambundu and Ambewa people of the Kongo plateau. Ntinu Wene strengthened his position by marrying a daughter of the *kitomi,* the "earth priest," who was custodian of spiritual rights over the land. When the kitomi accepted Ntinu Wene as his political overlord and consecrated him as the *manikongo,* or supreme chief, this legitimized his rule.

Ntinu Wene did not rest content with this success but continued to conquer neighboring lands, including the kingdoms of Mpangu and Mbata. He was recognized as overlord by these kings, and they were permitted to continue to rule their people according to their own laws and customs. Other neighboring kingdoms such as the Dembo, Matamba, and Okango also became vassal states of the manikongo. The Emperor of Kongo was always a descendant of Ntinu Wene. The manikongo was chosen by a kind of electoral college in which the kitomi held a veto. The king ruled with the assistance of an aristocracy in which all members were identified by the title *mani,* prefixed to their office. For example, *manilumbu* was governor of the king's quarters, *manivanguvangu* was first judge and specialist in cases of adultery, and *manisoyo* and *manimbata* were governors or kings of the provinces of Soyo and Mbata. The basic units of Kongo's political structure were the matrilineal family, the village, province, and kingdom.

In about 1482, during the reign of Nzinga Kuwu, the Portuguese came to the Kongo. Ambassadors were exchanged between the two countries, and before long the manikongo embraced Christianity. An era of contact with a European power was thus begun. Manikongo Afonso I, the Christian son of Nzinga Kuwu, made a genuine effort to westernize his country by opening schools, encouraging trade, and supporting missionaries. Despite this promising beginning, the Portuguese let him down. The missionaries sent to the Kongo were too few and many led dissolute lives. The Portuguese also became interested, chiefly, in personal gain through the enslavement of the Kongo people.

The greed and intrigues engendered by the slave trade resulted in bitter factions and rivalries. The capture and transportation of thousands upon thousands of African slaves caused fear and despair among the people of the land. In spite of the manikongo's efforts to stop this trade in human beings, slavery continued until the ruler's authority was undermined, and the land was depopulated. Another source of internal dissention and strife was the method of electing a new manikongo at the death of the old one. All these things resulted in the critical weakening of the Kongo state. Consequently the Kongo was powerless when the fierce Jaga people invaded their country from the east in 1568. These ruthless warriors were eventually dispersed in 1576 with the help of a Portuguese force under the command of the governor of Sao Tome, Francisco de Gouvea. Even though the Jaga invasion was turned back, the energy of the Kongo Empire had been exhausted. Its glory was a thing of the past.

Bunyoro and Buganda

In the east, around the great lakes, Bantu farmers were living north and west of Lake Victoria. They were joined by migrating Hima pastoralists and farther south, near Lake Kivu, by the Tutsi people. About twenty-five generations ago in the fifteenth century, the Chwezi (Bacwezi) and their now legendary parent dynasty, the Abatembuzi, appeared in this area and gained domination. It is they who are said to have built the 6½-mile-long trenches at Bigo and other spectacular earthworks at Musa and Kibengo. They organized the Kitara Kingdom.

The Chwezi were a pastoral aristocracy whose power lay partly in their strong clan and family cohesion, partly in their great mobility, and also in their ability to store large quantities of surplus food for use during the construction of large public works such as the dam at Ntutsi and the earthworks. Chwezi rule and power disappeared in time, probably because they had spread themselves too thin over too large a territory, permitting their subjects to develop a sense of cohesion independent of their rulers.

The disappearance of Chwezi power may have been hastened by an influx from the north, of the Luo whose influence spread through former Chwezi domains until the Kitara had been reordered to become the Bunyoro Empire. Several states, including Buganda, which at this time consisted only of five pre-Kintu clans, were loosely bound together in Bunyoro-Kitara. First, Bunyoro, controlling the grazing lands in western Uganda, gained ascendancy over other states, including Buganda and Ankole, and incorporated them within its boundaries. By the turn of the seventeenth century, however, Bunyoro's boundaries had shrunk even though she remained the strongest state. Buganda now asserted its independence and extended its boundaries to the Katanga in the south, the Nile in the east, and also brought Sesse Islands under Buganda rule. The states of Ankole and Mpororo also expanded into large units. Both Buganda and Ankole had highly centralized forms of government with very efficient local rule. They also had an agricultural-pastoral balance which gave an advantage over Bunyoro whose economy was dependent mainly on pastoral activities.

By the beginning of the nineteenth century, Buganda, Ankole, and other states had further extended their boundaries at the expense of Bunyoro, whose eclipse was accentuated by the development of the Arab slave trade. By the time the British arrived on the scene in the 1890's Buganda had become the largest and strongest state in this region.

Azania and Zanj

According to the *Periplus of the Erythrean Sea,* there was, at the beginning of the Christian era, an empire called Azania along the eastern littoral of Africa. Azania is the name some Africans would like to use for the present Republic of South Africa. Azania had many trading posts, the most southern of which was a place called Rhapta. At these ports, "corn, rice, clarified butter (ghee), sesame oil, cotton cloth (*monache,* which was fine cotton, and *segmatogenae,* coarse cotton), girdles, and reed honey called *sacharis,*"[2] ivory, turtle-shell, rhinoceros horn, coconut oil, and the like were exchanged for lances, axes, hatchets, awls, several kinds of glass, wine, wheat, and other stuffs.

Between about 975 and the arrival of the Portuguese in 1498, however, into the territory once occupied by the Empire of Azania, a new kingdom had arisen. Arab writers referred to it as the Land of

Zanj. The Zanj Empire was composed of "small towns, oligarchic in social structure trading in ivory and in slaves and using a currency of beads and rolls of cloth." [3] Sofala became the port from which gold and ivory from Zimbabwe was transported by sea, to Kilwa and on to the outside world. About these towns, Gervase Mathew, tells us: "Most of the medieval towns along the African coasts seem to have come into existence about the twelfth century and to have reached the climax of their prosperity about the year 1500.

"Small trading towns, probably mainly built of wood, turned into great merchant cities, with their own characteristic architecture, and with contacts throughout the Middle and Far East. In the ruined city of Songo Mnara on a coral island off Tanganyika, each pointed arch with its thin stone edging is reset within a rectangle of cut stone, and fluted demidomes rest on fluted pilasters. There is an intricate system of sanitation, with stone piping. Everywhere there is an evident delight in geometrical precision. I found scattered among the ruins, broken glazed pottery from the Persian area, stoneware from Burma and Siam, pieces of Carnelian, and amber, crystal and topaz and a mass of Chinese porcelain from late Sung to early Ming." [4]

Thus, long before the advent of Europeans along the African coast of the Indian Ocean, Africans had been in contact for centuries with other lands as far afield as China. A business language: Swahili, consisting mainly of Bantu and Arabic words, had developed along the coast and is now the *lingua franca* of some countries in eastern and central Africa.

The Rozwi Empire of Zimbabwe

In an area stretching from the Zambezi River in the north, beyond the Limpopo River in the south, and from the Indian Ocean on the east to the Kalahari Desert in the west, the Rozwi Empire of Zimbabwe flourished. Archaeological evidence shows this area to have been, not only the home of people of Bushmanoid stock, but also, to have been, from the beginning of the Christian era, continuously occupied by people skilled in the use of iron weapons and tools. These Iron Age people are believed to have entered the area in waves, the earliest of which was already in the country by

A.D. 300, while the last is thought to have arrived at the beginning of the second millennium.

Among the later immigrants were the ancestors of the Shona speaking people in the country today. Soon after their arrival, the Mashona gained domination of the area and became rulers of the land. They constructed several *dzimbawhe,* i.e., royal residences in stone, the largest and most famous of which is Great Zimbabwe, seventeen miles from Fort Victoria. Zimbabwe, "the big house of stone," is situated atop a hill in rolling country. It sits on this height like a citadel with walls built onto the granite rock. The entrances are openings, or breaks, in the wall, placed to be easily defensible. In the valley there is a great wall surrounding a huge conical tower and several buildings connected by a labyrinth of walled passages. The walls are thirty feet high and fifteen feet wide, built evenly and neatly of stone bricks, without mortar.

When Europeans first saw Great Zimbabwe in the nineteenth century, the ruins immediately became one of the wonders of the world. The question was, who built them? They were described as a mystery, a riddle, and an enigma. Their construction was ascribed to Phoenicians, Egyptians, Cretans, Etruscans, Sabeans, Persians, Sumerians, Dravidians—anyone, except the Mashona. But, as European understanding of African history developed, it was discovered—as Africans had known all along—that the Zimbabwe had been built by the Mashona. Europeans not only found that there were several other *dzimbawhe* in other parts of the country at Mapungubwe, Dhlo-Dhlo, Khami, Naletale, but also that some of these places had been occupied comparatively recently. Clearly, the mystery, riddle, and enigma of the Zimbabwe had existed only in European minds some of whose scholars, even today, still try to pretend that these *ma dzimbawhe* are not the work of Africans.

Edward Alpers points to what is perhaps the most remarkable aspect of Shona dominance over this area: "There is no indication that they achieved this dominance by violent means. In fact the archaeological record suggests exactly the opposite, for . . . Shona culture coexisted with earlier cultures and never completely replaced them. Similarly, the key to Shona dominance would seem not to have been superior military power, although this may have been a contributory factor, but rather the possession of superior organizational skill." [5]

The intellectual capacity and organizational skill of the Mashona is particularly demonstrated in their complex religious concepts connected with the worship of *Mwari,* the Supreme Divine Being. There was also a cult of worship through ancestors and tribal spirits, *mhondoro,* who spoke through mediums called *svikiro.* Since the power of Shona kings and chiefs was ultimately based on the influence and sanction of *Mwari,* the religious apparatus through which communication between the god and the people was maintained, furnished a potent instrument for the integration of social, political, religious, and economic factors in the society.

Shona organizational skill also showed itself in the economic sphere. Shona states had a firm economic base founded on agriculture and trade with Arabs from the east coast. This trade, which dates from the time of the Empire of Zanj, was primarily in copper and gold. African ivory was in great demand for the making of bracelets and trinkets in India where ivory from the native elephants was considered too hard and brittle. In exchange, the Mashona imported such things as glass beads, cloth, and porcelain. This long-distance trade was organized on a large scale and was facilitated by the ease and safety of movement secured by Shona rule.

Early in the fifteenth century, there arose a dynasty among the Mashona, later identified as the Rozwi. The two most able and adventurous of the *mambos,* or kings, earned the praise name *Mwene Mutapa,* meaning "master pillager." From about 1420 to the middle of the century, Mambo Mwene Mutapa Nyatsimba Mutota reigned over the empire. On account of overpopulation and a shortage of salt, the mambo embarked on a military campaign of conquest designed to ease congestion and control salt deposits. Mutota moved the capital from Great Zimbabwe to the north in Dande, southeast of Zumba. He was succeeded by his son, Mambo Mwene Mutapa Matope, who followed his father's expansionist policy until all land from the Zambezi to Mapungubwe beyond the Limpopo and from the Indian Ocean to the Kalahari Desert, was under his rule.

"The king was revered as a god," observes Robert July, "and lived on a most lavish scale with his court of wives, concubines, and officials. His audiences were held in public but he himself remained behind a screen which concealed him from suppliants who came creeping and clapping their hands to show proper homage. When the king died his queens and some of his ministers were dispatched to keep him company in the spirit world, while all the fires in the land were extinguished, for fire was associated with the royal authority and new fires could be kindled only with the flame of the new king. Yet this seemingly omnipotent personality was severely limited by tribal customs. As a god, the king had to be of flawless aspect; hence if he became seriously ill or deformed he was expected to commit suicide. The royal compound, situated behind a high fence, tended to isolate the monarch and make him dependent upon his deputies—the legion of officials, courtiers, and queens, into whose hands much actual power devolved. The royal office was therefore powerful but its power lay as much in its symbolic strength as in the authority wielded by the royal incumbent." [6]

Such a vast area could only be governed by means of virtually independent kings and governors. Accordingly, kings and governors were appointed at the old capitals: Great Zimbabwe, Mbire, Dande, Chidima, Manyika, Barwe, Uteve, and Madanda. And these, whether bound to the Mwene Mutapa, by consanguinity or other ties, toed the line only as long as the emperor had the personal qualities to command obedience and fear. Mutota and Matope were such emperors. Unfortunately, Mambo Mwene Mutapa Nyahuma, who succeeded Matope was not a man of such caliber. During his reign, Changamire who governed the south from the old capital of Great Zimbabwe, together with Togwa, ruler of the central state of Mbire, rebelled against the king and killed him in battle. Changamire became virtual emperor, after this, and his name is now a title of respect denoting a ruler, or lord, among the Mashona. In 1494, Nyahuma's son revenged his father's death by defeating and killing Changamire in battle. Changamire's son was, nevertheless, able to succeed his father and to keep control of the south and of Mbire. Later he obtained Uteve and Madanda, but Dande, Chidima, Manyika, and Barwe remained loyal to the Mwene Mutapa.

Thus, when the Portuguese came, at the beginning of the sixteenth century, the Rozwi Empire of Zimbabwe was virtually divided in two. At this time Changamire's dynasty controlled the larger and more important portion; its influence and strength grew from day to day.

On the other hand, the Mwene Mutapa's empire and power were shrinking. Portuguese designs and circumstances brought them into contact with the portion of the Rozwi Empire ruled by the Mwene Mutapa, and this ruler, understandably, tried to use them to retrieve the lost ground ruled by Changamire. About 1692, Nyakambira challenged the authority of the Mwene Mutapa who called on the Portuguese for assistance. Nyakambira solicited the support of Dombo, the reigning *Changamire*. Dombo's army marched to the Zambezi and forced the Portuguese to flee to Tete and Sena. After this, Dombo became the real heir to the Rozwi Empire while the Mwene Mutapa, although not completely powerless, was virtually a puppet of the Portuguese.

Rozwi-Changamire rule was eventually disrupted by the Ngoni warriors of Zwangendaba in 1830 and by the Amandebele under u Mzilikazi ten years later.

One of the things common to nearly all these empires and states is the institution, in various forms, of divine kingship. That this institution was so widespread among African kingdoms has surprised some European scholars who have immediately tried to find its source and to trace its diffusion to the various parts of the continent. Others have seen in it the influence of foreign conquerors. There are many institutions, practices, customs, and ideas held in common by Africans in areas remote from each other. For instance, there was the custom of holding at an emperor's court sons of vassal kings, ostensibly to be schooled in court etiquette, but really as hostages for the good conduct of their fathers. This arrangement was practiced by the emperors in such widely separated areas as Egypt, Mali, and Zimbabwe.

It would have been more surprising if Africans did not share such things. Africans were greatly influencing one another socially, politically, economically, and culturally long before the days of the radio and jumbo jets. In spite of the diversity of their cultural backgrounds, Africans manifest a remarkably similar attitude to life and people in general.

This, then, was the state of Africa on the eve of the advent of the white man and the slave trade. Yet, as Professor Jackson complains,

"The picture we get today of Africa in the past ages from the history taught in our schools is that Africans were savages and that, although Europeans invaded their lands and made slaves of them, they were in a way conferring a great favor on them; since they brought to them the blessings of Christian civilization." [7] Have the kingdoms and empires we have seen been those of savages? What did white men see when they came to Africa?

Leo Frobenius answered these questions with these words: "When they [the first European navigators of the end of the Middle Ages] arrived in the Gulf of Guinea and landed at Vaida, the captains were astonished to find streets well cared for, bordered for several leagues in length by two rows of trees; for many days they passed through a country of magnificent fields, a country inhabited by men clad in brilliant costumes, the stuff of which they had woven themselves! More to the South in the kingdom of Congo, a swarming crowd dressed in silk and velvet; great states well ordered, and even to the smallest details, powerful sovereigns, rich industries—civilized to the marrow of their bones. And the condition of the countries on the eastern coast—Mozambique, for example—was quite the same.

"What was revealed by the navigators of the fifteenth to the seventeenth centuries furnishes an absolute proof that Negro Africa, which extended south of the desert zone of the Sahara, was in full efflorescence, in all the splendour of harmonious and well-formed civilizations, an efflorescence which the European conquisadors annihilated as far as they progressed. For the new country of America needed slaves, and Africa had them to offer, hundreds, thousands, whole cargoes of slaves. However, the slave trade was never an affair which meant a perfectly easy conscience, and it exacted a justification; hence one made of the Negro a half-animal, an article of merchandise. And in the same way the notion of fetish (Portuguese *feticeiro*) was invented as a symbol of African religion. As for me, I have seen in no part of Africa the Negroes worship a fetish. The idea of the 'barbarous Negro' is a European invention which has consequently prevailed in Europe until the beginning of this century." [8]

NOTES

1. Jan Vansina, "Kingdoms of the Savanna," in *Problems*, p. 279.
2. *The Periplus of the Erythrean Sea*, as cited by Zoe Marsh, ed., in *East Africa Through Contemporary Records* (New York: Cambridge University Press, 1961), pp. 4-5.
3. Gervase Mathew, "The Land of Zanj," in *Dawn of African History*, ed. R. Oliver, ed. (New York: Oxford, 1968), p. 51.
4. Mathew, "The Land of Zanj," p. 50.
5. Edward Alpers, "The Mutapa and Malawi Political Systems," in *Aspects of Central African History*, ed. T. O. Ranger (Evanston, Ill.: Northwestern University Press, 1968), pp. 5-6.
6. Robert July, *A History of the African People* (New York: Scribner's, 1970), p. 132.
7. John J. Jackson, *Introduction to African Civilization* (Hyde Park. N.Y.: University Books, 1970), p. 292.
8. DuBois, *World and Africa*, pp. 78-79.

CHAPTER 14
The African Diaspora

"But it is time that we considered, however briefly, the contribution of the Negro Race, second only to the European in its dispersal over the world's surface," Dr. K. Onwuka Dike told an International Congress of Africanists meeting at Ibadan University, Nigeria, in 1960. While the European is found all over the world, primarily because his feet are always itching to travel; the African's dispersal is due mainly to about five hundred years of being chained and sold into slavery. Slavery has, therefore, been the main vehicle of the African diaspora. Through slavery, Africans went to Europe, Arabia, Turkey, Persia, India, North America, Mexico, Panama, Peru, the Carribean, and other parts of the world. In talking about slavery, however, it is important to bear in mind that slavery is something that did not begin and end with the enslavement of Africans. There were slaves in the empires of Greece and Rome long before Africans were taken in chains across the Sahara and the oceans. These slaves were not black men and women. They were white. As Denys Hay points out, the word *slave* itself "was derived from Slav prisoners, and owed its currency to those imported through Dalmatia in the thirteenth century," and he further explains, "*Sclavus*=slave (rather than Slav) is first found in the tenth century as a result of the trade in Slavs captured in the German expansion eastwards; they were sold mainly to Moslems in Spain. This trade and the word itself disappear in the early eleventh century to appear later." [1]

When it did appear, Europeans and white American captives arrived by the shipload for almost six centuries and were sold into slavery at the African ports of Salee, Tangier, Algiers, Tunis, and Tripoli.[2] Europeans sold as slaves were, at the beginning, non-Christians and Jews. But as the trade got brisk, European merchants in the business became less discriminatory and, in spite of papal objections, sold Christians. "All the great city-states of medieval Italy appear to have dealt in Christian slaves," says Davidson. "The Venetians and the Genoese were deep in the trade as early as the tenth and eleventh centuries. They continued in it, together with the Pisans and the Florentines and the merchants and mariners of ports as far apart as Lucca and Amalfi, until as late as the middle of the fifteenth century. Throughout the thirteenth century, European slaves were being carried in European ships to the Sultanate of Egypt despite all ecclesiastical rebukes and threats. 'The excesses of the traders,' Scelle records, 'were such that Pope Clement V excommunicated the Venetians and authorised all Christian people to reduce them in turn to slavery.'

"Little more than half a century before the launching of the oversea slave trade from Africa, Pope Martin V published a bull of excommunication against the Genoese merchants of Caffa, Genoese city-state on the Black Sea, for their persistence in buying and selling Christians. This was as ineffectual as the earlier excommunication of the Venetians, and in 1441 the laws of Gazaria (as the Genoese called their little trading "empire" on the Black Sea Coast) expressly provided for the sale and purchase of Christian as well as Muslim slaves." [3]

In an age when sea pirates were regarded as heroes, African Moslem seamen added to the numbers of white slaves with every European or Christian vessel that fell into their hands. Christian sailors shipwrecked along the coast of North Africa were treated the same. The Catholic Church founded two orders for the purpose of ransoming Christians enslaved by Muslims: the Trinitarians in 1198 and the Mercedarians in 1218. According to their records, these orders, between them, liberated over two million Europeans in five hundred years.[4] This figure does not include those ransomed by Protestant missions or the American government.

Within five years of the Pilgrims' landing on Plymouth Rock, American ships were being captured and a New Englander complained in 1680:

"The Turks have so taken our New England ships richly laden homeward bound, that it is very dangerous to goe. Many of our neighbours are now in captivity in Argeer (Algiers). The Lord find out some way of their redemption." [5] After Independence the American Congress entered into a treaty with the Bey of Algiers and not only ransomed its citizens but also agreed to pay an annual tribute of $700,000 to ensure their safety. A similar arrangement was concluded with the King of Tripoli. The Americans paid $50,000 to free their citizens and considered it politic to sign a peace treaty which expressly stated: "The Government of the United States is not in any sense founded on the Christian religion." [6]

There were white slaves exported directly to America. "By as early as 1501, only nine years after the first voyage of Columbus" Davidson tells us, "the Spanish throne had issued its initial proclamation on laws for the export of slaves to America—mainly, as yet, to Hispaniola (Haiti and the Dominican Republic today). These slaves were white—whether from Spain or North Africa—more often than black; for the black slaves, it was early found, were turbulent and hard to tame. How poorly grounded in fact was the old legend of 'African docility' may be seen from the events of 1503. In that year the Spanish governor of Hispaniola, Ovando, complained to the Spanish Court that fugitive Negro slaves among the Indians were teaching disobedience, and that it was impossible to re-capture them. Ovando asked for an end to the export of Negro slaves, and Queen Isabella consented. She seems to have decided to allow the export to the Indies only of white slaves, although her motive was no doubt different from Ovando's: she hoped that Christian slaves would help in the work of converting the heathen, not knowing, of course, that most of the heathen would soon be dead.

"Export of Christian slaves continued, though in small numbers, until the end of the seventeenth century; generally they were women, and they were for use but not for sale. Thus in 1526 a license was granted to a certain Bartolomeo Conejo for the opening of a brothel at Puerto Rico, and to Sanchez Sarmento for the establishment of another in Santo Domingo; and white girls were needed for these. A few years later the Spanish governor of Peru secured a license through his brother Fernando Pizarro for the import from Spain of four girls who, the license stipulated, 'must be born in Castile and

Christians baptized before the age of ten'—not, that is to say, converted Moorish or Negro women. This early white-slave traffic dwindled after the middle of the sixteenth century; yet as late as 1692 there is record of a permit issued for the export of four girls to Veracruz in Mexico." [7]

And yet, there are people who act and behave as if Africans were the only people ever to be enslaved and the word "Negro" or "Colored" has come to mean, among some Americans, "one who is descended from a slave." A native African is not described as a Negro by these peoples. A few years ago, a black woman with an African name surrendered her driver's license from an African country to receive one from Alabama. The Alabama police wrote on her new license "Not Colored Person."

What the Alabama police did not know was that she is a "soul sister," born and raised in Jackson, Mississippi (and one cannot be more "soul" than that), married to an African, and back in the United States after living in Africa a number of years. When is a Negro not a Negro?

Clearly, some people would like to see generations of black Americans identified until kingdom come as descendants of slaves. Let us make no mistake about it; there is nothing to be ashamed of in being a descendant of a slave. The point is that black people in America are not the only descendants of slaves. There are millions upon millions of white people descended from Europeans sold as slaves in Europe, Africa, America, and other parts of the world. Why should the black man in America be perpetually identified as the descendant of a slave when these others are not? This is one of the reasons, some black Americans no longer wish to be called Negroes.

In some respects the enslavement of white people by North Africans was different from the enslavement of black people by whites in the New World. North African white slavery was based on religion, not race. The Moslems were enslaving Christians—infidels. There was thus no question as to whether white people were human or not. In the eyes of the Moslems, white people were human beings who, unfortunately, qualified for slavery by being Christians and so, infidels. Europeans on the other hand, tried to convince themselves that the black men they were enslaving were not human beings at all.

Another difference was the purpose for the enslavement. The North African aim was to receive ransom for the enslaved while the transatlantic slave trade was intended to provide labor for the white man. Under these circumstances, North African slavery was geared to yielding and, in fact yielded, more slaves to freedom than its counterpart in the New World which, as a rule, destroyed men rather than free them.

The enslavement of white people by North Africans was, generally, much more humane than the enslavement of black people by whites. This is not to deny that, in countless instances, many white slaves were treated with brutality and cruelty. On the whole, however, it can be said that white slaves were better treated by Africans than African slaves were treated by whites. As a member of the British Embassy in Morocco reported to the British Government in 1727: "I am sure that we saw captives who lived much better in Barbary than they ever did in their own country. What ever money was sent them by their friends in Europe was their own, unless they defrauded one another, which had happened much oftener than by the Moors." [8]

Another white man defended African Moslems, the Moors, against charges of inhumanity made by a Father de Bourk saying: "Oh fie, Father! Though it is part of your function to make a dismal story of Slavery among *Infidels* (the very name of which is indeed bad enough) yet you should, methinks, adhere only to the truth. You came very lately from Marseilles where you must, or might, have seen the Turks, Moors, et cetera in much worse condition than the most unhappy beylical slave in Algiers. You likewise must needs have seen how slaves are treated in Spain, Malta, Genoa, et cetera. Thousands of Algiers captives live abundantly happier there (want of freedom excepted) than ever they can hope to do at home; and that very many are excused with a few bastinadoes for crimes for which they would have suffered the wheel in most parts of Europe, or at least have made their exit in a halter. Therefore I say again, Father, stick to the truth." [9]

It was the United States Consul at Tunis, General William Eaton, however, who made the most categoric defense of the Moors against charges of ill treating slaves. In 1799 he wrote his wife: "Truth and justice demand from me the confession that the Christian slaves among the barbarians of Africa are treated with more humanity than the African slaves among the professing Christians of civilized America."[10]

Wellard further explains, "Again, those captives who were opportunist or cynical enough to say the magic formula, 'There is but one God and Mohammed is His prophet'—to become renegades, as the expression was—often became rich, particularly as they were allowed to run the taverns, a lucrative trade, even if a despicable one in the view of orthodox Moslems. Several well-born renegades, on the other hand, rose to positions of great trust and power, among them the French nobleman Count Joseph de Saulty who eloped with his colonel's wife, hid out in Tunis until she died, then went to Morocco, became a Moslem, and was appointed commander-in-chief to the Sultan."[11]

It should be born in mind that serfdom, though not chattel slavery in the European sense, was known in Africa long before Europeans came. Europeans were mistaken when they described the serfs they saw in Africa as slaves. Some realized this and called the serfdom "African slavery" or "domestic slavery." Some loss of freedom, which it is an exaggeration to describe as slavery, was entailed when wars were fought and prisoners taken. These prisoners of war, inaccurately described as slaves by Europeans, were incorporated into their captors' tribal systems. Their women were taken as wives and their men and boys taught to fight in the armies of their conquerors. As individuals they retained their rights as human beings. They could marry and own property. They could not be killed at will by anyone. They were still human beings, not chattel. Many tribes augmented their numbers and strength in this way.

Sometimes, prisoners of war were sold to individuals who could afford them. Prisoners, purchased in this way became part and parcel of their purchasers' families. In many instances, such men married into a family and later rose to be the family head. However, such men were not free to return to their former homes, and, what was even more painful, they lost their identities to the extent that they had to worship through the ancestors of their new families. To older people, especially, this was the most unbearable part of being captured or sold into another family. The idea that a human being could be sold or bought by another did not originate with the coming of Europeans to Africa; it was already part of African culture when Europeans got there.

There were other circumstances in which people could be sold. Mungo Park who traveled in West Africa between 1795 and 1797 observed that people could become slaves not only through captivity but also through famine, insolvency, and crimes.

In time of famine, some men gave their daughters in marriage or their sons as laborers, in exchange for corn or millet to save their families from starvation. In the eyes of foreigners, the daughters and sons had been sold into slavery. Needless to say, Africans did not consider them as slaves. If a man contracted debts and became insolvent not only was his property sold to satisfy the demands of his creditors but also his person. According to Mungo Park, this was the commonest cause of "slavery" in Africa. People who committed such crimes as murder, adultery, and witchcraft could be sold also. The important point to remember here is that the selling and buying of human beings was not unknown in African society. So, when the European slave traders came, they had something to build on. They did not have to teach Africans something new or repugnant to their customs because the practice of selling human beings was already common practice among them.

In view of the oft-repeated assertion, mainly by white scholars, that in the business of slavery Africans are as guilty as white men because many Africans entered into partnership with slavers and sold their own brothers down the river; let us examine the methods by which white men procured slaves from Africa. Before doing this, however, let us see how and why Europeans came to Africa.

We know that Europeans wanted to find an alternative route to India and also get in on the rich gold trade for which West Africa was famous. In spite of a victory at Ceuta in 1415, the Portuguese had not been able to make any headway along the Mediterranean coast of Africa. We also know that far from gaining ground the Portuguese had met with disaster at Al Ksar al-Kabir in 1578 and had therefore been forced to explore the west coast of Africa in an attempt, ultimately, to get to India by this route.

Under the patronage of Prince Henry the Navigator, Portuguese sailors slowly explored along the western coast. By the time of Prince

Henry's death in 1460, Portuguese sailors had gone as far as Sierra Leone. In 1482 they completed the construction of Fort Salo Jorge da Mina, now known as Elmina, on the Gold Coast (Ghana), and continued to press on with their exploration, certain in the knowledge that Africa was circumnavigable. This information had been passed on to the Portuguese king by Abraham of Beja and Joseph of Lamego, Portuguese Jews, who had traveled through Egypt, Syria, and along the Persian Gulf.

The king of Portugal then sent two men—Pero de Covilham and Alfonso de Paiva—to India by way of Egypt and the Red Sea instructing them also to find out whatever they could about the mysterious Prester John—the legendary first Christian king of Ethiopia. They were to ascertain whether there were in the lands they traversed any neutrals or potential allies the king of Portugal could count on.

In 1487 de Covilham and de Paiva reached Egypt where they parted company, de Covilham going to India and de Paiva to Abyssinia, as Ethiopia was called then. Before he got to Ethiopia, de Paiva was killed near Suakin, but de Covilham made it to India, visited Madagascar (Malagasy), and Sofala before returning to Cairo where he met Abraham and Joseph and learnt of de Paiva's death. Sending Joseph with all of the information he had gathered to King John II, de Covilham and Abraham traveled to Mecca, Medina, and Zeila before going to Ethiopia. As a result, an Ethiopian envoy went to Lisbon in 1507 and a Portuguese embassy was sent to Ethiopia. One of the two priests attached to the embassy was Fr. Alvarez, writer of the interesting accounts to which we have already made reference.[12]

It was the information supplied by de Covilham which motivated the Portuguese to continue their naval expeditions until, at last, Bartolomeu Diaz rounded Africa in stormy weather without knowing it and found himself at Mossed Bay on February 3, 1488. He proceeded as far as the mouth of the Great Fish River before his sailors forced him to return home. Diaz named the terminal point of southern Africa, *Cabo Tormentoso,* the Cape of Storms, but his king changed it to 'Cape of Good Hope,' good hope to reach India. It was not until nine years later in 1497, however, that Vasco da Gama, by sailing to a point in the middle of the Atlantic and then eastward, also sailed around the cape and found himself in the Indian Ocean, along the east coast of Africa. It was Christmas day, and the circumstance inspired him to name this part of the coast Natal.

Vasco da Gama called at Sofala where he noted that Africans were not overawed by the appearance or size of his ships. Why should they be? Africans along this coast had been seeing foreign ships for centuries. In 1417 and again in 1422 Chinese ships had called on the east coast of Africa. So, when the Portuguese came, Africans saw nothing to be excited about. Vasco da Gama was taken to Malindi where he engaged an African pilot, Ibn Madjid who piloted him to India. This seaman was the author of a set of instructions on navigating in the capricious monsoon winds of the Indian Ocean, and he knew the Indian Ocean as the palm of his hand.[13] When da Gama returned to Portugal to report his success, a new era began on the east coast of Africa.

So, it was while searching for a new route to the East, for gold in West Africa, and for the legendary Prester John, that the Portuguese came into contact with Africans along the coast. How did they get their first slaves? by kidnapping and abduction. As Davidson recounts: "Having persevered southward for as far as he judged it was wise or useful to the winning of a reputation, the youthful Goncalvez conceived the idea of pleasing his royal master, Prince Henry of Portugal, by capturing some of the inhabitants of this unknown southern land. 'O how fair a thing it would be,' Zurara makes him say to his crew, 'if we, who have come to this land for a cargo of such petty merchandise, were to meet with the good luck to bring the first captives before the face of our Prince.'

"On the following night Goncalvez went ashore with nine of his men. 'When they were about a league distant from the sea they came on a path which they kept, thinking some man or woman might come by there whom they could capture; but it happened otherwise.' They pushed on for another three leagues, and there they 'found the footmarks of men and youths, the number of whom, according to their estimate, would be from forty to fifty, and these led the opposite way from where our men were going.'

"Should they persist or go back? Heat, fatigue, and thirst discouraged the raiders. They decided to give up. But while returning over sand-warm dunes to the sea,' they saw a naked man following a camel, with two assegais in his hand, and as our men pursued him there was not one who felt aught of his great fatigue. But though he was only one, and saw the others that they were many, yet [this African] had a mind to prove those arms of his right worthily and began to defend himself as best he could, shewing a bolder front than his strength warranted.

"'But Affonso Goterres wounded him with a javelin, and this put the Moor in such fear that he threw down his arms like a beaten man.' The Portuguese took him prisoner; then, 'as they were going on their way, they saw a Black Mooress come along and so they seized her too.'"

From abducting and kidnapping individuals, the Portuguese went on to attack and capture groups. We are told that Goncalvez and Nuno Tristao, "a youthful knight very valiant and ardent," were captains of an armed caraval with orders both to explore the coast and to take captives "as best he could." The two captains decided on a joint enterprise.

"'And so it chanced that in the night'—after their landing together—they came to where the natives lay scattered in two encampments. . . . 'And when our men had come nigh to them, they attacked [the natives] very lustily, shouting at the tops of their voices "Portugal" and "Santiago," the fright of which so abashed the enemy that it threw them all in disorder.'

"And so, all in confusion [the natives], began to fly without any order or carefulness. Except indeed that the men made some show of defending themselves with their assegais (for they knew not the use of any other weapon), especially one of them who fought face to face with Nuño Tristao, defending himself till he received his death. And besides this one, whom Nuño Tristao slew by himself, the others killed three and took ten prisoners, what of men women and boys. And it is not to be doubted that they would have slain and taken many more, if they had all fallen on together at the first onslaught." [14]

This story illustrates the second method by which Europeans got slaves from Africa, making war on villages and carrying the survivors into slavery.

When the demand for slaves increased as they were more and

more required for domestic purposes, not only in the Iberian Peninsula, but also for work on sugar plantations on islands along the African coast and in the New World, a third method was devised whereby Europeans involved themselves in African wars so as to take the vanquished into captivity. The activities of John Hawkins illustrate this method.

"In 1567 Hawkins set forth upon his third slaving voyage to the lands of Guinea and passed, as before, down the coast by what was now a familiar route: from Cape Verde to the Rio Grande (in the modern Portuguese colony of Guinea); thence to the Islands of the Idols (Ihlas dos Idolos, corrupted to Isles de Los, off the modern city of Conakry, capital of independent Guinea); and so onward, raiding for slaves all the way, to the coastland of Sierra Leone. By the time he had come as far as this he had collected 150 slaves and was ready, having suffered some losses, to sail with them to the West Indies and sell them there to Spanish planters. But events took a new turn.

"'And being ready to depart from the Sea coast,' runs the account of this voyage, 'there was a Negro sent as an Ambassador to our Generall, from a King of the Negroes, which was oppressed with other Kings, his bordering neighbors, desiring our Generall to graunt him succour and ayde against those his enemies, which our Generall graunted him thereto.' With reason—for the ambassador added a promise 'that as many Negroes as by these warres might be obtained, as well of his part as of ours, should be at our pleasure.' The local chief, in other words, cared nothing or knew nothing about any difference between the condition of African captives and that of captives who were sold to the Europeans. He considered selling prisoners to an ally who came by sea in the same light as selling them to an ally on land. Anyone who was not of his own people—a 'believer'—was fair game. The precedent would mark a fateful step.

"Hawkins thereupon took two hundred Englishmen ashore and joined the 'king of Sierra Leone' and the 'king of Castros' against the hostile kings 'Zacina and Zetecame'. The object was to storm and ruin a town which was said to have some eight to ten thousand inhabitants; and they marched on it forthwith, a curious army of mercenaries mingled with feudal vassals.

" 'This towne was built after the use of the countrye. very warlike, and was walled round with mighty trees bound together with great wythes and had in it soldiers that had come thither 150 leagues. The kings within it had in it of principall soldiers Negroes 6,000, besides thereof innumerable sight of other menne, women and children.' Eager for his booty, Hawkins pressed this feudal assault. But the taking of the town proved no easy matter, the beseiged having 'made many engins, as false ditches covered with light sticks, leaves and such trumpery, to overthrow our men in and with their envenomed arrows and darts so defended the walls, having made loopes in every place to shoot out at for their safety. . . .' In the end the English fired the town. There was great slaughter, and Hawkins eventually weighed for the Spanish Main with 470 captives."[15]

The fourth method was sometimes employed by white slave dealers who lived among Africans. Often a trader married one of the chief's sisters and so secured the protection of his person and effects while, at the same time, gaining the right to a voice and influence in tribal affairs. The slave dealer set one African chief against another so that when they came to blows he claimed the captives from both sides and sold them into slavery. One of the people we know who was captured and sold into slavery through the activities of a white slave dealer resident in Africa is Cinque.

On board the slave ship *Amistad,* Cinque successfully led a revolt, killed all except one of the crew, and ordered the lone white man to steer the ship back to Africa. During the day, the white man sailed, keeping the sun on his right as he had been instructed to do but turned the ship at night so that, eventually, it was found off the New England coast, where Cinque and his friends were arrested. A group of American citizens organized a committee which, in spite of strong opposition from the southern states, successfully fought the Africans' case in American courts. Cinque and his friends were freed and returned to their homeland.

The fifth method is one in which Africans sold other Africans in order to get European goods, particularly guns. Generally, they sold members of another tribe, or those with whom they had no special bonds of friendship, or those they regarded as enemies. In the end, it became simply a matter of looking after one's own skin, fighting, killing, capturing, and selling into slavery one's neighbors before they had a chance to do the same to one.

It will be seen that of these five methods used to get slaves from Africa, only one involved the voluntary participation of Africans. Since no one can say that this last method alone yielded more slaves than the other four put together, there is no basis for claiming that Africans were as guilty as Europeans in the crime of slavery. Furthermore, as we have seen, in selling each other, Africans were doing nothing new or repugnant to their laws and customs. The only new thing they did was to sell one another to men of a different race—Europeans. Europeans treated those they bought, not according to African values and ideas, but according to notions of their own culture. This is all understandable because Africans and Europeans had different cultural backgrounds. It was not to be expected that one group would know, or, want to behave according to the precepts of the other's culture. In this case the Africans' attitude towards people sold and bought was much more humane and civilized than that of the Europeans. How were they to know that the people they sold to Europeans would be treated as chattel and not human beings? To equate their guilt with that of Europeans when they, in fact, were incapable even of conceiving such notions of slavery as were held by Europeans, is to be both unreasonable and unfair to Africans. It is an attempt on the part of the white man to share his guilt with Africans even though they were unaware of his grotesque notion of what a slave was. He has succeeded in brainwashing some black people in America who are now heard saying, "I don't care a d— for these Africans. After all, it is they who, with 'Mr. Charlie,' sold us down the river!" Let the white man carry the cross of his guilt alone. Africans will have none of it. The only thing they did, not sanctioned by traditional practice, was to assume that white men were human and to sell other Africans to them. No one has seriously contended that this assumption was wrong.

When Europeans had kidnapped and abducted Africans, or attacked and burned villages capturing the survivors, or involved themselves in African wars and claimed the captives, or incited one tribe against another and claimed the surviving vanquished; they marched the victims to the coast. Whether it was to the

Atlantic coast, Indian Ocean, or across the Sahara, whether the slavers were white men or Arabs, the march to waiting ships and distant lands was the same. As Sir Harry Johnston recounts: "In these later days, when it was necessary to evade tiresome regulations or to carry on the trade in the face of direct prohibition, the sufferings of the slaves were so appalling that they almost transcend belief. It would seem as though the inhuman traffic had created in Arabs, Negroes and white men a deliberate love of cruelty, amounting often to a neglect of commercial interests; for it would obviously have been more to the interest of the slave raider and the slave trader and transporter that the slaves should be landed at their ultimate destination in good condition—certainly with the least possible loss of life. Yet, as the present writer can testify from what he has himself seen in the eighties and nineties of the last century, a slave gang on its march to the coast was loaded with unnecessarily heavy collars or slave-sticks, with chains and irons that chafed and cut into the flesh, and caused virulent ulcers. The slaves were half-starved, over-driven, insufficiently provided with drinking water, and recklessly exposed to death from sunstroke. If they threw themselves down for a brief rest or collapsed from exhaustion they were shot or speared or had their throats cut with fiendish brutality, I have seen at Taveita (now a civilized settlement in British East Africa) boys and youths left in the bush to die by degrees from mortification and protrusion of the intestines owing to the unskillful way in which they had been castrated by the Arabs, who had attempted to make eunuchs of them for sale to Turkish and Arab harims. Children whom their mothers could not carry, and who could not keep with the caravan, had their brains dashed out. Many slaves (I again write from personal knowledge) committed suicide because they could not bear to be separated from their homes and children. They were branded and flogged, and, needless to say, received not the slightest medical treatment for the injuries resulting from this usage."[16]

Along the coast, certain ports acquired a reputation for dealing in slaves. To these ports captives sold by other Africans were brought. Before the sale, some haggling between white men and black men over the correct price to be paid took place amidst much boozing and carousing. Davidson reports: "'On the twenty fifth in the morning,' runs the log of the *Albion-Frigate* in 1699, trading at New Calabar, 'we went ashore also to compliment the king, and make him overtures of trade, but he gave us to understand he expected one bar of iron for each slave more than Edwards had paid for his; and also objected much against our basons, tankards, yellow beads, and some other merchandise, as of little or no demand there at the time.' Such was the customary opening; the great thing was not to lose heart.

"'On the twenty sixth, we had a conference with the king and principal natives of the country, about trade, which lasted from three o'clock till night, without any result, they insisting to have thirteen bars of iron for a male, and ten for a female slave. . . .' This was too dear for the Europeans; they took supper with the king and went back to their ship.

"'The thirtieth, being ashore, had a new conference, which produced nothing. . . .' The king's representative held forth once again on his difficulties. 'He was sorry we would not accept of his proposals; that it was not his fault, he having a great esteem and regard for the Whites, who had much enriched him by trade. That [the reason why] he so earnestly insisted on thirteen bars for male, and ten for female slaves, came from the country people holding up the price of slaves at their inland markets . . . but to moderate matters . . . he would be contented with thirteen bars for males, and nine bars and two brass rings for females, etc. . . .' And at last, on the following day, they fell into agreement.

"Such haggling was accompanied, especially at prosperous harbors like New Calabar in the Niger delta, by a vast amount of entertaining, bestowal of gifts, argument, teasing on both sides, and alcoholic refreshment. On this particular occasion there was an almost riotous reception on board the *Albion-Frigate,* everyone being filled 'with drams of brandy and bowls of punch till night'; and the king was presented with a hat, a firelock, and nine bunches of beads. His various counselors and subchiefs, garnished in the slavers' records with a fine sequence of names and titles, benefited likewise. Thus: 'To Captain Forty, the king's general, captain Pepprell, captain Boileau, alderman Bougsby, lord Willby, duke of Monmouth, drunken Henry, and some others, two firelocks, eight hats, nine narrow Guinea stuffs. . . .'"

African potentates became adept at extracting tax and tribute from Europeans. It was "usual for Europeans to give the king the value of fifty slaves in goods, for his permission to trade, and customs, for each ship; and to the king's son the value of two slaves for the priviledge of watering; and of four slaves for wooding." [17]

While all these business arrangements were going on, the captives, we are told, " 'are put into a booth or prison, built for that purpose, near the beach, all of them together; and when the Europeans are to receive them, they are brought out into a large plain, where the [ships'] surgeons examine every part of every one of them, to the smallest member, men and women being all stark naked. Such as are allowed good and sound, are set on one side, and the others by themselves; which slaves so rejected are called Mackrons, being above 35 years of age, or defective in their lips, eyes, or teeth, or grown grey; or that have the venereal disease, or any other imperfection.' Only the best were good enough; and this is no doubt one reason for the often amazing resistance, physical and moral, of the slaves who reached the Carribean and the Americas.

" 'These being so set aside, each of the others, which have passed as good, is marked on the breast with a red-hot iron, imprinting the mark of the French, English or Dutch companies, that so each nation may distinguish their own, and to prevent their being chang'd by the natives for worse, as they are apt enough to do. In this particular, care is taken that the women, as tenderest, be not burnt too hard.

" 'The branded slaves, after this, are returned to their former booths,' where they await shipment, 'sometimes ten or fifteen days.' When that happens they are stripped naked before being put into the canoes 'without distinction of men or women;' but, adds Barbot, 'to supply which [deficiency of clothing], in orderly ships each of them as they come aboard is allow'd a piece of canvas to wrap about their waist, which is acceptable to the poor wretches." [18]

Often the slaves revolted but had no chance. They were put down with the ferocity and brutality of Captain Harding who "weighing the Stoutness and Worth [of the ringleaders] did, as in other countries they do by Rogues of Dignity, whip and scarify them only; while three other Abettors, but not Actors, nor of Strength for it, he sentenced to cruel deaths; making them first eat the Heart and Liver of one of them killed. The Woman [who had helped in the revolt] he hoisted up by the Thumbs, whipped, and slashed her with Knives, before the other Slaves, till she died." [19]

For what one thought and felt when one went on board a slave ship, we can do no better than turn to the narrative of Equiano, otherwise known as Gustavus Vassa, who, as a little boy, survived the transatlantic passage. He was a slave for many years and during that time he educated himself and ultimately bought his freedom. He lived long enough to campaign against slavery and to urge its abolution. He was prominent in the founding of Sierra Leone. In his autobiography Equiano wrote about the slave ship.*

"The first object which saluted my eyes when I arrived on the coast was the sea, and a slave ship which was then riding at anchor, and waiting for its cargo. These filled me with astonishment, which was soon converted into terror, which I am yet at a loss to describe, nor the then feerings of my mind. When I was carried on board I was immediately handled, and tossed up, to see if I were sound by some of the crew; and I was now persuaded that I had gotten into a world of bad spirits, and that they were going to kill me. Their complexions too differing so much from ours, their long hair, and the language they spoke, which was very different from any I had ever heard, united to confirm me in this belief. Indeed such were the horrors of my views and fears at the moment, that, if ten thousand worlds had been my own, I would have freely parted with them all to have exchanged my condition with that of the meanest slave in my own country. When I looked round the ship too and saw a large furnace of copper boiling, and a multitude of black people of every description chained together, every one of their countenances expressing dejection and sorrow, I no longer doubted my fate; and, quite overpowered with horror and anguish, I fell motionless on the deck and fainted. When I recovered a little, I found some black people about me, who I believed were some of those who had brought me on board and had been receiving their pay; they talked to me in order to cheer me, but all in vain. I asked them if we were

* Quotations from the *Interesting Narrative of the Life of Olaudah Equiano or Gustavus Vassa, the African* (Edinburgh: printed and sold by the author, 1792), pp. 46-52.

not to be eaten by those white men with horrible looks, red faces, and long hair? They told me I was not; and one of the crew brought me a small portion of spirituous liquor in a wine glass; but, being afraid of him I would not take it out of his hand. One of the blacks therefore took it from him and give it to me, and I took a little down my palate, which, instead of reviving me, as they thought it would, threw me into the greatest consternation at the strange feeling it produced, having never tasted any such liquor before. Soon after this, the blacks who brought me on board went off, and left me abandoned to despair. I now saw myself deprived of all chance of returning to my native country, or even the least glimpse of hope of gaining the shore, which I now considered as friendly; and I even wished for my former slavery, in preference to my present situation, which was filled with horrors of every kind, still heightened by my ignorance of what I was to undergo. I was not long suffered to indulge my grief; I was soon put down under the decks, and there I received such a salutation in my nostrils as I had never experienced in my life; so that, with the loathsomeness of the stench, and crying together, I became so sick and low that I was not able to eat, nor had I the least desire to taste anything. I now wished for the last friend, death, to relieve me; but soon, to my grief, two of the white men offered me eatables; and, on my refusing to eat, one of them held me fast by the hands and laid me across, I think, the windlass, and tied my feet, while the other flogged me severely. I had never experienced anything of this kind before, and, although not being used to the water, I naturally feared that element the first time I saw it; yet, nevertheless, could I have got over the nettings, I would have jumped over the side; but I could not; and, besides, the crew used to watch us very closely who were not chained down to the decks, lest we should leap into the water: and I have seen some of these poor African prisoners most severely cut for attempting to do so, and hourly whipped for not eating. This indeed was often the case with myself. In a little time after, amongst the poor chained men, I found some of my own nation, which in small degree gave ease to my mind. I inquired of these what was to be done with us? they gave me to understand we were to be carried to these white people's country to work for them. I then was a little revived, and thought, if it were no worse than working, my situation was not so desperate: but still I feared I should be put to death, the white people looked and acted, as I thought, in so savage a manner; for I had never seen among my people such instances of brutal cruelty; and this not only shewn towards us blacks, but also to some of the whites themselves. One white man in particular I saw, when we were permitted to be on deck, flogged so unmercifully with a large rope near the foremast, that he died in consequence of it; and they tossed him over the side as they would have done a brute. This made me fear these people the more; and I expected nothing less than to be treated in the same manner. I could not help expressing my fears and apprehensions to some of my countrymen: I asked them if these people had no country, but lived in this hollow place the ship? they told me they did not, but came from a distant one. 'Then,' said I, 'how comes it in all our country we never have heard of them?' They told me because they lived so very far off. I then asked where were their women? had they any like themselves? I was told they had: 'and why,' said I, 'do we not see them?' They answered, because they were left behind. I asked how the vessel could go? They told me they could not tell, but that there were cloth put upon the masts by the help of ropes I saw, and then the vessel went on; and the white men had some magic they put in the water when they liked in order to stop the vessel. I was exceedingly amazed at this account, and really thought they were spirits. I therefore wished much to be from amongst them, for I expected they would sacrifice me: but my wishes were vain; for we were so quartered that it was impossible for any of us to make our escape. While we staied on the coast I was mostly on deck; and one day, to my great astonishment, I saw one of these vessels coming in with the sails up. As soon as the whites saw it, they gave a great shout, at which we were amazed; and the more so as the vessel appeared larger by approaching nearer. At last she came to an anchor in my sight, and when the anchor was let go I and my countrymen who saw it were lost in astonishment to observe the vessel stop; and we were now convinced it was done by magic. Soon after this the other ship got her boats out, and they came on board of us, and the people of both ships seemed very glad to see each other. Several of the strangers also shook hands with us black people, and made motions with their hands, signifying, I suppose, we were to go to their country; but we did not understand them. At last, when the ship we were in had got in all her cargo, they made ready with many fearful noises, and we were all put under deck, so that we could not see how they managed the vessel. But this disappointment was the least of my sorrow. The stench of the hold while we were on the coast was so intolerably loathsome, that it was dangerous to remain there for any time, and some of us had been permitted to stay on the deck for the fresh air; but now that the whole ship's cargo were confined together, it became absolutely pestilential. The closeness of the place, and the heat of the climate, added to the number in the ship, which was so crowded that each had scarcely room to turn himself, almost suffocated us. This produced copious perspirations, so that the air soon became unfit for respiration, from a variety of loathsome smells, and brought on a sickness among the slaves, of which many died, thus falling victims to the improvident avarice, as I may call it, of their purchasers. This wretched situation was again aggravated by the galling of the chains, now become insupportable; and the filth of the necessary tubs, into which the children often fell, and were almost suffocated. The shrieks of the women and the groans of the dying, rendered the whole a scene of horror almost inconceivable. Happily perhaps for myself I was soon reduced so low here that it was thought necessary to keep me almost always on deck; and from my extreme youth I was not put in fetters. In this situation I expected every hour to share the fate of my companions, some of whom were almost daily brought upon deck at the point of death, which I began to hope would soon put an end to my miseries. Often did I think many of the inhabitants of the deep much more happy than myself; I envied them the freedom they enjoyed, and as often, wished I could change my condition for theirs. Every circumstance I met with served only to render my state more painful, and heighten my apprehensions and my opinion of the cruelty of the whites. One day they had taken a number of fishes; and when they had killed and satisfied themselves with as many as they thought fit, to our astonishment who were on the deck, rather than give any of them to us to eat as we expected, they tossed the remaining fish into the sea again, although we begged and prayed for some as well as we could, but in vain; and some of my countrymen, being pressed by hunger, took an opportunity, when they thought no one saw them, of trying to get a little privately; but they were discovered, and the attempt procured them some very severe floggings.

"One day, when we had a smooth sea, and moderate wind, two of my wearied countrymen who were chained together, (I was near them at the time), preferring death to such a life of misery, somehow made through the nettings and jumped into the sea: immediately another quite dejected fellow, who, on account of his illness was suffered to be out of irons, also followed their example; and I believe many more would very soon have done the same, if they had not been prevented by the ship's crew, who were instantly alarmed. Those of us that were the most active were in a moment put down under the deck; and there was such a noise and confusion amongst the people of the ships as I had never heard before, to stop her, and get the boat out and to go after the slaves. However, two of the wretches were drowned, but they got the other and afterwards flogged him unmercifully for thus attempting to prefer death to slavery. In this manner we continued to undergo more hardships than I can now relate; hardships which are inseparable from this accursed trade.—Many a time we were near suffocation from the want of fresh air, which we were often without for whole days together. This and the stench of the necessary tubs carried off many."

NOTES

1. Denys Hay, *The Medieval Centuries* (New York: Harper, Torchbooks, 1964), p. 44 *n.*
2. Wellard, *Lost Worlds,* p. 164.
3. Davidson, *Black Mother,* p. 22.
4. Wellard, *Lost Worlds,* p. 164.
5. Charles Sumner as quoted by Wellard in *Lost Worlds,* p. 185.

6. Theodore Lyman as quoted by Wellard in *Lost Worlds,* p. 186.
7. Davidson, *Black Mother,* pp. 45-46.
8. Henry Boyde as quoted by Wellard in *Lost Worlds,* p. 182.
9. Quoted by Wellard in *Lost Worlds,* p. 182.
10. Quoted by Wellard in *Lost Worlds,* p. 183.
11. Wellard, *Lost Worlds,* p. 183.
12. Sir Harry H. Johnston, *A History of Colonization of Africa by Alien Races* (London: Cambridge University Press, 1913), pp. 81-82.
13. Ronald W. Davis, "Negro Contributions to the Explorations of the Globe," in *The Negro Impact on Western Civilization,* ed. J. S. Roucek and Thomas Kiernan (New York: Philosophical Library, 1970), p. 33.
14. Quoted by Davidson in *Black Mother,* pp. 33-34, 35.
15. Davidson, *Black Mother,* pp. 81-83.
16. Johnston, *Colonization of Africa,* pp. 156-57.
17. Quoted by Davidson in *Black Mother,* pp. 88-90.
18. John Barbot as quoted by Davidson in *Black Mother,* p. 92.
19. John Atkins as quoted by Davidson in *Black Mother,* pp. 94-95.

CHAPTER 15

After the Slave Trade

The four hundred and eighty-nine years—between 1440, when Portuguese sailors began kidnapping and abducting lone African men and women into slavery, and 1929, when the last officially recorded caravan of slaves arrived at Mourzouk on the northern fringe of the Sahara desert—were fateful years for the continent and people of Africa. Prior to this period Africans and Europeans knew very little about one another, though they lived under feudalistic political systems with much in common and were, in terms of economic development, not very far apart. For centuries, the Mediterranean littoral of Africa had been in touch with Asia and Europe. The Moors had colonized Europe in the tenth century and had been driven back to Africa by the fifteenth. The eastern coast of Africa to which Vasco da Gama came had been "in direct contact with the southern shores of Arabia, southern Persia, western India and the islands of the Indonesian archipelago for over two thousand years."[1] At this time, Europeans nursed none of the ideas of racial superiority later to be characteristic of them, and Africans on their part did not suffer from any inferiority complex. If anything, Africans considered themselves superior as Father Cavazzi reported from the Congo in 1687, "With nauseating presumption, these nations think themselves, the foremost men in the world, and nothing will persuade them to the contrary. They imagine that Africa is not only the greatest part of the world but also the happiest and most agreeable. Similar opinions are held by the king himself but in a manner still more remarkable. For he is persuaded that there is no monarch in the world who is his equal or exceeds him in power or the abundance of wealth."[2]

During the slave trade, Europe benefited from the material wealth —gold, silver, ivory, ostrich feathers, palm oil, and other things she took from Africa. Money flowed into her coffers from the sale of sugar, tobacco, and other crops grown by African slave labor, and from industries expanded to manufacture goods demanded by the slave trade. Her population found employment in the various activities generated by the slave trade while her technological skills increased with every new challenge. White people were, however, brutalized by the experience and acquired notions of racial superiority.

Africa during this same period suffered from the systematic plunder of her material wealth. She suffered even more from internecine strife and from the selling of the cream, the ablest and fittest, of her sons and daughters into slavery. It is reckoned that during this period, 100 million Africans were enslaved. Over and above this figure are people who died on African soil in the wars of the slave trade and those who perished in transit—on the sands of the Sahara and the waves of the oceans.

Africa's economy was ruined, her nascent cottage industries—textile, iron, and others—were destroyed. Her once proud empires crumbled as slave traders armed vassals, upset the balance of power, and undermined imperial authority. Africa's once proud armies were shattered, as was the unity of her people. Only bitter divisions, mistrust, and suspicion of one another remained.

What did Africa have to show for all this? She had thousands upon thousands of rifles. In 1894 a British naval officer named Bedford reported inspecting Nanna's house "where large stores containing munitions of war and trading materials in very large quantities were found. . . . Scattered about all over town, and in large quantities, in the stores, were leg and neck irons, also handcuffs, evidently for use in keeping the large number of slaves owned by Chief Nanna in order by most severe means. . . .

"There were," Bedford continued, "a total of 106 cannon from 3-pounder to 32-pounder in size, including 'a large number of 9-pounders, very good-looking cast-iron guns,' and stores of powder made up in neat muslin bags and cylinders of split bamboo with iron balls and pieces of scrap iron, permitting rapid fire." [5] Africa had, also, another form of capital to show for her five hundred years of the slave trade—booze. The British naval officer found in Nanna's house 8,300 cases of gin. In each case were twelve bottles, making a total of 99,600 bottles of hooch." [3] To this impressive return can be added large quantities of rum and tobacco.

Africa's real and lasting benefit from the slave trade accrues from the nature and extent of her diaspora. Because the black man is now the second most widely dispersed human being on earth, African culture has influenced remote and widely diverse people. In some parts of the world, especially in the Caribbean and South American countries like Brazil, this influence is acknowledged with pride. In other countries, however, racial prejudice makes its recognition extremely difficult. In international affairs, the diaspora has also assured Africa of a sympathetic hearing and moral support in matters concerning her generally. And there is active support from countries with sizeable black populations. This is proving invaluable to African diplomacy because the spirit of unity among black people in various parts of the world stems from the fact that they acknowledge a common African ancestry and heritage.

By the end of the eighteenth century, some African rulers had become, for various reasons, strongly opposed to the slave trade. In 1526 the Manikongo Afonso wrote King John of Portugal "it is our will that in these kingdoms of Congo there should not be any trade in slaves or any market for slaves." In 1724 King Agaja of Dahomey sent a message to the British Government saying he wanted to "stop the export of people from his country." A Swedish traveler visiting Africa in 1789, reported that the Almamy of Futa Toro in northern Senegal, "had passed a law 'very much to his honour,' which declared that no slaves were to be taken through Futa Toro for sale abroad." [4] Captains of French slave ships begged him to change his mind but he refused and returned the presents they had sent to him saying all their riches would not make him change his mind. Clearly, some Africans had become aware of the differences between the African and the white man's concepts of slavery.

Even in Europe, decent men had become sick and tired of the bestial cruelties perpetrated in the interests of the slave trade. More and more questioned themselves and searched their consciences about the morality of treating human beings as chattel. In France opponents of the slave trade cited a royal declaration of 1571 permitting no slave in the country and a law of 1607 which not only confirmed the freedom of all people in the kingdom, but also declared free all slaves who set foot on French soil and were baptized. In England, Chief Justice, Lord Mansfield's judgment of 1772 was interpreted to mean that no man could be held a slave in that country. Consequently, fifteen thousand black people became free though destitute and were known as the Black Poor. And in the United States of America, more than sixty thousand black men managed to gain their freedom while many more took up arms for freedom in the Caribbean.

As European industries expanded, employing more and more people, they needed raw materials, such as palm oil, used in the manufacturing of soap. From their contact with Africa through the slave trade, Europeans knew that many of the raw materials required for their industries were obtainable in Africa.

Furthermore, the slave trade had also demonstrated the potentialities of Africa as a market for European goods. The idea that it would be more profitable to engage in legitimate trade than in slave trade began to gain ground. A movement for the abolition of slavery gathered momentum, led by white men as well as black men like Equiano, Frederick Douglas, and Ottobah Cugoano who wrote a book entitled, *Thoughts and Sentiments on the Evil and Wicked Traffic of Slavery and Commerce of the Human Species.*

Europeans were so impressed by the immense possibilities for legitimate trade with Africa and its potential as a source for raw materials that they supported three schemes for the repatriation of black men to Africa so that they could become a nucleus for such trade. From England the Black Poor, from Canada black soldiers promised land that was never given, and from the West Indies the Maroons were tricked into leaving their strongholds and sent to Sierra Leone. In the United States, wealthy Afro-Americans, like Paul Cuff, financed voyages of black men returning to Africa while prominent black and white Americans sponsored the American Society for Colonizing the Free People of Color, which led to the founding of Liberia. Under French auspices, Libreville, in Gabon, was also founded as a settlement of former slaves.

Denmark has the distinction of being the first European country to abolish slavery. Led by Britain, other countries followed her example. Many ships of countries that outlawed the trade, nevertheless, continued to deal in slaves until the British Navy made the business unprofitable for them.

Because Africa emerged from the slave trade depopulated and divided, its people weak and suspicious of one another, it fell easy prey to the mechinations, colonization schemes, and armies of Europeans.

"To trade effectively, or be able to stake their claims with any degree of accuracy, European powers needed to know more about Africa; its geography, natural resources and people. So, travellers and explorers, backed by organizations and people of varied interests and motives, went into the interior of Africa to augment the scanty and sketchy coastal knowledge of the continent, sailors and traders provided. The journals of Mungo Park, David Livingstone, Herbert Stanley, Richard Burton, Heinrich Barth, Speke, Rene Caillie, Paul Soleillet, and many others record the remarkable journeys and 'discoveries' of these men. As feats of endurance, the remarkable journeys are truly remarkable but, perhaps, even more remarkable are the discoveries; for, how does one discover, as Livingstone is said to have done, something like the Victoria Falls which millions and millions of other people have known for generations as *Mosi oa tunya*—the smoke that thunders?

"The journeys had another merit: they portrayed Africa as virgin land for the planting of Christianity (and some would give the word 'planting,' here the meaning it has in detective stories). So, European missionaries went to Africa to preach the Gospel. They wore out soles saving souls; but too often found themselves the agents of life through death, peace through war, accord through discord, education through westernization, civilization through dehumanization, and construction through destruction. For they were soon persuaded that only through waging ruthless wars of conquest—or pacification, as such wars are euphemistically called—could peace reign in Africa. Only through discord, inherent in the injection of Christianity and the rejection of traditional African ideas of God, could accord be achieved. Only by keeping Africans ignorant of the good in their culture and the greatness in their history, by teaching them Western values and the superiority of Europeans, could they be educated. Only through the abandonment of a native culture based on humanistic, family and tribal ties, responsibilities, and sanctions, and the imposition of a dehumanizing, individualistic, and materialistic one; could Africans be civilized. Only through the total destruction of African ideas, values, and mores could a new Africa be built.

"Missionary accounts of the white man's formidable task in Christianitizing, civilizing, and educating Africans often couched in picturesque hyperbolic terms, were calculated to gain financial and popular support for them in their homelands. The reports also attracted an assortment of adventurers, prospectors, traders, concessionaires, and fortune hunters to Africa. These were followed and backed by multifarious syndicates and chartered companies. The presence in various parts of Africa of agents of European business interests made way for the involvement of European governments on the grounds that they were protecting the commercial concerns of their nationals.

"The scramble for Africa thus began. The possession of colonies in Africa was regarded by European powers as a means of acquiring national prestige, mollifying wounded national pride, and keeping the scales of the distribution of power in Europe even. Africa was, as a result, drawn into the struggles for power in Europe; so much so that it is essential to study European politics of this period in order to understand why certain countries in Africa became colonies of certain powers in Europe and why arbitrary boundary lines were often drawn which put people of a single tribe into different states, or would lump together into one state peoples who should have been in separate states. Some of these boundaries, drawn in the nineteenth century and dictated, primarily, by considerations of the power struggle, are a source of friction today. Indeed, some of Africa's present major problems can be traced to decisions taken in Europe at this time.

"Actual colonization was, as a rule, undertaken not by governments but by private companies organized specifically for the task. The legal fiction under which such companies operated was that they were not representative of the governments from which they derived their charters. Their actions, therefore, did not necessarily have the agreement and sanction of their governments. This fiction enabled the chartered companies to rush in where governments feared to tread. They were financed privately, at no cost to the taxpayer; so, according to the fiction, governments could not scrutinize or control the details of their operations. In actual fact, governments could and did interfere with the companies. It sometimes suited governments to seem to be powerless because the corporations could be useful tools. They could be disowned, conveniently, when they failed to pull off such a scheme as the Jameson Raid in southern Africa which caused more than mere ripples of diplomatic embarrassment to the government of the country in which the syndicate was registered. On the other hand, territory in which a company operated was almost invariably taken over by a European government and turned into a protectorate, colony, or overseas province when this was considered convenient.

"Often, on the basis of fraudulent treaties and bogus purchases of land from unsuspecting African rulers, a European power would claim a vaguely demarcated sphere of influence in which to exercise exclusive trading rights. In this manner protectorates and colonies were carved on the map of Africa. There was a mad rush for territory. The cupidity, intrigue, cutthroat competition, and rivalry that characterized the activities of many of the foreign agencies generated friction, hatred, and animosity not only between themselves but also between Africans and the nations involved. To bring some sort of order into this chaos, the European powers decided to lay down some ground rules to govern the staking of claims and carving of colonies in Africa.

"The Berlin Conference of 1884-85 was convened to formulate these rules. It was decided that all future claims to colonies or protectorates in any part of Africa should be formally registered and notification given to members of the conference and that each claim should be backed by effective authority in the areas concerned. Furthermore, there was to be freedom of navigation along the Niger and Congo rivers. Thus, the idea of exclusive trading areas was frustrated. In spite of the conference decision requiring effective occupation of areas before claims could be recognized, most claims were not, in fact, based on demonstrable effective authority or occupation but on concessions and treaties of very doubtful and questionable validity. The impressive point, however, is that European powers agreed to base their partition of Africa on a set of rules acceptable to them all and thus avoided coming to blows with one another in the scramble.

"With this accord in Europe, the age of colonialism began in Africa. Europe was no longer content to take Africans as slaves into far off lands; they laid claim to the very soil of Africa and took possession of the land itself. In 1880 more than ninety percent of the continent of Africa was ruled by Africans, but by 1900—a mere twenty years later—only a tiny fraction, Ethiopia and Liberia, was ruled by Africans. In the scramble Europeans carved up Africa fast. Sixty years later, they were to scram out of Africa even faster. The original scramble lasted twenty years. It took most European powers half that time to scram out of Africa when colonialism was challenged.

"What was Africa's response to the conspiracy of the Berlin Conference of 1884-85? Was there concerted African action to meet the European threat to the land? It is safe to say that Africans, in general, knew little about Europe and even less about Berlin. After all, the days when radio, television, and jumbo jets would facilitate the formation of an Organization for African Unity were still far away. Yet, in spite of the weaknesses of African armies, the division and suspicions consequent upon the slave trade, the inability of African rulers to consult together and agree on a common strategy, African response to the European menance can be described in one word: resistance! They stood up and fought. Uncoordinated though they were, African wars of resistance were fought all over the continent. Africans stood up, grabbed their spears, and fought like men. The European invaders enjoyed the advantage of a superior and more deadly weapon: the gun, but that was the only advantage they had. In all other aspects of the conflict, the African more than held his own.

"In these encounters, Africans, usually armed only with spears, displayed greater bravery and valor than Europeans firing guns from a safe distance. For, as Mzilikazi, King of the Amendebele once observed, the gun is a weapon which must have been invented by a coward. In the sphere of strategy and battle tactics, Africans more than held their own against graduates of the best military academies in Europe.

"What, then, turned the scales in favor of Europeans enabling them eventually, to colonize Africa? It was the assistance Europeans received from other Africans. Although Europeans enjoyed the advantage of more deadly weapons, Africans enjoyed greater numerical strength. European armies had to depend on Africans for actual soldiers and carriers, for intelligence and food supplies. Without other Africans supplying these services, Europeans would never have been able to mount the campaigns by which they conquered the continent.

Even today in Zimbabwe (presently called Rhodesia), South Africa, Namibia, Angola, and Mozambique where armed resistance to white rule is taking place, the success of the white man in suppressing this resistance is due, in no small measure, to the extent and manner in which he has been able to make use of Africans as soldiers, secret agents, and intelligence gatherers, on his side. Perhaps this part of our history illustrates the point of the Zulu saying: *Isitha somunthu nguye uqhobo lwake,* "the enemy of an African is he, himself." There can be no doubt, however, that these early wars of resistance to European rule in Africa were a source of great inspiration and spiritual strength to the generation of Africans whose destiny it was to carry on the fight against European colonialism and, from the late 1850's on through the 1960's, eradicate it from most of the soil of Africa.[5]

Europeans still impose minority rule in a minority of states in Africa. For the sons of the soil in these white-dominated states, there is great disappointment at not being free and independent like others on the rest of the continent. They often ask: Why are we not free? What did we do wrong? Are we any different from other Africans now free? Will we ever get our freedom? When? Even though disappointment is understandable, it should be remembered that the problem pockets of white minority rule in Africa is not the first challenge of this kind to confront Africa, neither is it the most formidable. Problems like the slave trade and colonialism appeared insoluble or ineradicable in their day. In due course, both were eradicated. Admittedly, it took time: about five hundred years in the case of slavery, half a century for colonialism. In terms of an individual, five hundred years is a long time. But, in terms of a people, a nation, a continent, such a span is no more than a moment in its history. These pockets of white minority rule in Africa will be eradicated. When they will disappear, no one can say, but one day they will go, and Africa will be free from European rule as Asia is today. Those living at present would like to see with their own eyes the coming of freedom to Zimbabwe, Namibia, Angola, Mozambique, and Azania (South Africa). Naturally, they would like to celebrate the occasion, perhaps because they have seen others celebrate their *uhuru*. Still, many an African who hoped, fought, and fervently prayed for an end to the scourge of the slave trade or colonialism was not alive when that day dawned many years later. Let the march of history run its course. Suffice it to know that "We shall overcome," and that one day Africa shall be completely free from European rule.

Today, most of Africa is, thank God, ruled by sons of the soil. Europeans have not, however, completely relaxed their grasp. In various ways, they have substituted neo-colonialism for older, franker colonialism. Even though they no longer claim ownership of the African cow, they continue to milk it and to make and eat the butter, while the owners go hungry and die of starvation. The economy of many African states is still controlled and its fruits enjoyed mainly by Europeans. Economic colonialism still exists. Fortunately, African leaders are dealing firmly with this problem, and steps are being taken to facilitate the participation of Africans in the ownership, management, and working of their commerce and industry.

Another area in which colonialism still exists is the educational sphere. The educational systems of most independent African states are modeled after those of the former colonizing powers. Most government officials and other leaders are products of these systems and still look up to Oxford, Cambridge, the Sorbonne, for "standards." Although there is, at present, a lot of heartsearching and new thinking about this problem, there is no running away from the fact that we are still mentally colonized and will probably continue to be so until we have developed the perspicacity to discern what must be preserved in African culture. This also means discovering what in Western culture must be eschewed. In a world increasingly dominated by machines and with personal relationships becoming ever more mechanical, Africa's major contribution may well be her sense of *hunhu* or *ubuntu,* i.e., "humanness" which her people have developed over the centuries.

NOTES

1. James S. Kirkman, *Men and Monuments on the East African Coast* (New York: Praeger, 1966), p. 15.
2. Davidson, *Black Mother,* p. 10.
3. Davidson, *Black Mother,* p. 269.
4. Davidson, *West Africa,* p. 296.
5. Stanlake Samkange, "Wars of Resistance to European Rule," in *Horizon African History* (New York: American Heritage Publishing Company, forthcoming).

BIBLIOGRAPHY

The following list of additional titles is submitted not as a comprehensive or exhaustive bibliography on Africa but merely as a guide to some of the books the reader might find useful for further study.

Chapter 1

Baker, J. N. L. *A History of Geographical Discovery and Exploration.* New York: Cooper Square, 1937.

Boyd, Andrew, and Rensburg, Van P. *An Atlas of African Affairs.* rev, ed. New York: Praeger, 1965.

Fage. J. D. *An Atlas of African History.* New York: St. Martin's Press, 1958.

Kimble, George H. *Geography in the Middle Ages.* Reprint. New York: Russell & Russell [1938] 1968.

Stamp, L. D. *Africa: A Study of Tropical Development.* 2nd ed. New York: Wiley, 1964.

Thompson, J. O. *A History of Ancient Geography.* Cambridge: The University Press, 1948.

Chapters 2 and 3

Campbell, Bernard C. *Human Evolution: An Introduction to Man's Adaptations.* Chicago: Aldine Publishing Company, 1966.

Clark, J. Desmond. "Prehistoric Origins of African Culture." *Journal of African History* 5 (1964), 163-82.

Clark, Grahame. *World Prehistory*. London: Cambridge University Press, 1969.

Clark, Sir W. LeGros. "The Humanity of Man." *Nature*, no. 4702 (1961).

Leakey, L. S. B. *Adam's Ancestors: The Evolution of Man and His Culture*. New York: Harper, Torchbooks [1953].

McBurney, Charles Brian Montague. *The Stone Age of Northern Africa*. Baltimore: Penquin Books, 1960.

Morris, Desmond. *Naked Apes: A Zoologist's Study of the Human Animal*. New York: McGraw-Hill, 1967.

Pilbeam, D. M. "Man's Earliest Ancestors." *Science Journal* 3 (1967).

Ogot, B. A., and Kieran, J. A., eds. *Zamani: A Survey of East African History*. New York: Humanities Press, 1968.

Posnansky, Merrick, ed. *Prelude to East African History*. New York: Oxford University Press, 1966.

Chapters 4 and 5

Childe, V. G. *New Light on the Most Ancient East*. 4th ed. New York: W. W. Norton, 1969.

Edwards I. E. S. *The Pyramids of Egypt*. rev. ed. Baltimore: Penguin Books, 1961.

Frankfort, Henri. *The Birth of Civilization in the Near East*. New York: Doubleday, Anchor Books, 1968.

Hayes, William C. *The Scepter of Egypt*. 2 pts. Cambridge, Mass.: Harvard University Press, 1953, 1959.

Malcolm X *On Afro-American History*, Chicago: Merit Publishers, 1967.

Chapter 6

Arkell, A. J. *History of the Sudan from the Earliest Times to 1821*. 2nd ed. New York: Oxford University Press, 1961.

Budge, E. A. W. A *History of Ethiopia, Nubia and Abyssinia*. New York: Humanities Press, 1966.

Garstag, J. A. H.; Sayce, A. H.; and Griffith, F. L. L. *Meroe: The City of the Ethiopians*. Oxford: Clarendon Press, 1911.

Holt, P. M. *A Modern History of the Sudan*. New York: Praeger, 1963.

Shibeika, Mekki. *The Independent Sudan*. New York: Robert Speller & Sons, 1959.

Chapter 7

Bucholzer, John. *The Land of Burnt Faces*. Translated by Maurice Michael. New York: Robert M. McBride, C., 1956.

Czeslaw, Jesman. *The Ethiopian Paradox.* London: Oxford University Press, 1963.
Greenfield, Richard. *Ethiopia: A New Political History.* New York: Praeger, 1965.
Huggins, W. M. and Jackson, J. G. *Introduction to African Civilizations.* New York: Negro Universities Press, 1937.
Lipsky, G. A. *Ethiopia: Its People, Its Society, Its Culture.* New York: Human Relations Area File Press, 1962.
Pankhurst, Sylvia. *Ethiopia: A Cultural History.* London: Sidgwick & Jackson, 1955.
Ullendorff, Edward. *The Ethiopians: An Introduction to Country and People.* London: Oxford University Press, 1961.
Wright, A. W. *Ethiopia Stretching Forth Her Hand: The Black Man of Today, A Vindication of the Afro-American Race.* Morgantown, W. Va., 1899.

Chapter 8

Bates, Oric. *the Eastern Libyans.* New York: Barnes & Noble, 1914.
Breasted, J. H. *A History of Egypt from the Earliest Times to the Persian Conquest.* New York: Scribner's, 1909.
Emery, W. B. *Archaic Egypt.* Baltimore: Penguin Books, 1961.
Kwapong. A. A. "Carthage, Greece and Rome." In *The Dawn of African History,* edited by Roland Oliver. New York: Oxford University Press, 1968.
Lhote, Henri. *Search for the Tassil Frescoes: The Story of the Prehistoric Rock-paintings of the Sahara.* Translated by A. H. Brodrick. New York: E. P. Dutton, 1959.
Steel, Ronald, ed. *North Africa.* New York: H. W. Wilson, 1967.
Villard, H. S. *Libya: The New Arab Kingdom of North Africa.* New York: Cornell University Press, 1956.
Warrington, B. H. *The North African Provinces: Diocletian to the Vandal Conquest.* Cambridge: The University Press, 1954.

Chapter 9

Black, M. *The Historian's Craft.* Manchester University Press, 1954.
Collingwood, R. G. *The Idea of History.* New York: Oxford University Press, 1946.
Gooch, George P. *History and Historians in the Nineteenth Century.* Boston: Beacon Press, 1959.
Greenberg, J. H. *Studies in African Linguistic Classification.* New Haven: Compass Publishing Co., 1955.
Lystad, R. A., ed. *The African World: A Survey of Social Research.* New York: Praeger, 1965.

McCall, D. F. *Africa in Time Perspective: A Discussion of Historical Reconstruction from Unwritten Sources.* New York: Oxford University Press, 1969.

Vansina, Jan. *Oral Tradition: A Study in Historical Methology.* Translated by A. M. Wright. Chicago: Aldine Publishing Company, 1965.

Vansina, Jan; Mauny, Raymond; and Thomas, L. V., eds. *The Historian in Tropical Africa:* Studies presented and discussed at the Fourth International African Seminar at the University of Dakar, Senegal, 1961. London: Oxford University Press, 1964.

———*Journal of African History* 3 (1964). Special Number: Third Conference on African History and Archaeology, School of Oriental and African Studies, London, July, 1961. London: Cambridge University Press, 1964.

Chapters 9, 10, 11 and 12

Ajayi, J. F. A., and Espie, Ian, eds. *A Thousand Years of West African History.* New York: Humanities Press, 1969.

Bovill, E. W. *The Golden Trade of the Moors.* 2nd ed. New York: Oxford University Press, 1970.

Chu, Daniel, and Skinner, Elliot. *A Glorious Age in Africa: The story of Three Great African Empires.* New York: Doubleday, 1965.

Davidson, Basil. *African Kingdoms.* New York: Time-Life, 1966.

Davies, Oliver. *West Africa Before Europeans Came.* New York: Barnes & Noble, 1967.

Fage, J. D. *A History of West of Africa: An Introductory Survey.* 4th ed. New York: Cambridge University Press, 1969.

Forde, Daryll, and Kaberry, O. M., eds. *West African Kingdoms in the Nineteenth Century.* New York: Oxford University Press, 1967.

Hogben, S. J., and Kirk-Green, Anthony H. *The Emirates of Northern Nigeria: A Preliminary Survey of Their Historical Traditions.* New York: Oxford University Press, 1966.

Naiane, D. T. *Sundiata: An Epic of Old Mali.* New York: Humanities Press, 1965.

Novels:

Amadi, Elechi. *The Concubine.* New York: Humanities Press, 1966.

Beti, Mongo. *Mission to Kala.* New York: Humanities Press, 1966.

Ekwensi, Cyprian. *Burning Grass.* New York: Humanities Press, 1966.

Oyono, Ferdinand. *Boy* (original title *Houseboy*). Translated by John Reed. New York: Macmillan, 1970.

Chapter 13

Cameron, Verney L. *Across Africa.* New York: Negro Universities Press, 1877.

Childs, G. M. *Kinship and Character of the Ovimbundu.* New York: Humanities Press, 1970.
Colson, Elizabeth, and Gluckman, Max, eds. *Seven Tribes of British Central Africa. New York: Humanities Press,* 1959.
Davidson, Basil. *A History of East and Central Africa to the Late Nineteenth Century.* New York: Doubleday, Anchor Books 1969.
Greenberg, Joseph. *Languages of Africa.* 2nd ed. Bloomington: Indiana University Press, 1966.
Guthrie, Malcolm. "Some Developments in Prehistory." *Journal of African History* 3 (1962).
Wills, A. J. *An Introduction to the History of Central Africa.* 2nd ed. New York: Oxford University Press, 1967.
Novels:
Mofolo, Thomas. *Chaka the Zulu.* New York: Oxford University Press, 1967.
Ngugi, James. *A Grain of Wheat.* 2nd ed. New York: Humanities Press, 1968.
Rubadiri, David. *No Bride Price.* Evanston, Ill.: Northwestern University Press, 1967.
Samkange, Stanlake. *On Trial for My Country.* New York: Humanities Press, 1966.

Chapter 14

Birmingham, David, *Trade and Conflict in Angola: The Mbundu and Their Neighbors Under the Influence of the Portuguese.* New York: Oxford University Press, 1966.
Curtin, P. D. *Africa Remembered: Narratives by West Africans from the Era of the Slave Trade.* Madison: University of Wisconsin Press, 1967.
Dike, K. O. *Trade and Politics in the Niger Delta 1830-1885.* New York: Oxford University Press, 1956.
Morel, Edmund. *The Black Man's Burden.* Chicago: Afro-Am Books, 1970.
———. *Red Rubber.* History and Culture Series, no. 100. New York: Haskell House, 1970.
Park, Mungo. *Travels in the Interior of Africa.* London: Cassell and Company, 1900.

Chapter 15

Hargreaves, J. D. *Prelude to the Partition of West Africa.* New York: St. Martin's Press, 1963.

Hoskins, H. L. *European Imperialism in Africa.* Reprint. New York: Russell & Russell [1930] 1967.

Jones, Gwilym I. *Trading States of the Oil Rivers: A Study of Political Development in Eastern Nigeria.* New York: Oxford University Press, 1963.

Ranger, T. O. *Revolt in Southern Rhodesia 1896-97.* London: Heinemann, 1967.

Samkange, Stanlake. *Origins of Rhodesia.* New York: Praeger, 1969.

General

Clark, Leon E., ed. *Through African Eyes,* Vols. III and IV. New York: 1970.

Davidson, Basil. *Africa in History.* Rev. ed. New York: Macmillan, 1969.

———.*The African Past: Chronicles from Antiquity to Modern Times,* London: Longmans, Green, 1964.

———.*A Guide to African History.* Garden City, N. Y.: Doubleday, 1965.

DeGraft-Johnson, J. C. *African Glory: The Story of Vanished Negro Civilizations.* New York: Praeger, 1954.

Gailey, H. A. *The History of Africa in Maps.* Chicago: Denoyer, 1967.

McEwan, P. H. M., ed. *Africa from Early Times to 1800.* London: Oxford University Press, 1968.

INDEX